SUBPOENA DUCES

UNITED STATES OF AMERICA
NATIONAL COMMISSION ON PRODUCT SAFETY
1016 Sixteenth Street, N. W.
Washington, D. C. 20036

To ~~Edward M. Swartz~~

~~53 Beacon St., Boston, Massachusetts~~

DISCARDED

Pursuant to the authority contained in Public Law 90-146 (81 Stat. 466), you are hereby required to appear before the National Commission on Product Safety, or any two Members thereof, at ~~John F. Kennedy Federal Building~~

in the City of ~~Boston, Massachusetts~~

on the **17-19** day of ~~December~~ , 19**68**, at **9:30** o'clock **a.** m. of that day, to testify **on hazards to children** ~~and others in connection with the~~ ~~manufacture and sale of toys and related products.~~

and you are hereby required to bring with you and produce at said time and place the following books, papers, and documents:

All relevant documents

Fail not at your peril.

In testimony whereof, the undersigned, a Member of the National Commission on Product Safety, has hereunto set his hand this 12th day of Dec., 1968.

Arnold B. Elkind   Commissioner

Toys That Don't Care

Toys That Don't Care

Edward M. Swartz

Gambit
INCORPORATED
Boston

1971

© Copyright 1971 by Edward M. Swartz
All rights reserved, including the right to reproduce this book
or parts thereof in any form
Library of Congress Catalog Card Number: 70-140966
Printed in the United States of America
SECOND PRINTING

WRITTEN FOR, AND DEDICATED TO, CHILDREN EVERYWHERE, WITH THE PRAYER THAT THIS BOOK WILL CONTRIBUTE TOWARD MAKING THEIR WORLD SAFER, HAPPIER, AND MORE SECURE.

Acknowledgments

IN LARGE PART THIS BOOK BECAME A REALITY BECAUSE OF TWO very special people—James Swartz, age five, and Joan Swartz, age four, whose playful exuberance and insatiable curiosity were instrumental in demonstrating to their father their very special need for protection from toys that don't care. I hope they will forgive Dad for the times he thought their playthings were better placed in his Boston office and in this book than in their toy box. To Linda, my wonderful wife, my thanks for her patience and understanding and for the sacrifices she made by allowing the extra time, which would have been family time, for the writing of this book. I would also like to thank her for her valuable ideas and contributions, particularly with reference to Chapter Seven. To my brother, Joseph Swartz, still a teenager, my thanks for his toy-shopping help.

The author wishes to acknowledge the valuable editorial assistance of John Corrigan, Paul Daw, Jeffrey Woolf and Mark Knoll.

To the countless attorneys, physicians and academicians from virtually every part of the Country who so generously aided this study, the author's deepest appreciation for their valuable and unselfish contribution.

To his brother, Attorney Fred Swartz, he extends his thanks for expertly attending to the many extra problems that became his in a busy law office while the author was busy collecting

ACKNOWLEDGMENTS

source material and writing this book. Celeste Royall and Karen Goldberg have my deep appreciation for their attention to the typing of the manuscript and for their valuable suggestions.

My mother and father, Mr. and Mrs. Jacob W. Swartz, have my thanks for teaching me that above all else it is important to serve society well. I hope that in some small way this book contributes to that important goal.

E.M. S.
Belmont, Massachusetts
November 24, 1970

Contents

Acknowledgments   *vii*

Introduction   *1*

PART ONE

1   Toy Merchants vs. Toy Consumers   7

2   How Toys Are Unsafe   20

3   Toy Industry Self-Regulation: *The Fox Attempts to Guard the Henhouse*   76

4   Watching the Watchmen: *The Testing Agencies*   94

5   Governmental Action and Toy Safety   *123*

CONTENTS

6	Toys in the Courtroom	152
7	Is This Toy Necessary?	187

PART TWO

8	Shopper's Guide: *Toys to Avoid or Discard*	201

A Buyer's Guide to Toyland

Babies' Playthings	204
Candy "Toys"	208
Catapult Toys	210
Chemistry Sets	210
Clothes, Clothing, and Burns	213
Dolls and Stuffed Animals	218
"Educational" Toys	220
Electrical Toys	222
Exploding Toys	226
"Feeding Time" Playthings	227
Games	228
Hobby and Craft Toys	230
Hypodermic Toys	232
Musical Toys	233
Jewelry and Cosmetic Sets	234
Party Favors and Decorations	235
Playground and Outdoor Equipment	237
Premiums: Free Toys	241
Riding Toys	243
Swimming Pools and Swimming Toys	245

CONTENTS

Trains, Trucks, Automobiles and Flying
   Machines — 248
War Games — 250
Weapons — 251

Some General Rules and Suggestions — 254

Conclusion — 267

Bibliography — 271

Index — 279

Introduction

MY INTRODUCTION TO THE FRIGHTENING WORLD OF DANGEROUS toys came about in the course of my work as a lawyer, when several clients came to me to begin proceedings in the courts to recover legal compensation for injuries suffered by their children as a result of playing with hazardous toys. These incidents alerted me to the possibility that my own children were—unknown to me or my wife—running totally unreasonable risks of grave physical and psychological harm. Their toy box might well have been a death trap.

So I began to look very carefully at all of the toys already there and at those still coming into the house—elaborate gifts from friends and relatives, simple trinkets picked up as an afterthought at a supermarket, more thoughtful presents for holidays and birthdays. What I found appalled me.

Again, as a lawyer, I have had occasion to look into the network of common and statutory law that affords parents and children protection from dangerous toys. The law can have a preventive effect on toy accidents and injuries, and it provides a degree of redress to the injured once an accident has happened. I found a confusing labyrinth of federal and state agencies, enormous loopholes in the laws, and a morass of technical obstacles woven into the actual process of bringing suit against makers or sellers of dangerous toys. Again, I was appalled.

The immediate stimulus for this book was a summons (see endpaper) that came to me in December, 1968, to appear before the National Commission on Product Safety (NCPS) to give testimony concerning the legal protections from dangerous toys provided for children in this country. At those hearings I presented a lengthy written analysis of the legal doctrines currently in force in the field of consumer protection, together with some suggestions for legal reforms in this area. I also demonstrated to the NCPS how easy to get and how dangerous are those consumer products that perhaps we tend to take most for granted.

All I had done was to make a brief, one-man shopping tour in a major Boston toy store. In that short trip, I spotted, and bought, more than a dozen toys and playthings that I considered dangerous and totally unfit for open marketing. I took them with me to the hearings and showed them to the commissioners, their staff assistants, and the press. They, too, were appalled.

As a result of the publicity that attended this demonstration at the hearings, at least one toy—a dangerously flammable cloth tunnel—was ultimately taken off the market by governmental order. (Three months after the hearings, I was still able to order one at the toy industry's annual trade fair in New York.) A number of parents had been alerted, at least, to some of the dangers to be found in a very few of the thousands of toys for sale across the land.

It is vital to attract public attention specifically to the dangers of many toys if parents are to be well informed enough to protect their children from unreasonable risks. But, although the media have generally been very diligent in their coverage of such matters, continuing attention in the press and on television is unavoidably limited. Thus, neither informing the parents of specific toys nor checking toys already on sale is enough. Recall by the manufacturer, even under governmental compulsion, is not the answer either, for at best it can only bring back the items not yet sold. The fact that by the time this book is read a few of the toys mentioned may have been modified or discontinued by the manufacturer is not very reassuring since many toy boxes will continue to contain the earlier versions or models. The real solution, as this book will argue, lies in premarket testing. This, however, is for the future. The reader will have to make his own decisions, with the help of this book, about toys already in his home.

Given the limited usefulness of news coverage and the industry's own lethargy in the matter of strict safety controls, it is clear that something must be done.

It seems plain to me that as many people as possible should be informed about the dangers of injury, and even death, that many toys bear with them. This warning should be on as broad a basis as possible, and not limited to just a few specific items. It seems equally plain that the public should know just how limited is the protection that our present laws afford to the consumer, who in this case is the child. Most of us believe that patently dangerous items are banned from the market. As we will see, this is not true—especially with respect to toys. And the protective effect that a successful lawsuit against the maker or seller of a dangerous toy might have is all too often diluted by the fact that such suits can still be won or lost on technical grounds entirely unrelated to the merits of the case itself. Therefore, there is a special need for general public debate on reform to protect the child consumer and on reform of the common law governing manufacturers' and sellers' liability for the injuries their products cause to children.

This book, an answer to that need, has its limitations. Many toys other than those specifically mentioned contain obvious or latent hazards and are sold. Because I call some toys dangerous, however, does not imply that those *not* named are safe. Whether or not a toy is safe is a question that should be studied very carefully in each particular instance. The message of this book is to parents: Be careful, be suspicious—of every toy—from every country—from every manufacturer.

Most of us have neither the expertise nor the leisure to undertake safety studies on every possible toy we might come across or buy. The crying need is not merely for a heightened parental sensitivity to potential dangers. The need is for a fundamental reform in the whole pattern of toy marketing in this country. The federal government must undertake to provide compulsory premarket testing of all children's items. Such testing has been initiated in other areas. We have, for example, federal meat inspectors to check every piece of meat that moves in interstate commerce. Why not federal toy inspectors, too?

Parents *must* learn something about the hazards present in toys in order to guard against them as much as they possibly can. We *must* all make a concerted effort to call public and congressional attention to the need for remedial legislation, to the need for a strong and vigorously enforced set of premarketing safety standards.

If only one parent is alerted to the dangers of only one toy, if only one child is spared the mental or physical suffering or disfigurement that can be inflicted by one toy, the effort that has gone into this study will be justified.

Part 1

1

Toy Merchants vs. Toy Consumers

NOTHING CAN COMPARE WITH THE CLEAR, PURE JOY OF CHILDREN playing. We love to watch them: little girls splashing in the surf, boys in blue jeans racing after lazy fly balls in the summer sun, babies gurgling with delight over flashy, noisy rattles. And almost every one of us has, tucked away in the back cupboards of his mind, his own set of favorite childhood memories—the special toys that were, at least for a time, our own keys to a private world of innocent serenity, of mystery and adventure, and of happiness.

But this magical mystery world of toyland is also an enormous and successful business. In the United States today, the annual dollar volume of the toy industry is close to three billion. Toys are sold through every kind of retail outlet imaginable: the corner drugstore, where playthings turn up between the patent medicines and the tobacco counter; the supermarket, where toys are set up next to the check-out counters, ready to be dropped into the shopping bag on top of the breakfast cereals or under the cranberry juice. They can be found in sporting goods shops, hardware stores, department stores—even automobile supply houses. Toys are everywhere.

Toys are often, or even most of the time, a mixed blessing. Just as most of us have some special memories connected with the toys of our childhood, most of us also carry some long-forgotten scars, physical or psychological, caused by toys that gave us insult or injury in return for our affection. The United States Public Health Service has estimated that toys alone injure some 700,000 children in this country every year. Another half million are hurt by swings, and 200,000 more by slides. Of these injuries, many are not serious, of course; but far too many are. The face and head of the injured child take the brunt of a toy-related injury about forty percent of the time, the arms and legs about twenty-five percent, the hands in seventeen percent, and the eyes and feet each in four percent of the time. Besides very frequent cuts and bruises to the extremities and face, there are thousands of burnings, blindings, permanent disfigurements, puncture wounds, fractures, dislocations, poisonings, strains and sprains, and far too many deaths.

Toys with sharp cutting edges, easily shatterable parts, high explosive potential, lethal electrical hazards, dangerous flammability, unnecessary psychological risks, suffocation or strangulation capabilities, or fatally poisonous potential can be found by the dozens.

Parents are generally uninformed about these dangers, most of which are totally unnecessary and many of which are simply unknown to, or hidden from, the consumer. Retailers disclaim responsibility on the grounds that the variety and complexity, as well as the high volume and high turnover of toys, and the fact that most of them arrive in the store in an already prepacked form, make it impossible for the retail dealer to inspect, for safety and quality, those he sells. Of course, it is just as impossible for the customer. The toymakers themselves have taken only the most timid and tenuous steps toward imposing and observing voluntary safety standards; independent safety organizations are handicapped by many of the same factors that the retailers cite in self-exoneration; and governmental presence in the field is largely nonexistent. Yet the toy industry is booming.

If we turned the clock back to colonial America, we would find a nation in which toys themselves were rare, either homemade or imported from Great Britain or the Continent. But as industrial America expanded and metal production of all kinds of items developed, during and after the Civil War, toy manufacturing began to come into its own. Still, up to World War I, retail toy sales continued to be dominated by European imports that were chiefly German. However, when war broke out, American families constituted a large and growing market for toys—and foreign competition was reduced to nothing. Thus began the great development of the native toy industry.

The dimensions and pace of the growth of the domestic toy manufacturing industry are hard to measure, because statistics with any degree of reliability have been available only since 1954. The conditions that had prevailed since World War I—growing market and minimal foreign competition—continued in 1954. During that year, the domestic toy industry's dollar sales volume, at wholesale, was $516 million. But by 1969, the dollar volume of toy sales, at wholesale, was well over $2 billion, reflecting a dramatic fourfold increase. And this latter figure, viewed conservatively, indicates that the annual *retail* volume of toy sales is now not less than $3 billion.

Between 1955 and 1965, the toy industry was one of the fastest-growing industries in America. Stimulated by the postwar baby boom and by the rising standards of living and of leisure to which the American consumer had so quickly become accustomed, the industry expanded vigorously. The number of children was increasing very rapidly, and their parents had more spending money than ever before. This buying spree has not abated, and in the last five years the toy industry has been growing at more than ten percent per year —an astonishing fifty-four percent increase in that short period. Despite the general economic slump on Wall Street, the toy industry reported in December of 1970 that business was seventeen percent ahead of 1969.

Such phenomenal growth has resulted in handsome financial rewards to the toymakers. Traditionally, the toymaker has been the prototypical little man—the independent manufacturer with a good idea and a rugged determination to make a go of it. And the growth potential in the industry has been such that if the idea were *really* good and the determination *really* rugged, the independent man could strike it rich. This is exemplified by the story of Berkeley Compton. In 1964, Compton couldn't afford to buy Christmas presents for his twelve children, but by 1969 he was a millionaire. His company, Funtastic, which makes "Jupiter and the Go-Go Gun"—a contemporary version of an old American Indian stick-and-propeller toy—was started with $5,000 capital and three employees. The "Jupiter and the Go-Go Gun" went on the market in 1965, caught on, and made Compton rich. Or consider the even more impressive history of the Mattel Company, which began as a husband-and-wife team that put toys together out of metal scraps in the years just before World War II. Today, Mattel is the largest toy company in the world, with a work force of more than 14,000 persons and an annual income of more than $200 million. There are many other toy companies, moreover, that could tell similar success stories.

The scope of the industry can be further illustrated by the fact that in November and December of each year, six out of every ten adults in the United States purchase at least one toy. This, of course, is the peak buying period for children's things, since Christmas has become a major commercial season. More than half of all the dollars spent each year on toys are spent in this two-month period, in which almost half of all the toys bought annually are purchased. The extent of the rush on toys during this season is so great that one prominent toy retailer once thought it well to advise his fellow merchants not to lose sales through inadvertence. He had found that by providing much larger shopping carts for his customers, the volume of business shot up dramatically—the toy buyers were buying as many toys as would fit into the carts. Changing the size in no way diminished their enthusiasm, and they continued to fill the buggies up to the brim.

Today, the average American over sixteen years of age spends about $21 a year on toys. In sales volume, the toy industry ranks with new car purchases. Detroit, of course, has to comply with federal safety regulations, while the toymakers have nothing at all comparable to contend with. On the highways, strict traffic rules control the flow and interaction of vehicles and require that anything on the road at least meet minimal performance standards. In the home, where many more accidents occur than on the roads, there is almost no protection written into law that has been effective in reducing the hazards associated with dangerous playthings.

Comparing the regulations applicable to automobiles and toys leads to further understanding of the vastness of the toy industry. For it is not usually very difficult to classify a given piece of machinery; it is either a vehicle or something else. But what is a "toy"? If we begin with the assumption that a toy is anything a child is apt to play with, then we open up an almost illimitable field of articles. Is a blanket a toy? What about air rifles? Archery sets? Are they toys, or sporting equipment, or weapons? Or all three? The courts have run into enormous analytical problems in trying to classify and categorize the less obvious playthings.

Toys can be anything from teething rings to chemistry sets. Nightlights carry the familiar face of Mickey Mouse—does that make them toys? What about toy stoves, which get hot enough to sear the flesh right off the hands of the children who touch them? I have seen a number of toys advertised both in the children's section and in the household or sporting goods sections of major mail-order catalogs, and the logic of this duplication is clear enough: the greater the exposure, the greater the sales. And this principle extends to items as potentially lethal as crossbows, a weapon once banned by medieval popes as inhumane, but now to be found in toy departments.

This confusion of categories contributes to the vastness of the industry and allows toys to turn up for sale in almost every conceivable retail outlet. They are even given away as prizes or premiums, and I know of toy parties run along the lines of the more familiar women's cosmetics parties, in which the hostess gets a free set for herself while the company salesman uses the occasion to promote his products to her invited guests.

In addition to the baby boom, the relatively high standard of living in America, and the uncommonly varied number of retail outlets available to toy manufacturers, advertising has helped make the toy industry such an economic success. All parents who own a television set must be aware of the impact advertising has on toy sales. Saturday mornings are especially filled with children's programs, and the programs themselves are crammed with advertising. Every sophisticated Madison Avenue technique available is brought into play, and the sales pitch is directed straight at the child. It is a startling phenomenon that children are much more likely to follow the commercials than they are to be interested in the show itself. In any case, television advertising for children hits the mark, and the result is that children display an amazing ability to recognize and to demand from their parents the items that they have been conditioned to "need" by hard-sell Saturday morning toy advertising.

The greatest danger in this process is that the child's feeling of "need" makes the parent's purchase of the "needed" toy nearly inevitable; the pressure on the parents is almost irresistible. But this means that parents are shopping for toys, not on the basis of their own mature and considered judgment as to what is best for the child and most reasonable in terms of the family budget, but on the basis of the demand created by the media. It is easy to see how, in the unfolding of this process, safety considerations carry no weight at all.

Estimates made at the time of the Toy Fair held in New York City in March, 1969, indicated that, for example, the Mattel Company was planning to spend $11 million on advertising, Ideal Toy Corporation $8 million, Remco Industries, Inc., $5 million, Kenner Products at least $5.5 million, and Hasbro about the same.* These enormous budgets—mostly spent on television advertising—are worked out with superb skill and tested on panels of selected children before being put on the air. Most of the TV spots are broadcast during the three or four months before Christmas. The fundamental philosophy of such advertising was expressed in a comment by the advertising director for Ideal, who told *The New York Times,* "We'll pound away at the kids for thirteen weeks, hoping to build some memorability."

"Memorability" works, and it is a startling fact that an astonishing number of American children buy their own toys. An exhaustive study commissioned by the Toy Manufacturers of America (TMA) reported that children themselves buy one-third of all the toys sold in America, while—according to the same study—only three percent of the parents reported that their children bought their own playthings regularly, and only thirty percent had any knowledge of their children buying toys on their own at all. Hence, while the industry knows quite accurately that children themselves are a direct market for at least one-third of the three-billion-dollar American toy business, the parents are not fully aware of this.

Many parents thus know little or nothing about the toys their children are buying. This leaves the marketing experts at liberty to devise a sales message that will appeal directly to the child—free from the interference of mature adult judgment. The implications of this for toy safety are unsettling.

* *The New York Times,* March 16, 1969.

For the toymaker is presently free to sell directly to the child and to sell him almost anything, no matter how intrinsically hazardous it may be unless it is used according to precise instructions. At the same time, the industry assumes that children's toys are, and should be, used only under parental supervision; that parents should not, and do not, let their children play with toys that are "too advanced" for them (meaning, usually, "too dangerous"); and that, in cases where injuries do occur, the resulting harm must have been the fault either of the child who "abused" the toy or of the parent who was not concerned enough to watch over the child who was using it. How anyone can expect a young child to have any "legitimate" use for a two-dollar chemistry set that includes poisonous substances packaged in candy-wrapped containers, or to be comfortable with an electric metal-casting set that can burn him to the bone, is incomprehensible. But the sales pitch and the high-pressure advertising are aimed at this unsuspecting market, and made as directly attractive as possible.

Besides the dangers inherent in direct selling to children, the multitude of confusing and misleading claims—this time, aimed at adults—which are put out by toy manufacturers in order to stimulate sales to grown-ups, is at least equally irresponsible. Since seventy percent of all toys are purchased by adults, the child is in the unique position of being a "captive consumer"—most of his possessions are bought for him by someone else. The captivity of the ultimate consumer is all the more important when we consider that forty percent of all toys are bought for children under five years of age and that eighty percent of all toys are bought for children under ten.

Parents of very young children are normally concerned about two things when they buy toys: that the toy be fun, and that it also be safe. No parent would willingly buy his child something harmful, nor do parents buy things they feel would simply bore the child. The sales pitch to parents is therefore tailored with this two-fold requirement in mind. The most thrilling and exciting toy is also advertised as "completely safe" or "harmless" or "supersafe." The thrill instinct is to be aroused while the safety instinct is satisfied. What too often happens is that the thrill is real enough, while the safety characteristics are illusory.

This two-pronged and often contradictory sales approach is geared especially to impulse buying. Impulse buying is cultivated, nurtured, and encouraged to such a great extent that one is tempted to ask why the toy industry is afraid to let its customers think the matter over for a little while. The wrapping is made as seductive as possible, and usually it cannot be opened for inspection.

Impulse buying is a puzzling phenomenon, and the toy industry is well aware that the motivations of parents who buy their products are often very subtle and complex. Most toy buyers say that they buy what they do because the child wants it. This is so at least half the time (and it incidentally proves the value of advertising to children directly), but most toy buyers have personal reasons as well. Some look for playthings that "take me back to my own childhood." Others are hoping to find something that "will keep the children quiet and occupied for a while"; still others are mainly looking for toys that are fun, or for "educational" playthings. The use of contemporary marketing analysis and sales promotion techniques to satisfy as many as possible of these various desires has been brought to a very high level of sophistication by the toy industry, which also realizes that safety is among those qualities most parents like to find in everything they buy for their children.

The TMA study referred to earlier disclosed that most of us who buy toys do it fairly haphazardly. When going into the store, twenty-four percent of toy buyers have no intention of buying a toy at all, while another nineteen percent have no particular toy in mind and have only a vague intention of buying a toy of any kind. Sixty-three percent of all the adults who buy toys start out with no particular price range in mind. Over a given year, more than half of all the toy buyers make their decision after they have browsed around awhile in the store, and eighty-five percent of the people who set out to shop for toys visit only one store.

This tendency toward impulse buying accounts for the efforts toymakers make—very successful efforts, by the way—to distribute their wares among as many different types of stores as possible. There is a belief in the toy industry, and one which seems to be verified by experience, that putting toys in locations where parents shop regularly, like drugstores and supermarkets, has benefits even greater than those normally associated with immediate impulse sales. Regular proximity to the toy counter—passing it every time you check out of the supermarket or stop to pick up aspirin—creates a familiarity with and eventually a "need" for the playthings. This is a practical application of a standard advertising ploy: Keep reminding the consumer of your product, and sooner or later, he'll want to try it out.

Because so many toys are bought on impulse, safety considerations are usually ignored by buyers. Most of us tend to think that toys are usually safe anyway, and we don't anticipate that any real or serious risks to our children's health or lives will result from the toys we buy for them. This is a fundamental mistake. In addition, the impulse buyer is not a comparative shopper. He reaches for the toy that "looks good right now."

Even those of us who do have a minimal safety standard in the backs of our minds are routinely satisfied if the toymaker has put a safety claim on the box, or has included some expression like "educational" or "creative"—words we associate most with intellectual pursuits.

The toy industry is further shaped through an abnormally high incidence of planned obsolescence. Far too many toys are very cheaply built and very expensively sold. The toy that quickly breaks creates a need for a replacement. If a toy has broken, to little Harry's great and vocal disappointment, it is natural for Harry's mother to replace it as soon as possible. Toys which break easily, however, often break dangerously; parts come flying off into eyes, or end up being swallowed. Plastic edges cut. Moving parts catch fingers when the covering materials fail. All of these are dangerous situations.

Since there are relatively few staple toys, the strongest competition among the toy manufacturers is to search for a new twist to an old plaything. Consumers get used to this "neophilia" and pick up the habit of browsing regularly through the toy department looking for the latest idea. Hence there are constant changes in design, in coloring, in packaging, all aimed at turning what is fairly old hat into something new and different and exciting—the very conditions on which impulse buying thrives.

High turnover is essential to the toy industry, for if the same long-lasting toys were in the stores year in and year out, retail toy sales would drop off drastically. The problem for the industry is that children don't really need a constant parade of new and different toys. Most of us know how a three-year-old can be delighted with and absorbed in a cardboard carton or a rag doll, but few of us realize that many complex and highly sophisticated toys—those that look so interesting to us in the store—may really only bore our children. The reason why they find them less than captivating is that when the toy does all the playing, then their developing skills and inventive imaginations are crowded out of the field. This can have the undesirable effect of turning the active child into a passive onlooker.

Parents ought to demand a greater degree of sturdiness and durability from their children's toys, as well as suitable interest-sustaining characteristics and over-all safety. But as we have seen, the marketing practices of the toy industry are all geared to precisely opposite requirements. This should not surprise us, for if toys were safer, sturdier, and could keep our children amused far longer, then the toy sales curve would begin to dip and profits would unavoidably decline.

Novelty is a constant theme in the articles and advertisements that fill trade journals and magazines. New products are promoted by their manufacturers to retail dealers as "irresistible" or "sure to sell on sight" or "new and different." Some companies make a special point of stressing that "we sell parents" or of ballyhooing (and inflating) the extent to which their newer products are or will be heavily advertised on television.

Just as impulse buying has dangers because of the lack of inspection by parents before buying, so the same dangers are present when toys are bought and sold by mail. Here again, the pitch is usually made directly to the child. Mail-order toy advertisements are found in comic books, in popular children's magazines, and in many adult periodicals. The items you can order by mail include guns, knives, fireworks, and explosives; and they are often advertised as "thrilling" or "fun" or "exciting."

In summary, the toy industry is vast and growing, and it works chiefly through impulse buying based on hard-sell advertising directed at the children themselves and on sophisticated packaging intended to capture the parents' immediate interest. We can't blame the toymakers for trying hard to sell their wares, but we have a right to be angry when we find that the wares in question have been shoddily or dangerously produced, or advertised in a fraudulent and misleading way. Still, all too many of us remain children when it comes to buying toys for our own youngsters, and we are too easily seduced ourselves by bright colors and exaggerated promotional claims.

Every toy buyer must be alert to the dangers associated with the millions of toys produced by the $3-billion-a-year toy industry. This is a powerful economic concentration using all the modern sales and marketing techniques at its command to maintain its phenomenal rate of growth. We—the consumers—are up against a giant, and the giant holds most of the cards.

We, however, hold a trump: caution. There must be strict and effective governmental control over the toy industry, but the primary effort in ensuring our children's safety right now will have to come from us. Armed with a knowledge of the dangers many toys present, we can all be more careful shoppers and more attentive parents; and until the government begins to exercise its proper responsibilities for children's health and welfare, we can try to protect our children from the "toys that don't care" as best we can.

2

How Toys Are Unsafe

I am not pretending for one moment that there are not unsafe and hazardous toys on the market. . . . We think they are being kept to a very, very low percentage. . . . But there are hazardous toys coming on the market today.
                        Jerome M. Fryer
                        Toy Manufacturers of America
                        May 22, 1969
                        Hearings before House Subcommittee on Commerce and Finance, p. 148.

Too many unreasonably hazardous articles for children are for sale in the marketplace today. Hardly any industry standards exist to deal with their design and manufacture.
                        Arnold B. Elkind, Chairman
                        National Commission on Product Safety
                        May 20, 1969
                        Hearings before House Subcommittee on Commerce and Finance, p. 15.

IT WILL PROBABLY MATTER VERY LITTLE TO THE MOTHER WHOSE daughter has just had her eye shot out by a "harmless" plaything to say that it is difficult to set up formal categories and classifications of the many ways in which toys and other children's articles can be unsafe. The permutations are limitless.

TOYS THAT DON'T CARE

A toy that is dangerous because it is poorly designed may be even more so when badly made, or misleadingly advertised, or inaccurately labeled, or foolishly and irresponsibly sold to or for children who are far too young to appreciate, or to defend themselves against, any of these multiple hazards.

The toy industry allows children to flirt with pain, injury, psychological damage, and death in many ways. Many dangerous and unsuitable toys may already have found their way into your home.

In selecting or reviewing new or favorite toys, here are some questions to ask about them:

(1) Are necessary warnings omitted, improper directions provided, or misleading advertising used in connection with the toy?

(2) Is this toy's basic design fundamentally safe?

(3) How well is the toy put together—was a safe design properly executed, or has it been "adjusted" in order to save a little money along the production line? (This question will probably be impossible for most parents to answer—but it suggests one very important way in which toys become dangerous.)

(4) Is the toy inherently dangerous (a firecracker, for example) or is it dangerous if sold or given to children too young to understand its hazards?

(5) Is it likely to break or fall apart, and if so, what dangers will the pieces or materials present?

(6) Is it easily turned from its advertised purpose into creative but dangerous misuse?

(7) Is it poorly packaged—is the box confusing or misleading—or dangerously marketed?

(8) Could this toy be carrying disease?

(9) Could the psychological effects of the toy be disturbing or damaging?

These questions tend to overlap, but as the following examples make plain, each of them makes us freshly aware of certain danger zones. The wise parent will do his best to keep these questions in mind the next time Christmas or a family birthday rolls around.

(1) INADEQUATE WARNINGS, IMPROPER DIRECTIONS, AND IRRESPONSIBLE ADVERTISING

Impulse buying stimulates marketing practices that make dangerous toys even more dangerous and that leave fundamentally safe toys open to dangerous misuse. While it is difficult to see why the toy merchants *must* sell dangerous playthings, it is even harder to understand why they persist in doing so without adequate warning to the public.

The junior Von Braun or Fermi with his rocket fuels or chemistry set, the young Davy Crockett with his air rifle, and the little Miss Homemaker with her "make-believe" but functioning electrical appliances are dangerous people. No sane parent would send his son to play in a university chemistry laboratory, nor would a thinking mother let her little girl run loose in the kitchen to play with the electric stove. But by failing to warn parents of the clear and obvious dangers of buying toys for children too young to use them safely, the industry is encouraging just this kind of danger-fraught mistake. My study has convinced me that most children are definitely too young for many of their playthings.

The tension between sales and safety that is implicit in this problem becomes clearer when we remember that more than eighty percent of all toy recipients are younger than ten years old. The intelligent toymaker knows that he isn't going to sell very many working electrical toys, or chemistry sets, or other sophisticated (and expensive) items, if he is constantly conveying the message to parents that they should not be given to children who are too young for them. And so, generally speaking, we simply cannot depend upon the toy retailers or manufacturers to get this information out to those who need it most. Their business is selling toys, not giving the kind of advice that, in their view, might "needlessly" cut down their market and otherwise decrease sales. For when it comes to a choice between ethics and profit, toymakers fully appreciate that you can't be a model of business ethics if your ethics have put you out of business. This sort of conflict is one of the most compelling arguments for mandatory and government-supervised premarketing controls and official safety standards. Controls like these would tend to eliminate the dangers *before* the toys come on the market and are sold—and sold hard—to the public at large.

There are many instances, including some that have come to my attention as a lawyer, in which failure to give adequate warnings about the dangers of toys led to tragedy or near tragedy.

One such case involved two little girls playing with a Kenner "Easy-Bake Oven." The Easy-Bake uses a 100-watt light bulb as a source of heat, and while the children were taking the toy apart, one of them stuck her hand in the empty bulb socket while the oven was still plugged in. Result: damaging electrical shock and burns. The Topper Corporation of New Jersey makes a similar oven, and has the effrontery to call its product the "Suzy Homemaker Super-Safety Oven."

When a major manufacturer of electrical appliances sells ovens or other potentially harmful apparatus, as a rule it will provide careful instructions to the customer. The dangers are obvious to anyone, and everyone knows that electricity is not something to fool around with. Not so the toy industry. The advertising and the packaging for toys like these often go to great lengths to assure parents that these items are acceptable gifts for small children. This approach is diametrically contrary to that of several national safety organizations, which have gone to enormous lengths to provide proper cautions for families with both young children and real household appliances—recommending, for instance, that all household electric outlets be capped when not in use, that cords and connections be regularly inspected for fraying and other wear and tear.

The only electric plaything I found that contained any acknowledgment that such toys are real electrical appliances with real life dangers was an item called " 'Snippy' Safe Electric Paper Scissors"! Even this item, however, gave safety cautions second or third billing at best. The outside of the cardboard box it came in announced that the contents were "Safe—NO SHARP POINTS!" (Fig. 1) Underneath, where it could be read, but only after the unit was removed from the box is: "Caution! The National Safety Council warns never to use any electrical appliance in or near water, or with wet hands. Remember, Snippy is an electrical appliance just like a radio, iron or electric razor." (Fig. 2)

It is common practice for the outside packaging of such items to stress the safety of the product. Warnings of hazards, if any are given, are usually hidden elsewhere.

In this connection, the "Magic Cool Oven," which the author demonstrated before the National Commission on Product Safety, is but one of many examples. A large blurb on the box containing the toy oven says, "Outside safe for little fingers to touch." This stove is metal and uses heating coils instead of light bulbs. Hidden on the inside of the oven was a warning, stamped in the metal and only barely legible, that said, "Caution, contact with hands inside of oven or inside of cooling chamber may cause burns." Elsewhere on

Fig. 1. "Safe" electric play scissors.

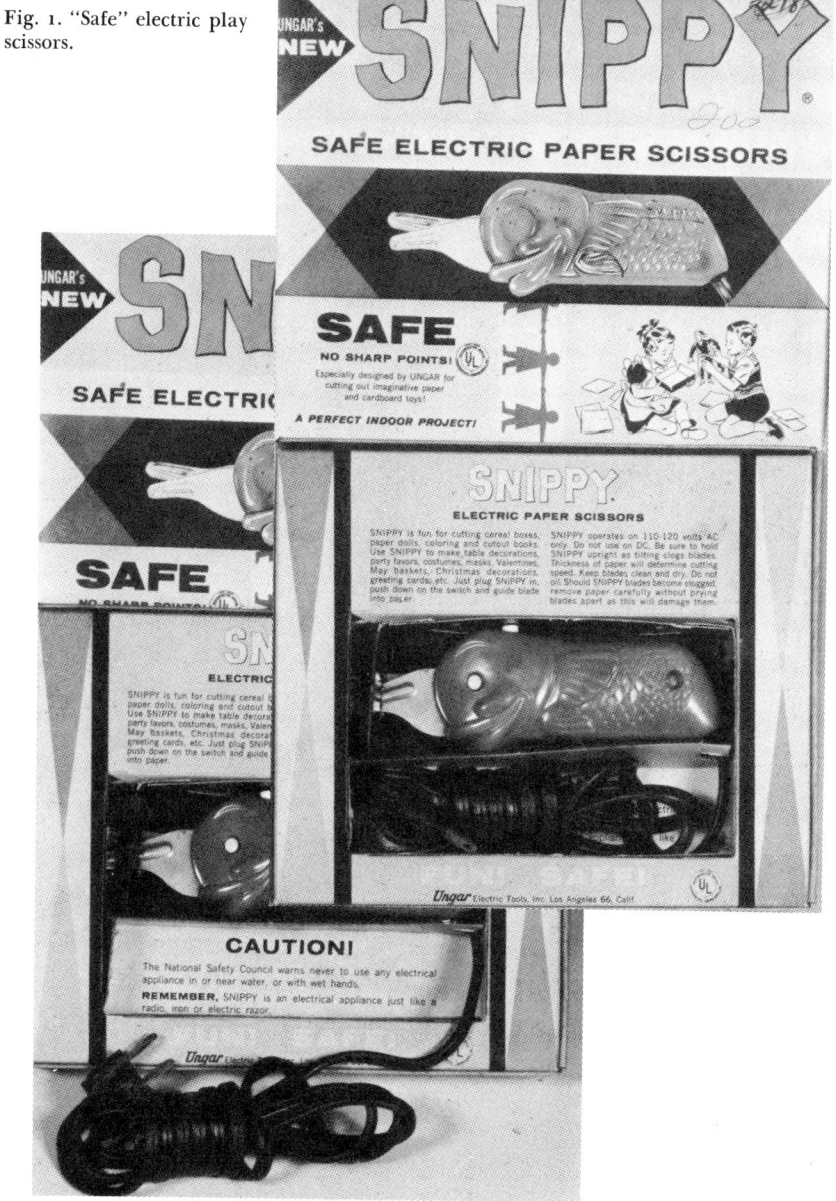

Fig. 2. "Safe" electric play scissors' container with cord removed disclosing warning of hazards.

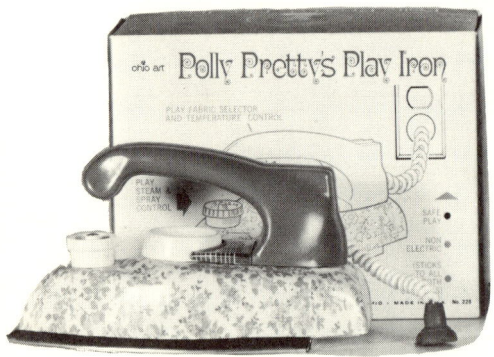

Figs. 3–6. 110-volt household current—"Safe" play irons.

the product, it said, "Remove plug before cleaning"—but can we count on tots to do that? And if you tipped the oven completely over, you would find on its bottom the statement, "Do not immerse in water and clean with damp cloth only." This was certainly a *minimal* and functionally useless set of warnings.

Electrical toys—almost without exception—carry no age recommendations on them whatsoever. To do so, of course, would at once cut down their sales potential by almost eighty percent. Electrical toys are sold because the parents who buy them believe that they are safer than the real things, which all of us appreciate can be lethal to unattended children. The manufacturers, by suggesting that the toys are safer than the real things, help to create a "need" for the toys. If parents realized that these toys were just as dangerous, they wouldn't buy them. Any prudent mother would rather teach her daughter how to cook on a real stove and under her own supervision than let her play, unsupervised, with a toy stove that is at least as dangerous. But in the economics of the toy industry, the practice is first to create the need ("safe and just like Mother's"), and then to sell the product that fills the need.

The same criticism applies equally to some makers of chemistry sets, who all too often market their products with no age recommendations, for the same profit-oriented reasons.

Some manufacturers of electrical toys, in addition to the negative failure to make any mention of age limits or of the dangers that could result from use of these appliances, are also fond of a positively misleading advertising gimmick: the abuse of the Underwriters' Laboratory (UL) seal of approval. The author has seen electrical toys that carry the UL seal and are labeled as "safe" or even "supersafe" and that deserve neither the adjectives nor even the seal itself. Some of them utterly fail to meet the UL standards; others meet them in part but use the seal misleadingly in their advertising and packaging; others still are inherently dangerous in ways that the seal does not purport to deal with. The confusions, mistakes, and misconceptions that bother so many shoppers trying to figure out just what exactly it means to have a UL seal (or a *Good Housekeeping* or *Parents' Magazine* seal of approval) are so fascinating and so widespread that they form the basis of a separate chapter, Chapter Four.

As a further illustration of misleading advertising and packaging, it might be well to mention another electrical toy which, like the ovens, is potentially dangerous. The Ohio Art Company puts out a plaything called "The Westinghouse Play Electric Iron," which comes in a box proclaiming: "You can be *sure* if it's Westinghouse," and going on to state, in large print, "THIS TOY IRON REALLY HEATS AND IRONS, BUT WILL NOT GET HOT ENOUGH TO CAUSE BURNS." They're right in saying that it doesn't get very hot. But it also lacks a "safety guard" around the plug to prevent the child's fingers from coming into contact with the live outlet to which the iron is to be connected. (Fig. 3) Other companies provide the guard; this one—Ohio Art—does not. Why not? Ohio Art certainly recognizes the risks of their electric play iron since they make another version entitled "Polly Pretty's Play Iron," which is advertised as "safe" because it is *"non-electric."* (Fig. 4) In view of their position that a non-electric iron is safe, consider yet another Ohio Art creation called "Miss Petite Electrical Iron," which uses real live household current and on the carton emphasizes its use as "safe play." (Fig. 5)

Or consider the "Beauty Queen Electric Iron" manufactured by Gabriel Industries, Inc., of New York. The packaging for this beauty says "Safe Play," displays the UL seal, and comments that the item is "safety designed." And to make sure the child knows it's the real thing and to ensure many trips to the wall outlet for the child, the package also has a drawing showing a plug inserted into a 110-volt outlet. (Fig. 6) The promotional material for these irons, as well as for other electrical toys, employs a favorite toy merchants' gimmick. It stresses one safe feature, the iron's moderate temperature, while ignoring more serious hazards.

Further, the sellers of electric toys rarely bother to inform the parent that safety plugs and—best of all—converters are available. The converters change high voltage AC house current at the wall outlet to safer, cooler low DC power. (Britain requires conversion devices on all electric toys that use household current.)

Another warning case, one in which the author was personally involved as a trial lawyer, involved BB guns. The Daisy Air Rifle Company, in its national advertising geared to young boys (in *Boy's Life,* for instance), has for years promoted the indoor use of their BB guns and suggested that such use was perfectly safe. Simply set up a target—a box—in the basement and fire away. No mention of the possibilities of ricochet. The obvious happened, and one of the two youths involved (a bystander at the time) lost an eye.

Subsequently, and possibly after other accidents of a like nature, Daisy modified the indoor-use ad by advising boys to stuff the target box with rags. The advertising still neglects to mention the dangers of ricochet, and of course, the danger is just as great once you admit the possibility that not every shot will hit the rag-stuffed box. Even marksmen occasionally miss. In this situation, every bystander, including the supervising parent in the room, is still in danger if the young Daniel Boone is content to follow Daisy's recommendations.

One hospital alone—the Charlotte (N.C.) Eye, Ear and Throat Hospital—reported 81 cases of eye injuries due specifically to BB guns over a nine-year period (1953–62). A significant number of these injuries resulted from ricochet. Yet Daisy continues to recommend the indoor use of air rifles. I doubt that a weapon like this, sold as a toy in many places, should *ever* be used indoors. But Daisy differs and its advertising encourages youngsters to use the air guns indoors: "Now rainy days can be fun days"; "Daisy has asked us dealers to let parents know about family BB-gun shooting indoors or outside." It is certainly hard to argue under these circumstances that the consumer has been properly educated by the company with respect to the dangerous propensities of its product.

For those who still think that air rifles are toys that can be safely used by youngsters—at least by youngsters of a certain age—without constant supervision and careful safety measures, one further note is in order. Officials at the Daisy Company have testified under oath in court that when they test fire their guns in their own plants by shooting them at concrete walls, the company marksmen are *required* to wear safety glasses. Safety for the plant, but not for the kids who read *Boy's Life*. Now, Daisy has at last come out with one model in its air-rifle series that is sold with accompanying safety goggles. And why only *one* model?

The point of these cases—and there are hundreds of others like them—is that advertising copy, whether in catalogs or on television, in magazines or printed on the package itself, is not designed to promote safety, but to promote sales. Advertising and promotional material are not turned out by safety engineers, but by writers and craftsmen whose expertise is in the art of persuasion. Their job is to make the toy *interesting* and *salable*, to overcome buyer resistance. And as a result of this narrow approach to the marketing of playthings, unsafe toys continue to be promoted and sold as "safe," "harmless," and so on.

When the toymakers are confronted with these specific abuses and with the general allegation that they don't often give adequate warnings to parents and buyers, one of their stock replies is that their playthings would be "perfectly safe if the directions were followed." This view has flaws.

For one thing, an essential requirement of any adequate

set of directions for use of sophisticated toys is an intelligent recommendation as to the age of the child who should be allowed to play with them. Any directions that leave this out are inadequate from the beginning, since a partial or incomplete warning or direction is often worse than none at all. Furthermore, children are not cautious toy users. They are often too young to read or to understand these directions, instructions and cautions that do come with their toys. And when they can read and understand them, the prohibitions often operate as temptations: the unlimited ingenuity and natural contrariness of children is a combination that frequently leads them to try out the forbidden just because it *is* the forbidden; and forbidding something, of course, is the best of all possible ways to plant something in a child's mind.

Children are like the rest of us in that we tend to disregard complex brochures and directions so long as everything is working; only when something goes wrong do we turn to the directions. This sort of self-dispensation from instruction (and from the delay in play that learning *how* to play involves) is endemic to human nature, and small wonder that children are not immune from it. The danger is that the "something going wrong" may have already maimed the youngster *before* he got to look it up in the little booklet.

A different, and more frequent argument put forth by toy industry spokesmen is that the major share of the blame belongs to parents. Many injuries, they say, could have been avoided with greater parental vigilance and supervision. This is undoubtedly true, and it is one of the aims of this book to stimulate that vigilance. However, most toymakers are well aware that as a practical matter of fact, it is often the case that parents do not, and cannot, watch over their children at all times. The toy manufacturers know this, but they ignore it and go ahead with the design, production, and sale of toys that are so dangerous that they are not safe unless used *only* with a parent there to supervise.

Certainly the toy merchants have an obligation to work harder to awaken parents to the dangers their products present. If the parents *do* wake up to the dangers some kinds of toys present, perhaps the makers of such toys will be compelled to stop making them. In any case, part of the process of growing up and vital to the very essence of play, is being left to one's own devices, to have fun, to imagine, and to learn. Toys that can burn, blind or kill have no place in this process.

It is one thing not to give necessary warnings or directions; it is a worse practice to seduce parents into a false sense of security with positively misleading advertising. Thus, dangerous items are labeled "safe" or "harmless" or contain misleading directions for use, and the hard sell is used to move them off the retail shelves and into the playrooms of unsuspecting families.

Mr. William G. Cole's son, Donald, was the victim of just such a misleading practice. Nine-year-old Donald was permanently blinded in one eye by an exploding cap device advertised as "harmless." The device was "played with" by throwing a feathered projectile into the air with one or several caps inside that exploded on contact with the ground. Mr. Cole, the father, told the National Commission on Product Safety how, after the tragedy, he went to the retailer from whom the toy was purchased and asked that it be taken off the shelves. However, checking at a later date, he found the item still being offered for sale.

Although one tragic story like the Coles' should be lesson enough, here are a few more examples of potentially dangerous toys that have been misleadingly promoted:

• A boomerang (originally an Australian weapon designed for killing small game), comes from the Wham-o Manufacturing Company in a box with no directions but these: "Returns to you! Hold with flat side down and experiment!" This heavy plastic model, with its sharp edges, requires—like all boomerangs—a large open space for use. What is more natural for a child than to try it out in the schoolyard or the local park? Directions to "experiment" are not likely to induce prudent use or to prevent the easily foreseeable accidents that such a device can cause.

There are, for example, boomerang-type toys sold which, while probably not completely safe, are made of lighter and therefore safer plastic than others. For example, I purchased one in a five-and-dime store for nine cents that came embossed with the following instructions: "Caution: throw in open area away from windows and other children." If this lighter and softer, and more inexpensive boomerang can carry a warning, why can't the more dangerous and more expensive ones?

• A "Zooper," another projectile toy, derived from the boomerang, comes from PBI, Inc., with directions which include the note that "Your Zooper is a versatile flying toy. Use your ingenuity to find new ways of flying it"—accompanied by a picture of a father and several small children throwing Zoopers at one another. While the Zooper is relatively light, it still has sharp edges and for this reason it is potentially blinding. The packaging gives the impression that it is safe for kids "of all ages" and offers a pictorial inducement to mayhem. In advertisements forwarded to the trade, the manufacturer expressly states it is safe. (Figs. 7 and 8)

• An archery set, sold by F.A.O. Schwarz in their nationwide chain of stores and imported from Arco Falc of Milan, Italy, contains a fiberglass bow and wooden arrows with removable rubber tips. It comes in a box with a picture on it of small children standing between the archer and his target. It is bad enough to make a bow strong enough to put an untipped arrow through the double thickness of two sides of a corrugated box (figs. 9 and 10), but the irresponsibility involved in the picture—which induces a totally false sense of security and constitutes an open invitation to accidents—is beyond belief. (Fig. 11) In its catalogs, F.A.O. Schwarz has run a color advertisement of the set with the proclamation that it is "harmless"; and in case I hadn't seen the catalog, my *sales slip* said it again: "a harmless" archery set! (Fig. 12)

I wrote to the then-president of F.A.O. Schwarz, Mr. Charles Vesey, about this questionable advertising. After some delay, he acknowledged my letter but made no commitment to correct the copy either in the catalog or on the box. The same set is advertised—still as harmless—in the 1970–71 winter edition of the F.A.O. Schwarz catalog. By the way, you will note the retail catalog price is $8.95; at the TMA Toy Fair I learned the wholesale price was under $2.00. Not a bad markup! The Winter 1971 Catalog did make some concession to child protection. The new president, Ernest M. Thauer, in a catalog letter to parents, announced that for the first time F.A.O. Schwarz "can provide for your child . . . life insurance" [!]

There is a further problem related to the sale of archery sets—and other weapons—to children: These articles are not toys. Properly used by people who have been trained by competent instructors and who are carefully supervised while shooting, those weapons can indeed be instruments of sport and skill. But they are not something for children to play with, uninstructed and unattended. I would favor legislation that would severely restrict the sale of any form of weaponry for children—bows and arrows, real or air guns. And such a law could easily be enacted in the many states that do not yet have one. The Massachusetts Act (General Laws, Chapter 269, Section 12A, 12B) is an example. Section 12A forbids the sale of an air rifle to any person under sixteen or the furnishing of one to such a minor except by "the parent, guardian or adult teacher or instructor," while 12B forbids persons under eighteen to be in the possession of an air rifle while in a public place unless duly licensed or accompanied by an adult.

Fig. 7. "Zooper"—"The amazing new outdoor toy" advertised to the wholesale trade as "safe, flexible plastic."

Fig. 8. "Zoopers" shown thrown and flying in all directions on package for retail trade.

Fig. 9. Author taking aim with so-called "harmless" bow and arrow set at hearings of National Commission on Product Safety.

Fig. 10. The result of author's shooting "harmless" arrow with the easily removable suction tip missing.

810-228 HARMLESS ARCHERY **8.95**
...e of the world's oldest sports, still pop-
...r and a challenge to all ages. Young
...bin Hoods will have fun galore shoot-
... the four 26" arrows at the colorful
... square bullseye target. 54" fiberglas
...w. Target has removable wood legs.
...nport) Ship. wt. 5 lbs.

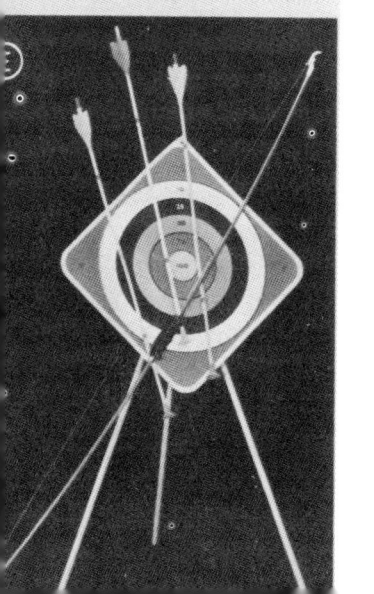

Fig. 11. Picture on box of bow and arrow set, showing children by-standers in unsafe position.

Fig. 12. Catalog entry describing potentially dangerous bow and arrow set as "harmless."

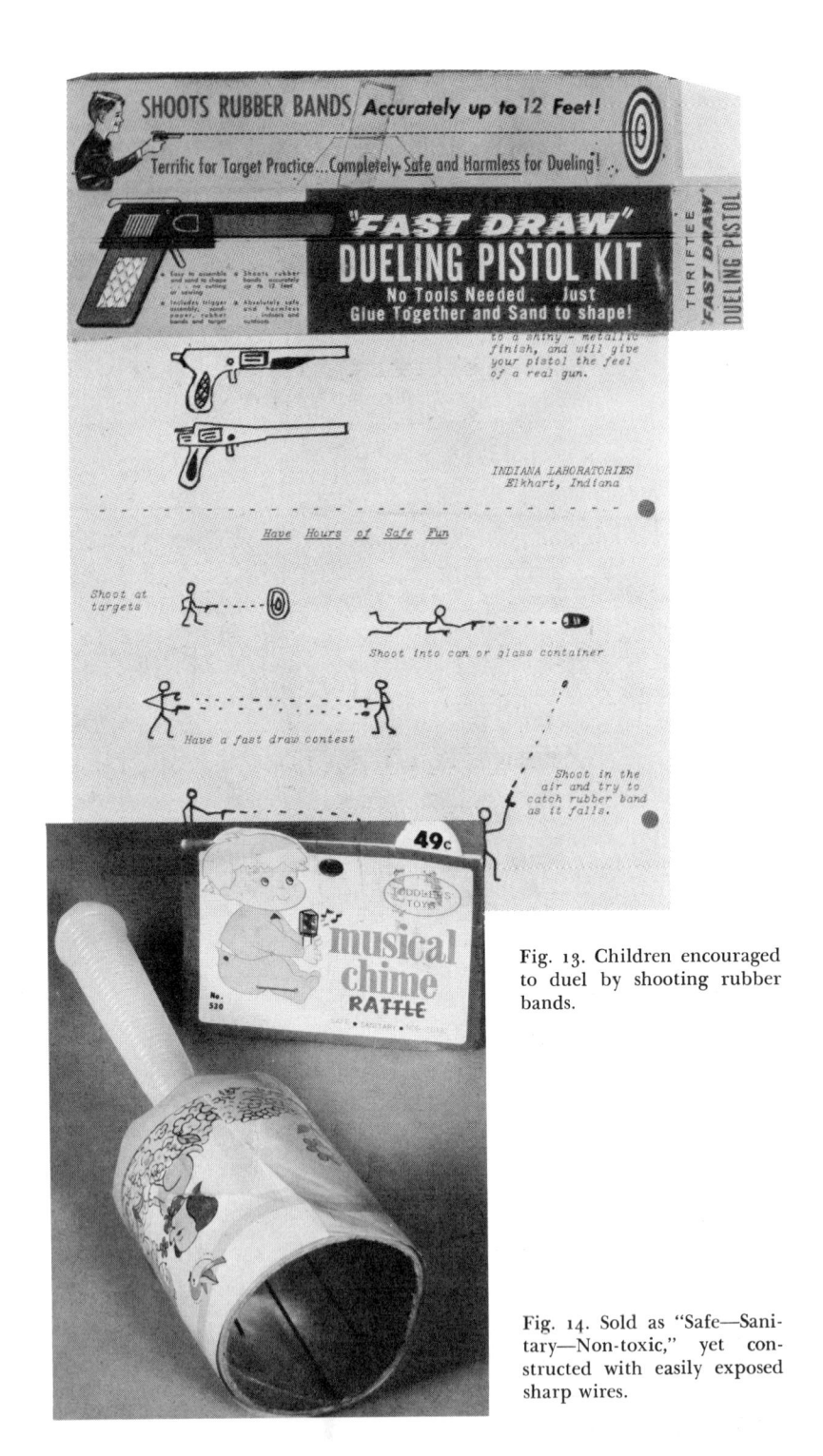

Fig. 13. Children encouraged to duel by shooting rubber bands.

Fig. 14. Sold as "Safe—Sanitary—Non-toxic," yet constructed with easily exposed sharp wires.

TOYS THAT DON'T CARE

- The Chemical Sundries Company markets a "Pea Shooter Game" at ten cents a crack which reminds the young consumers that "it's more fun to play safely" and has on the package, "PAPER TARGET FOR SAFE FUN." But, as any child knows, it's more fun not to play safely; the best fun is in shooting at one another. The paper target, which is printed on the bag containing the peas, is an awesome three inches wide —obviously too small and too hopelessly impractical to be used for target shooting. Furthermore, pea shooters are so intrinsically dangerous—because of the possibilities of injury to both "targets" and to "shooters" (who may inhale the pellets they are shooting, which could be stones or other sharp objects, once the peas have all been lost)—that they are illegal in several states, including Massachusetts (G.L. Chapter 264, Section 12). So, even though this company *must* know that anyone who buys a pea shooter is going to wind up shooting at people sooner or later, and possibly blinding them, they *still* make it, and sell it under the camouflage of providing "directions" and a "target."

- The Ohio Art Company makes a toy that their public-relations men named the "Safe-Play Dagger and Sheath." The very name suggests its innocence. The packaging claims that it has a "rolled safety-edge belt loop" on the sheath and a "rubber vinyl [blade] and sturdy metal sheath." While the dagger itself is made of vinyl, and does bend, it still has a sharp point stiff enough to hurt when used to jab with. It would put out an eye with no difficulty at all. As for the metal sheath, it is rolled, or turned under, only in one part: the rest has several edges still sharp enough to cut, pinch, or scrape. It is sturdy all right, and in fact it seems to be sturdy enough to inflict a puncture wound should a child fall upon it. My impression of this device is that the company invested more time in figuring out how to overcome natural buyer resistance to such a dangerous weapon than it did in trying to make and to market a safe and harmless toy.

- For the more industrious child there is a kit on the market called the "Thriftee 'Fast Draw' Dueling-Pistol Kit." This one must be assembled and glued together from the parts provided by the toy merchant. It is designed to "shoot rubber bands accurately up to twelve feet." In case the children have any doubts about the safety of aiming and shooting rubber bands at one another, the directions illustrated in the exhibit, under the caption, "Have hours of safe fun," clear up that little point by showing two children having a "fast-draw contest." In case the child or his parents still have doubts, the package assures him that the product is "completely safe and harmless for dueling." (Fig. 13)

The foregoing examples deal with weapons that explicitly or implicitly claim to be safe and secure playthings when they unavoidably are not. But deceptive toy-marketing practices are not at all limited to weapons or to complex electrical and mechanical equipment. When I called the attention of the National Commission on Product Safety to the extreme fire hazard posed by certain flammable cloth "toy tunnels," the demonstration model, which I tested at the NCPS Boston hearings, had—bravely enough—"educational" safety slogans printed on the cloth itself. Words and phrases such as "be careful" and "safety pays" were worked into the fabric design of the tunnel despite the fact that a child inside of one of these play tunnels, should it come into contact with a source of ignition, would be burned to a crisp before he could get out.

Overcoming buyer resistance by making exaggerated safety claims is characteristic of the entire industry. Some of the most outrageous examples can be found in the field of infant's playthings and products. Parents of babies are likely to be especially concerned about the possibilities of their children being poisoned or choked to death. The advertising and packaging of infants' toys is designed to allay these fears. Here are some typical examples:

TOYS THAT DON'T CARE

- Childhood Interests/Alan Jay puts out the "Little Angel Swing Me Suction Toy," which is a rubber baby sitting on a swing and designed to be mounted within reach of the infant. As the doll is swung, two little bells, one at the end of each of the ropes of the swing, jingle merrily. On the package: "soft— flexible— safe" (front); and (on the back) a lengthy passage, including this:

> This baby product has been made with your baby in mind. It is safe, durable, washable and manufactured of the finest nontoxic materials.

The merry bells, however, are easily pulled off the ropes, and could easily be swallowed by an infant. (What baby can resist putting something shiny and jingly in his mouth?)

- A "Toddlers' Toy Musical Chime Rattle" made by the Stahlwood Toy Manufacturing Company, is merely a cardboard tube mounted on a polyethylene handle with a flimsy plastic top. I bought one and as I was taking it out of the package, the flimsy top came right off. With the top off, a set of sharp wires that constitute the heart of the musical mechanism within were exposed. These spikes were not only sharp, but rusty, adding the threat of tetanus to that of puncture wounds. On the package: "SAFE—SANITARY—NONTOXIC"! (Fig. 14)

- The Reliance Products Corporation of Rhode Island makes a baby rattle that is unnecessarily hazardous. Inside the rattle are sharp, inflexible metal prongs that protrude from a disk inside the handle. The handle is made so that the prongs are surrounded only by a thin cardboard and plastic cylinder. The rattle sells for approximately forty-eight cents, and makes the following claim: "This toy is made of the purest materials and [is] unconditionally guaranteed to be completely safe."

These first two examples highlight one of the toy merchants' favorite sales slogans: "nontoxic." Almost every plaything a child could possibly put in his mouth is called nontoxic, and it seems as though "nontoxic" is a close third (behind "safe" and "harmless") as a selling point for toys. There is a hidden premise here that should be exposed.

Most of us associate the word "toxic" with poison, and feel accordingly that what is "nontoxic" is not poisonous or dangerous. This is not necessarily so, in terms of current law affecting toy advertising. The old Federal Hazardous Substances Act is the source for the toy manufacturer's definition of "nontoxic." Section 2(g) of the Act provides that "the term 'toxic' shall apply to any substance (other than a radioactive substance) which has the capacity to produce personal injury or illness to man through ingestion, inhalation or absorption through any body surface."

Certain manufacturers have made peculiar use of this statutory definition to overcome buyer resistance. Consider the packaging of the "Kookie Kamera," manufactured by the Ideal Toy Corporation. It states:

> The Kookie Kamera process uses a developing solution which, while nontoxic,* is not intended for internal consumption. Do not swallow. If taken internally will cause nausea and discomfort. If spilled will stain. Wash affected area immediately with soap and water.
> *According to the definition of the Federal Hazardous Substances Labeling Act.*

Apparently the Ideal Toy Corporation has decided that nausea and discomfort are not comprehended within the meaning of illness. Nor does it, in these instructions, provide the buyer with the chemical formula for its developing solution, information that might prove invaluable to physicians treating children who have swallowed it. Nausea, which may lead to vomiting and even asphyxiation due to blockage of the trachea in small children, is *not* a minor medical problem. It ought to be considered an illness. Yet, the manufacturer has apparently made a deliberate effort to minimize the impact of the Hazardous Substances Act and to turn its cautionary provisions into an endorsement of the product's safety.

The "Kookie Kamera" representations and other similar promotional messages naturally do not explain what precisely the definition of nontoxic in Section 2(g) involves. But this is certainly something to think about in connection with any toy that claims to be nontoxic—"Fun Straws," certain modeling-clay sets, teething rings, rattles. For even though they may be nontoxic by the Section 2(g) definition, there may still be precautions that should be taken in connection with their use. If so, what precautions? And how do we know how nontoxic any of these things really are? It is plain that existing regulations and, especially, existing marketing practices do not ensure that even those toys which do come under some minimal federal control are free from danger or that their safety claims are not misleading.

After "safe," "harmless," and "nontoxic," probably the fourth most strongly pushed sales slogan is "as seen on TV." Some mysterious power of approval seems to be implied by this phrase. That TV and the toy industry get along well together is undisputed: Millions of dollars in toy advertising are spent annually both on the networks and on spot announcements on local stations. According to statistics from the Television Bureau of Advertising, the TV advertising budget of the toy industry came in 1968 to $42.6 million—about $19.3 million in local spots, and the rest ($23.3 million) over the full networks. This was a $2.5 million increase over the advertising bill for 1967, a growth rate of over six percent in one year.

The guiding principle behind TV advertising of toys is saturation. Saturation is a tactic that aims not merely at having *everyone* see an ad, but at having him see it *over and over* again. As Remco Industries, Inc., made plain in a catalog they distributed to retail stores who were deciding whether or not to stock up on Remco's "Land of the Giants" toys:

> Now the highest rated children's show on TV, *Land of the Giants* has only scratched the surface as a merchandising medium. The adventures of the crew of the space liner Spindrift hold a vast nationwide audience of eager youngsters enthralled week after week. You can get your share of this network exposure and promotion with Remco's Land of the Giants toys!

Once we've seen and heard the commercials over and over again and the products have come to sound familiar to us, we are reminded in the store and on the packaging that the toys we're looking at are all just "as seen on TV." This is our clue that the item in question is indeed the one the children keep telling us they need, the one they saw on television. The most ominous insinuation is that the magic phrase "as seen on TV" constitutes some kind of assurance both of quality and of safety. After all, we believe that television programs and commercials are reviewed by the network and (in the case of spot announcements) the local stations, and so, we feel, the products advertised must be "right" for youngsters. But we are mistaken, for this is not the case.

It is true that television advertising censors do review toy commercials, as they do all other commercials, but their function is only to make sure that there are no obviously deceptive claims and that the commercials themselves comply with certain broadcasting standards. There is no attempt made to evaluate the safety of the playthings that the commercials are pushing, and in this sense, the safety claim that seems implicit in toy advertising on TV is even less reliable than the use of brand names and seals of approval. A recognized brand name usually means that the company is a going concern and is at least able to survive from year to year. But all that the claim "as seen on TV" indicates is that we've been, or the toymaker assumes we've been, sufficiently brainwashed by saturation advertising to buy toys on that basis alone.

Because so much TV advertising is directed at the children themselves, it's worth taking a closer look at some of the different strategies of exploitation involved. Some TV toy advertising simply displays the product during the times when children are most likely to be watching. But much of it is more emotional and more seductive. Thus the product brings the program to the child, building up his loyalty to the toy or game, as he establishes a connection between his favorite heroes and their "favorite" products. Or, in programs where children participate and play, such as *Romper Room,* it is not at all uncommon that the toys the fortunate kids use on the air are the very same ones the program is pushing.

Toy advertisers connect their product even more directly with TV shows by licensing both program names and program-related items. This is true, for instance, of "Fun Straws" and "Loonie Straws," plastic drinking straws wound in spirals and often seen on children's TV shows and featured in many spot TV ads. Their packaging proclaims, "as seen on TV." Thus, one of these straws is called the "Romper Room Fun Straw," in a shrewd and typical capitalization on the popularity of the well-known televised kindergarten activity class.

All of these straws (or "crazy straws" as some are called) claim to be washable. But there is a difference between flushing cold or warm water through a straw and actually cleansing it. Straws like this cannot be sterilized, or even put in an automatic dishwasher, because water that is hot enough to do the job will make them lose their spiral shapes. At the same time, these spiral curls are potential germ traps. For just as the shape of the straws prohibits thorough cleaning and drying, so it tends to encourage the accumulation of residues in the spiral curls. Hence, while the repeated advertising claims urge that they are "safe" and "sanitary," the fact is that they are neither, and the repetition merely tends to foster a casual and relaxed attitude about reusing them. For example, the Newman Company of New York puts out a "Loonie Straw" with the instructions, "Do not use hot water to clean straw." But they still insist on the fallacious assertion that the product is "safe" and "sanitary." Milk, of course, is what kids are most likely to be drinking through these straws; and milk, bacteriologists tell us, can be a fertile breeding ground for germs. Thus a milk residue trapped in the curl of the straw would be potentially unsafe. In spite of these dangers, straws like these are heavily promoted to children and their parents through hard-sell television advertising and through identification with favorite characters and programs. (Fig. 15)

Other and equally dangerous products make even more direct use of the child's love of certain TV shows. There are, for example, certain accessories designed to let the child "participate" in the action of his favorite programs, like *Batman, Star Trek,* or *Man from U.N.C.L.E.* Ray Plastics, Inc., for example, makes a "Star Trek Rapid-Fire Tracer Gun," which fires up to twenty hard plastic disks, all colored a bright and attractive red. The disks are stiff and small and come shooting out of the weapon fast enough to hit a child in the eye before he even has a chance to see them coming and to react. The possibility of accident is increased by the package's instructions, which recommend shooting the disks at an angle in order to watch them curve off to one side: For a youngster needn't aim directly at a playmate to risk hitting and hurting him. Furthermore, there is the obvious danger that a younger child, attracted by their small size and bright color, could choke while attempting to swallow one of the disks.

An ophthalmologist from the Boston Children's Hospital was so concerned about this product that he wrote to the manufacturer of the tracer gun directly:

December 8, 1969

Ray Plastic, Inc.
Winchendon Springs
Massachusetts 01477

RE: Star Trek Jet Disk Toy

Dear Sir:

I recently witnessed the near-tragic injury of a child's eye secondary to the innocent use of your Star Trek Jet Disk toy. Later inspection of this toy reveals it indeed very capable of producing significant ocular injury in the hands of an unsuspecting child. On the basis of my own experience with one child and later experimentation with this toy, I believe it is clearly dangerous and should not be presented to the public at large as a plaything. Possibly it might have some other use in other than a child's hands.

It is difficult for me to imagine how your company in good conscience manufactured and distributed this toy. I feel that you would serve your young consumers best by recalling any of these toys now distributed to retailers and certainly by manufacturing no more of them. I would appreciate learning what your plans are for this toy, which hopefully will be the discontinuation of its production.

Very truly yours,

David S. Walton, M.D.
Associate in Ophthalmology

DSW/cmt

After receiving a telephone response from the company the doctor wrote a second letter:

December 12, 1969

Mr. Downey
Ray Plastic, Inc.
Winchendon Springs
Massachusetts 01477

RE: Star Trek Jet Disk Toy
Item No. 35

Dear Mr. Downey:

Thank you for your phone call of December 11, 1969, and for your sincere concern that a child might have been injured by your company's Star Trek Jet Disk toy.

I was very disappointed to learn your company's present posture as presented by you in regard to the safety of the Star Trek Jet Disk toy, which you are now manufacturing as a plaything. It is my understanding that your company has done no testing to establish its safety; that you have no intention of stopping its distribution until its safety is established; and that you are unwilling to take whatever steps are necessary in the immediate future to establish that the toy is not a dangerous plaything. It is my understanding that you plan its continued distribution in its present packaging without any suggestion of a limitation of its use or warning of its potential danger.

I am truly amazed that your company in good conscience has manufactured and distributed this toy without making any attempt to establish its potential for injury. In my opinion your company will be held responsible for any injury encountered during the ordinary use of one of these toys. At no time in history is the public more aware of the manufacturer's responsibility for his products, a responsibility recognized by the legislature in its recent passage of the Consumer Protection Act.

Thank you again for your phone call and for the measure of concern expressed for one child.

Very truly yours,

David S. Walton, M.D.
Associate in Ophthalmology

DSW/cmt

The company's attitude is an excellent example supporting the view that governmental premarket testing is needed.

The fascination with gadgetry that grips the average child-viewer was perhaps best illustrated by the success of *Batman* among the younger set. As we know, the dynamic duo dash

Fig. 15. "Safe—Sanitary" re-usable straw which cannot be adequately cleaned.

Fig. 16. Doll whose ribbon is attached by a long, spikelike pin.

about doing good with the aid of all sorts of elaborate devices. At the heart of their operations is the Bat Cave, and ferrying them from place to place is the infinitely versatile Batmobile. It is hardly surprising therefore that one canny toymaker put out a plaything called the "Batman Cave Tunnel" and sold it by suggesting that to play in and with it was just like "being" Batman or Robin, "as seen on TV." The problem with this tunnel was that the child would more probably go up in flames than achieve identification with the dynamic duo—for the tunnel was extremely flimsy, highly flammable, and so absurdly easy to set on fire with the smallest careless spark.

Stephen Bluestone, toy editor of the Code Authority, National Association of Broadcasters, in a debate published in a trade magazine *Toys & Novelties,* March, 1970, on the ills of TV toy advertising, urged reform with the following admonition to toy merchants:

> Within a few weeks, work on 1970 toy commercials will have begun and it might be well to keep in mind that students throughout the country have been awakened and are actively striving for an improved society. Some are reading, some are writing, and some are marching. How would toy manufacturers handle marching five-year-olds?

And march they ought, if Dr. Moisey Shopper, psychiatric consultant at the Cardinal Glennon Children's Memorial Hospital in St. Louis, is correct. Writing in the December, 1968, issue of *Today's Health,* he had this to say about television toy advertising:

> Television advertising is too often fraudulent. It amounts to a rape of the child, using his naïveté and innocence to sell him a bill of goods. Some advertising magnifies the good points, while omitting to mention the limitations of the toy; some deliberately misleads.

The examples set forth in this section are only a sampling of the many potentially death-dealing or injury-producing playthings purchased each year by parents gulled by deceptive claims or pressured by hard-selling television advertising. They and their children are smooth-talked into believing that these items are safe or harmless or nontoxic and "just as seen on TV"—while in fact they may be unsafe, harmful, possibly poisonous, inadequately explained to parents and children alike. Examples of such items are legion; you will find dozens identified by name in Part Two of this book.

(2) BASIC DESIGN DANGERS

Many playthings are fundamentally unsafe because of flaws in their basic design. Here are some typical illustrations.

Fifty years ago, most dolls were stuffed or carved; today, they have shiny plastic faces, cute button eyes, elaborately styled hairdos with jewellike hairpins and ribbons, and the latest in current fashions to wear. Every one of these innovations has introduced new and serious dangers.

The cute little button eyes can be plucked out and swallowed by little children, and this can lead to death by choking. The wigs and hair ribbons are often fastened on with long tapered nails that can easily be pulled out and used as daggers or ingested by babies. I brought before the members of the National Commission on Product Safety several dolls with hairpins that could be pulled out and with ribbons spiked on instead of sewn on. (Sewing, which is safer, raises the production cost per unit, and apparently it was felt by some that safety was too expensive.) (Fig. 16) The clothing, hair, stuffing, and even the plastic smiles of other dolls have, in many cases, been found to be extremely flammable, liable to burst into flames if touched by a match or even a cigarette end.

In 1967, for example, authorities in Brooklyn seized 47,000

highly flammable dolls imported into the U.S. by A. D. Sutton & Sons. U.S. marshals in New Jersey confiscated another 37,000. Smaller lots of the dolls were similarly seized in other cities and states. For these dolls were made in part of cellulose nitrate, or "guncotton," which bursts into flames when exposed to the slightest source of ignition.

But it could have been too late, since toys, unlike defective automobiles or industrial or home appliances, do not carry serial numbers; they cannot be successfully recalled when a safety hazard is discovered. And even if the purchaser could be found, recovering the toy itself is still a difficult matter. For children often trade toys, lose them (to be found by other children), leave them at friends' homes; and parents may have given them to relatives or friends. They are commodities among children. Once an unsafe toy has left the shelf and gone into the mainstream of commerce, all we can really do is pray that nothing tragic will occur. Since there is no effective way to recall them, and no way to reverse the distribution cycle of unsafe toys, it is all the more imperative that they be kept from people in the first place.

Another example of a dangerously designed toy was the "Hooper-Dooper," which Amsco Industries, Inc., produced. Amsco's brainstorm was to introduce a variation on the hula hoop by stringing a plastic disk in the center of a hoop with several rubber bands. When the Hooper-Dooper was being used, the tension on the rubber bands increased and, in the case of one six-year-old, one of the bands snapped and put out one of his eyes. An expert toy designer later said that Amsco should not have tampered with the original; the ordinary hula hoop was safe enough. In the Hooper-Dooper, use of rubber bands under tension made the product inherently dangerous, the consequence of poor design. Incidentally, it is important to note that rubber bands are generally not a good idea in any toy, for just this reason.

There are also cases where the manufacturers simply refuse to modify toys that are inherently unsafe through poor design. The "tracer gun" that Doctor Walton complained about is one example. Here is another:

The Ohio Art Company introduced the extremely successful "Etch-A-Sketch" in 1963. In its first year, it earned $4.3 million, which was thirty-four percent of the company's sales total for that year. Five years later it was still going strong—and this in an industry where novelty is at a premium and the market popularity of almost every item drops annually. Against the odds, Etch-A-Sketch, which is fairly simple and consists of a panel-shaped box filled with aluminum dust, remains a best-selling drawing toy. There is a stylus equipped with horizontal and vertical control dials with which to guide the line traced on the window of the box. To erase the tracing, the child simply turns the panel upside down and shakes down the dust on the drawing.

The window panel appears to be plastic, but actually is made of plate glass, which is a very dangerous material to use in any toy, of course, because of its notorious fragility. A youngster who leaned on the panel while working on his drawing could easily break it and slash his arm. The cut might heal well enough, though the metal dust in the wound could slow this process and even generate an infection. It could also lead to disfiguring scars caused by the intrusion of foreign bodies under the skin, or even result, through the same process, in leaving large and blotchy "tattoos." Yet despite the many complaints made to the company about these dangers, and the lawsuits filed against it by several angry parents, the design of the Etch-A-Sketch remained substantially the same. Recently the manufacturer indicated a willingness to change the glass panel to plastic. Assuming the manufacturer belatedly changes the glass to suitable plastic —what do we do with the approximately 20 million glass-topped Etch-A-Sketches already sold to an unsuspecting public? On the back of the cardboard carton in which the glass edition of the toy comes packed is the advice, "The screen is made of glass and reasonable care must be taken to protect this toy." That takes care of the toy, I suppose, but who is going to protect the child? Nowhere on the toy itself, in its box, or in the package inserts will you find any warning of hazards to the children for whom it is designed—despite the many reported injuries.

Another group of toys with foolish designs is the series of hypodermic needles marketed as "Hippy-Sippy," "Hypo-Phony," and "Hypo-Squirt," and apparently intended to inspire children to imitate their drug-conscious parents or peers. Setting aside for the moment the obvious psychological dangers which these toy "needles" present, we consider here only their defective design.

The "Hypo-Phony" has a retractable needle that recedes into the syringe on impact. The metal needle is quite sharp and therefore capable of causing both deep scratches and potentially infected puncture wounds. The "Hypo-Squirt" is much larger than a syringe—about twelve inches long—and is designed to be used as a squirt gun. It is made of brittle, easily breakable plastic that, if shattered, might easily present jagged edges and the danger of serious injury to a child who fell upon it. Moreover, it is lubricated with a type of jelly which, in normal use, may be a natural medium in which germs can thrive. We all know that children shoot water into their mouths from squirt guns, and this raises—especially with the added factor of lubricating jelly—obvious sanitary problems. (The "Hypo-Squirt" I purchased at a Boston department store suffered from another, although not especially dangerous, design defect: It didn't work.)

Similarly, war toys, which also present psychological dangers that will be taken up later on, often have dangerously faulty design problems as well. The "U.S. Air Force Surface-to-Air Missile" is made by the Processed Plastic Company and consists of a ten-inch-high plastic rocket in four stages. The first two stages are dummies, but the third is a spring launcher and it, in turn, fires stage four, a hard nose cone, straight up into the air. It is clear that a curious child is likely to be looking down on the rocket at the moment he touches the trigger mechanism off and that he could lose an eye in return for his interest. Furthermore, the launcher will fire pencils, nails, and other similarly shaped objects, just as well as it will launch the nose cone.

A more modest weapon—for use, one supposes, where surface-to-air missiles are too cumbersome—is the "Green Beret Pistol and Target Set," Item No. 216 of the Parks Plastic Company. This is a standard dart gun, target, and darts outfit, with the standard chatter: "Shoots 4 harmless darts, Soft Vinyl-Tru-Flite Darts." As with most of these sets, the rubber tips are easily removed from the darts, leaving the dangerously hard plastic ends exposed.

Especially ironic is the Louis Marx & Co., Inc., version of the M-1 rifle. The "M-1 Rifle No. 232, the GI's Combat Weapon," is supposed to shoot soft bullets and to fire "harmless" explosive caps. Like the "Surface-to-Air Missile," this firearm is spring-loaded, and it, too, is capable of shooting nails and pencils. It is also capable of firing real, live ammunition! Moreover, a child with enough curiosity to put his finger in the firing chamber would be in for an unpleasant and painful surprise, for the force of the spring-loading mechanism is considerable. The irony, however, lies in its actual performance, more than its design, for like the controversial M-16 used in Vietnam, this plastic model of the M-1 does not function very well: The plastic bullets supplied by the manufacturer do not slide smoothly down the barrel; the trigger mechanism is subject to intermittent jamming; and there is occasional difficulty involved both in loading the bullets and in cocking the trigger. But the package does say, after all, "authentically modeled."

Often the chemical design or the composition of the toy's

TOYS THAT DON'T CARE

ingredients present unreasonable hazards. The grouting materials used in some mosaic tile kits (Fig. 17) have been found to contain irritating Portland cement. Professional tile grouting, used by the trades and homeowners, almost always contains the warning depicted in fig. 18 or one similar to it. It seems incredible that a toy tile kit could be marketed which on analysis was found to include grouting composed of 52.1 percent Portland cement and yet did not provide any warnings to the parents or children expected to buy it. (Fig. 19)

Another example of product design presenting unnecessary hazards is the so-called "Bird of Paradise," which is a slingshot-type device. The "Bird" has a razor-sharp metal beak enclosed in a flimsy plastic case. The case would crumble under slight contact or pressure and, even if it did not, it would still not be sufficient to protect against serious eye injury to anyone in the path of the bird's flight. (Fig. 20)

Many of the toys that I have examined that have a protruding edge or knob or fin were designed so that it was made of breakaway plastic, or of flexible rubber which gave way should someone fall on it.

But some space-age toys potentially involve greater risk to our tots than the real things do to our safety-conscious astronaut teams. Consider the space rocket with rigid metal fins pictured in fig. 21. The fins on the rocket, unfortunately, are real, honest-to-goodness hard metal fins. They don't give at all, and they are dangerous.

It is interesting that the new federal regulations covering the automobile industry recognize the dangers of protrusions. But children are the most traumatized individuals in our society. Toddlers fall countless numbers of times each day, and if they are given anything that has protrusions on it, the risk of injury is seriously increased. Yet although we have passed federal laws requiring the knobs in cars to be flat or flexible and forbidding sharp protruding edges in automobile design, some toy merchants feel children don't need the same protection from similar dangers.

Indeed, the possibilities of hazardous design seem nearly endless. Kites using copper wire can lead to electrocution. Some tops come with unnecessary nail-like protrusions in their bases. Children have been impaled on poorly designed portions of playground equipment. There are "safety" blowguns which, instead of preventing accidental inhalation of the darts, tend to lead to it. There are toy edibles—realistically designed to look like food—that many children have found tempting enough to eat. In many of these examples, a simple change in the original blueprints for the toy could be an easy way to avert tragedies. Others are beyond help and shouldn't be sold no matter what changes are made.

(3) DEFECTS IN MANUFACTURE AND DEVIATION FROM DESIGN STANDARDS

Section (2) describes cases where a toy is perfectly made according to imperfect plans. Consider the reverse: toys that may be designed according to reasonable specifications but are defectively produced. Deviations from specified design and manufacturing criteria can be just as dangerous as the faulty criteria themselves. An eleven-year-old boy lost the sight of one eye when his brand new pogo stick blinded him: A defective spring worked loose and hit him in the eye. Another boy lost part of his vision when a plastic slingshot snapped as he drew it back, and one arm of the weapon flew back into his face. There are many cases of riding toys, from bicycles to hobby horses, that have fallen apart because of defects in materials or in construction, with resultant injury; gym equipment has collapsed because of weak chain links; toy hammer heads have flown off because they were improperly fastened. And, as we will see when we come to discuss the testing agencies, there have been many, many electrical toys which—although they

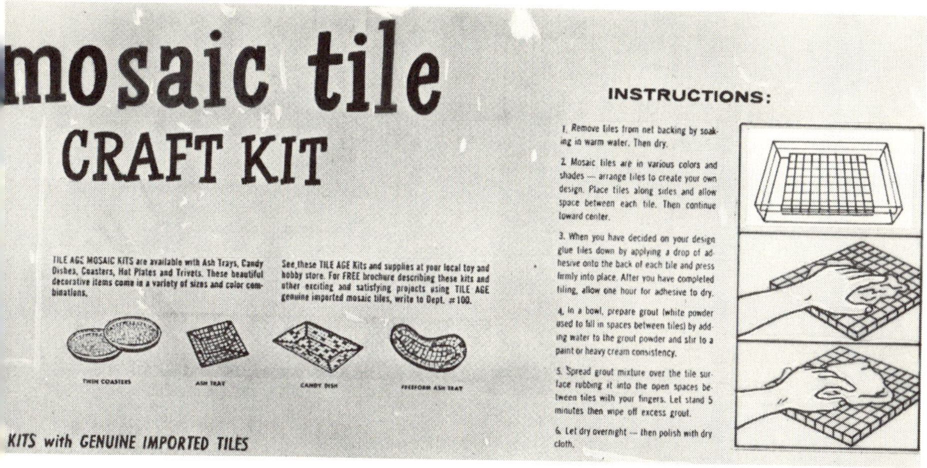

Fig. 17. Label, with no warning, from toy mosaic tile kit containing Portland cement.

Fig. 18. Label, complete with warning, from professional tile grouting package.

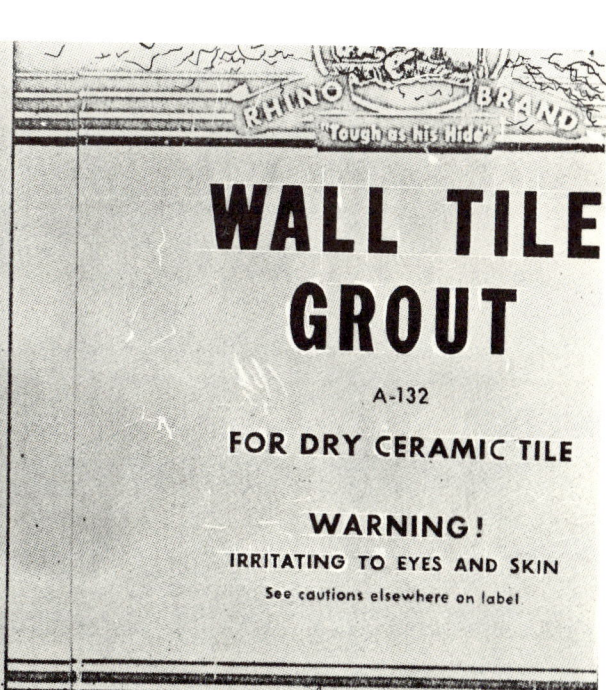

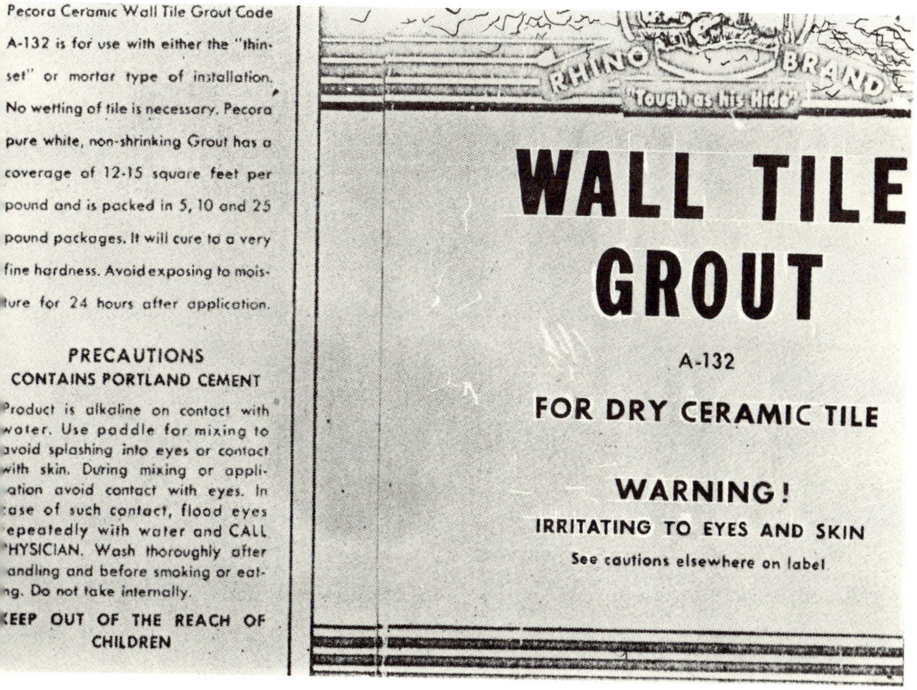

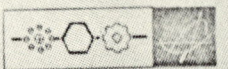

FOSTER D. SNELL, INC.
chemists · engineers · biologists
a subsidiary of
BOOZ · ALLEN APPLIED RESEARCH INC.

NEW YORK   WASHINGTON
CLEVELAND   CHICAGO
LOS ANGELES

29 WEST 15th STREET
NEW YORK, N.Y. 10011
924-9800
AREA CODE 212

February 6, 1967

Sample of: Grout from Mosaic Tile Craft Kit

Submitted by: Client

Sample Number: 7486-2

Marking: None

Sampled by: Client

QUANTITATIVE DATA:

pH of water slurry	12.0
Total alkalinity as hydrated lime	68.85%
Loss on ignition	4.47%
Acid insolubles	11.15%
Total silica	22.53%
Soluble silica	11.02%
Calcium oxide	63.48%

DISCUSSION:

From the above data we estimate the composition of this sample to be:

Portland cement	52.1%
Lime (CaO)	11.2%
Hydrated lime (Ca(OH)$_2$)	25.5%
Silica	11.2%

Respectfully submitted,

Chester A. Snell
FOSTER D. SNELL, INC.

Chester A. Snell, Ph.D.
Director, Analytical Dept.

FM:CAS:vm

Fig. 19. Analysis of toy tile kit depicted in fig. 17 with a finding that toy kit was composed of 52.1% Portland cement.

Fig. 20. "Bird of Paradise" with excessively sharp and pointed metal beak.

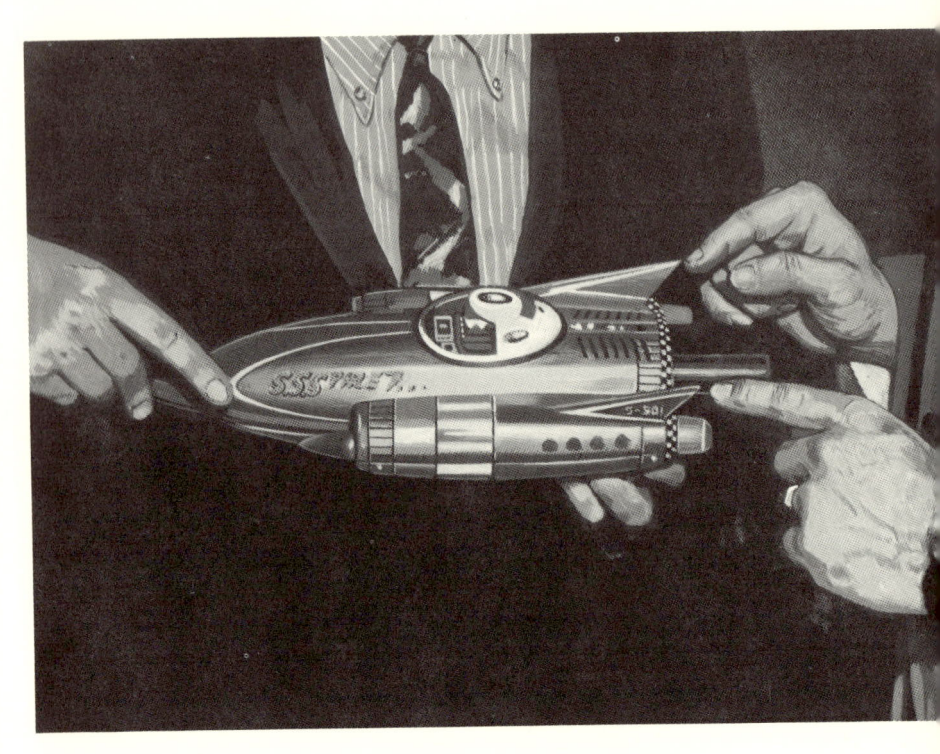

Fig. 21. Space rocket with rigid metal fins.

carried the UL seal of approval—did not meet the safety and performance standards that the display of that seal suggested.

(4) INHERENTLY DANGEROUS TOYS; TOYS SOLD TO CHILDREN TOO YOUNG TO USE THEM SAFELY

Some toys are well designed and are made correctly, but still remain inherently dangerous. Because of this intrinsic potential for harm, they should not be sold as toys at all. This category includes most electric toys and all firecrackers, plastic caps (which explode much more vigorously and dangerously than paper caps), metal-turned darts, whips, weapons (whether or not in so-called "safe" or "child-sized" versions) such as guns, crossbows, air rifles, bow-and-arrow sets, swords, peashooters, boomerangs, slingshots. All of these toys have been argued over in courts of law for years, the issue being whether they are "inherently dangerous instrumentalities" and not toys at all. Also, manufacturers are required to accept a greater burden of responsibility for their production and sale and to warn every purchaser of the potential dangers involved. Some of them are so dangerous that they ought not be sold at all. Many of the most dangerous ones cost under a dollar and are usually purchased and played with by children themselves without the intervention of an adult—save, of course, the seller.

Almost all of us at one time or another in our childhood either suffered ourselves or knew playmates who suffered accidents of varying severity with these toys. The procession of children killed or maimed by these items goes on: One cogent article on eye injuries from BB guns, for instance, reported that over forty percent of the victims surveyed became legally blind; in 12.5 percent of the cases the damaged eye actually had to be removed.*

* Kreshnon, Martin J., M.D., "Eye Injuries Due to BB-Guns," *American Journal of Opthalmology*, Vol. 48, No. 5, November, 1964.

But it is necessary to point out very clearly that in addition to these obviously dangerous playthings, there are other equally inherently dangerous toys that are not usually so regarded. One of the most popular of these items is the chemistry set.

As our educational theorists properly continue to stress the indispensable role of science in the contemporary world, the chemistry set has become virtually a fixture in the homes of families with young sons. This is a mixed blessing. One company's sets, for instance, gave instructions for making raspberry gelatin without warning that the resulting compound was neither gelatin nor edible. Most sets, however, do not suffer from such inadequacy of direction, nor, as a rule, do they include dangerous chemicals if safer substitutes are available. It remains true, nonetheless, and is a constant source of concern, that if the junior wizard is to be able to perform interesting and educational experiments, a certain number of potentially hazardous substances must inevitably be used. This means that chemistry sets should always be considered inherently dangerous and never proper for use by young children. "Never proper for use by" should be understood as "unavailable to," for any child will play with anything, if it is around the house and within reach.

Similarly, electrical cooking appliances and high-temperature metal-casting sets should also be kept out of homes where there are small children; nor should they be used by older children, except under supervision.

Besides playthings that are inherently dangerous because of the possibility of misuse (the BB gun, for instance) or use by children too young to appreciate the hazards involved (the chemistry set, for instance), there are other items so dangerous that they belong in no home under any circumstances. Chief among these are highly flammable articles, which—despite federal legislation—present a grave and pressing danger. The present legislation is discussed in Chapter Five, and a more detailed list of dangerously flammable products is to be found in Part Two.

(5) STURDINESS AND DURABILITY AS SAFETY FACTORS

Once my wife Linda and I began habitually to take a hard, long look at the toys available for our children, the toy buying in our own family was measurably curtailed. Well-meaning relatives and friends nonetheless continue to ply our children with tokens of their genuine affection: wind-up trains, planes, go-go cars, "Hot Wheels"—all have found their way through our front door (and sometimes, I suspect, through the back door as well). What I find especially discouraging is that after I have given these gifts a check for safety, and have passed them on to Jamie and Joanie, my wife and I still find that after a few go-rounds, many of these mechanical ingenuities quickly break down. A child's frustration in the face of a toy that "won't go, Daddy" is one that every parent well appreciates and learns to dread.

This is not merely a case of American (or foreign) industry falling down on its reputation for sound production. For the bond that children have to their toys is more than a mere consumer-to-product relationship. Toys are more than played with; they are loved and cared for. For proof of this, each one of us can refer to his or her own childhood, and how we refused to give up battered and broken dolls or trucks. Toys, even though they may be bought and sold in commerce, are not necessities of life, but embellishments of it. Toys, dolls, electric trains are not possessed for a practical reason, but for an emotional one. Hence, we do not measure their worth to us, nor do our children, by their efficiency. We don't toss them out at the first signs of wear and tear, nor do we hasten to replace them with later and more up-to-date models. We expect our toys to last, and we want them to, and toymakers should but do not respect this feeling.

They should respect it by making toys that are sturdy and safe, not just for the short run, but for the long run; not just when used in an artificial situation by demonstrators in a department store, but also when used in a real way by real, live, active children. But as we shall see, too many toymakers do not give much evidence of any awareness of the need for durability.

Hundreds of thousands of children suffer injuries from toys that cannot withstand normal play activity. A San Francisco mother bought a plastic top, called "Blo-Yr-Top," at a local supermarket and took it home in her grocery bag. Almost immediately after her teen-age daughter began to play with it, the top exploded, cutting the girl's face and putting out her right eye. The girl sued, and the defendants argued (successfully) that they were absolved of responsibility because there was no evidence that the toy when first used was in the same condition as when bought; it might have been damaged when transported from the store to the home in the grocery bag. So the girl lost her suit and recovered nothing in recompense for her disfiguring and disabling injury. (See also Chapter Six.)

The point of this case is that the defendants' argument implies that they were relieved of fault because the toy could, as a matter of course, have been damaged by resting under some groceries in a shopping bag. Yet it seems clear that the toy industry ought to make playthings durable enough at least to withstand a trip home from the store, and that they should make things that do not become safety hazards if they do break down. Surely this top could not have been that roughly handled in transit; no more, at least, than it would by being dropped by a child, or stored in a toy box with other playthings on top of it. In any of these instances, it probably would still have put out the young girl's eye.

Examples abound of toys similarly deficient in durability. Both the "Roly-Poly" doll, once exhibited at the Brooklyn

Museum for sale as part of a fund-raising drive, and the "Toddlers' Toy Musical Chime Rattle," which the Stahlwood Toy Manufacturing Company makes, are easy to crack open. When they do break, stiff, pointed and rusty wires (the sound-producing devices) are exposed. Yet both of these are advertised as being safe and nontoxic.

Very popular with children are flexible figurines that can be bent into a variety of postures. These dolls maintain their poses by virtue of a wire skeleton running through the hands, arms, legs, and torso, and the danger they commonly present is that the skeleton easily works through the soft plastic "skin" of the doll, exposing the wires, which may then cause scratches and puncture wounds. Included among these items are the "Slick Chick" doll by Topper Corp., "Gumby's Pal Pokey" by Lakeside Toys, and the "Twistee-Softee" by Jolly Toys, Inc. The same dangers are also present in some miniature dolls sold as accessories to dollhouses.

Rigid plastic is another source of serious cuts and lacerations, and all toys made of this material are likely to become safety hazards in the course of their normal use. Some companies, for example, manufacture plastic crash helmets and goggles for children in imitation of the ones worn by racing drivers. The idea behind this is fine indeed: to get children accustomed to using protective devices. But the execution of the concept is another matter. A friend gave my four-year-old son a plastic helmet and goggles set of this type. My child soon easily broke the goggles, which splintered into sharp and jagged pieces. Had he been wearing them when they broke, he could possibly have cut his face or even lost an eye. (Fig. 22)

Another toy I threw out of the house was a plastic "educational" animal house put out by Lakeside Industries. The house consists of a rigid white wall with a blue plastic base and a removable roof. The set includes four polyethylene animals, which the child is supposed to slip into four geometric holes in the wall. The aim of the game is to teach the child to associate the geometric shapes with the names of the animals. The latter are safe enough, soft and too large to be swallowed, but the danger lies in the house itself. Like the goggles, it is made of rigid plastic, and like them, it broke into several jagged sections when it was damaged in play. But in this case, the toy was not even really safe to begin with, for the roof was not attached permanently to the wall and merely rested on two plastic supports. These were two-inch, diamond-shaped, speartip-like protrusions that were very sharp to the touch. A child who fell on one of them would be lucky to escape with a minor injury, for it would be like tumbling onto a two-inch spike. (Fig. 23)

When an otherwise harmless-looking toy falls or shatters there is always the possibility that a piece or pieces will find their way into a child's mouth. This is a very common hazard. Consider the list of objects recovered from the lungs and stomachs of children, as reported to the Congress by the National Commission on Product Safety. (Figs. 24 and 25)

There is simply no excuse whatsoever for such a lack of safe design and durable construction in toys like these. Toy manufacturers ought to realize that their products are not complex machines like automobiles or television sets, designed to be taken to expert repairmen at the first hint of undue wear or substandard performance. But the industry doesn't seem to understand this at all, and meanwhile children everywhere are discovering with unsettling frequency that some of their toys just don't care.

(6) CHILDREN'S CREATIVITY AND SAFETY HAZARDS

It doesn't require a great deal of experience or imagination to appreciate that children are very easily able to find unorthodox ways to use toys. Just as one toy may be dangerous because it is too easily broken, so another may be dangerous

Fig. 22. Easily shattered plastic goggles presented to author's son as a gift.

Fig. 23. Educational "Animal House," with spear-type design, eliminated from author's son's toy box.

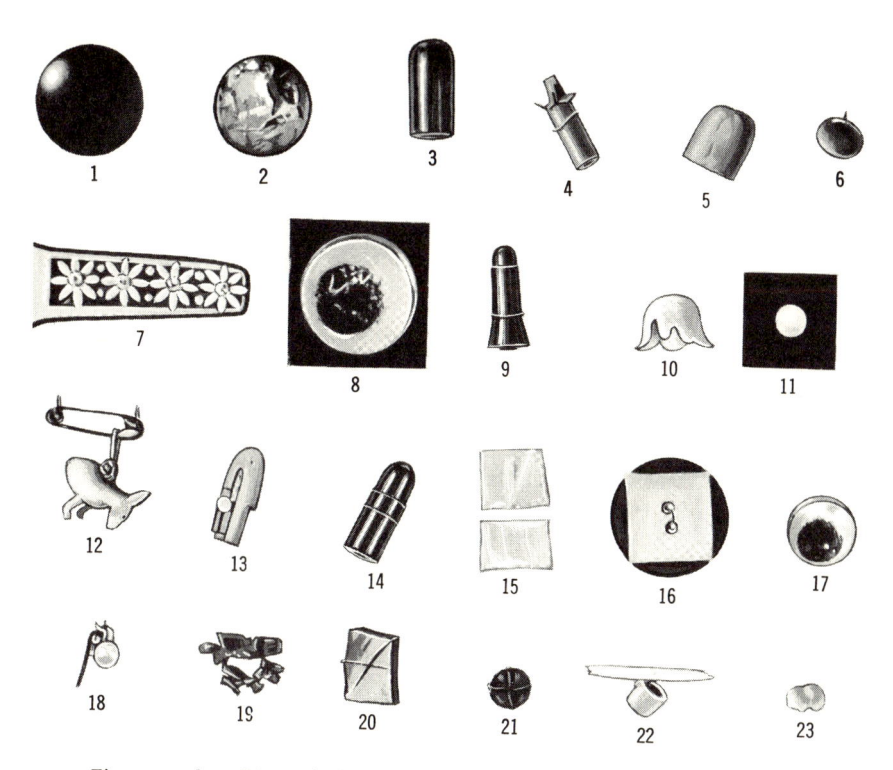

Figs. 24 and 25. List and pictures of objects recovered from gastrointestinal tracts of children.

Items 1 through 23:

1. celluloid button, esophagus
2. celluloid eye of toy rabbit, upper thor. esophagus
3. cap lipstick tube, rt.m.br.
4. whistle, rt.m.br.
5. plastic toy lipstick, lt.l.l.br.
6. plastic toy thumbtack, esophagus
7. plastic bobby pin passed by bowel
8. celluloid eye from toy doll, upper esophagus
9. plastic bullet, rt.l.l.br.
10. plastic flower, rt.l.l.br.
11. bead, lt.l.l.br.
12. celluloid donkey with string and safety pin, cerv. esophagus
13. plastic bullet, rt.l.l.br.
14. plastic bullet, lt.l.l.br.
15. two pieces of celluloid, upper trachea
16. celluloid button, esophagus
17. toy eye, celluloid, esophagus
18. bead with pin, from doll, rt.br.
19. fragments of wax, stenosis esophagus
20. piece of plastic toy, cerv. esophagus
21. piece of plastic, lt.l.l.br.
22. plastic fragment toy airplane, rt. stem bronchus
23. celluloid tooth, lt.m.br.

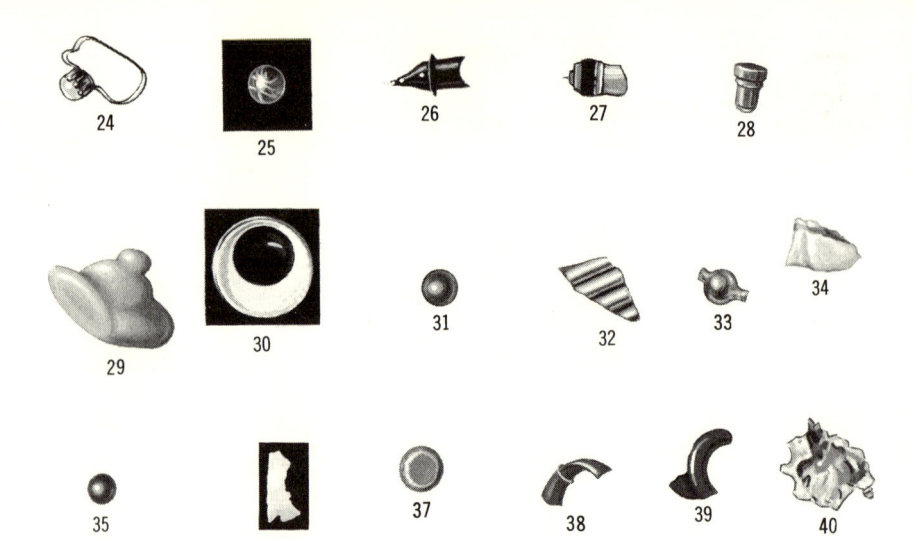

Items 24 through 40:

24. earring, esophagus
25. pearl bead, rt.br.
26. frag. glass ornament, lt.l.l.br.
27. frag. plastic toy, rt.tem.bronchus
28. plastic plug ballpoint, subseg. rt.l.l.
29. plastic port. toy bottle nipple, thor. inlet esophagus
30. celluloid eye toy rabbit, cerv. esophagus
31. bead, lt.m.br.
32. frag. toy—asbestos shingle, rt. lung
33. bead, rt.br.
34. piece of celluloid, sub-glottic larynx
35. pellet, rt.l.l.br.
36. port. Christmas tree ball, trachea
37. hollow plastic toy hat, lt.l.l.br.
38. fragment plastic, lt.br.
39. plastic portion button, trachea
40. crumpled fragment celluloid, sub-glottic larynx

because it is too easily adapted to dangerous uses—as the following examples illustrate.

Most children's darts, rockets, arrows and other projectile weapons have soft rubber tips, intended to blunt their impact and so to reduce injuries and damage to person and property. Most of them have two problems, however: Either the tips are so flimsy that the wooden or plastic shafts poke right through them on forceful impact, or they come off very easily in play, leaving the shafts directly exposed. Furthermore, children are likely to undertake variations on the suggested themes by putting pins, needles, and nails onto the tips in order to make the projectile "stick better." The first two are problems of design or manufacture; the third is one of creativity.

The same problem often arises with indoor and outdoor gymnasium and playground equipment. Playgrounds are naturally and normally the safety valves for children's excess energy—energy which occasionally includes a degree of hostility and aggressiveness. For instance, it is common to find children "dueling" with playground swings or using them for "target practice." For reasons like these, some designers of playground and gym equipment have tried to make their products "childproof," not only in the sense of being well built and safely designed, but also in the sense of being unamenable to creative misuse. One such innovation has been the construction of swings that can only move back and forth and that cannot be put into a side-to-side pattern; this eliminates collisions between swings, whether intended or accidental. Unfortunately, however, freely rotating swings are being revived: one such is the "Monkey Swing" produced by 20th Century Varieties, Inc. This set consists of a heavy wooden disk and a nine-foot rope, which the manufacturer recommends should be tied to a tree limb or a gym bar. The promotional material stresses the great strength of the rope, but overlooks the real danger involved, which is that because the swing is free to move in a 360° orbit, it could easily hit a bystander. The disk itself is hard; its edges are unbuffered; and its impact might readily break a head or an arm.

Only slightly better is the Irwin Corporation's "Swing Ring," a modern version of the old auto tire in the backyard, this time made of plastic, or rubber, and fitted out with handles. The same 360° orbit is possible, and the handles and heavy plastic invite similar dangers.

Another variation, *apparently* safer, also presents a series of hazards; this is the "Swing-A-Ling" by Moulded Products, Inc. The "Swing-A-Ling" looks like a tub or rowboat swinging open-side out. The child rides while sitting cross-legged, and he can hold on to holes cut in the sides. However, it remains a free-swinging vehicle, and therefore dangerous to bystanders, and has two further problems: (1) the child has no control over, nor can he see, where he is going; nor can he easily use a hand or foot to avoid colliding with someone or something; and (2) should he strike a tree or post, or a person unprepared, he might simply tumble out the open side, if the shock or surprise were enough to make him let go of the sides. On the whole, therefore, free-swinging swings should simply be avoided.

(7) TOYS THAT COME IN UNSAFE PACKAGES

Even if a toy is well designed, well constructed, and accurately promoted, and even if it is not subject to misuse and is psychologically acceptable, the toymaker's responsibility does not stop there. He should be careful to see that the package the toy comes in is also safe.

The natural desire to see what we're buying, and the need to reduce breakage before sale, and even shoplifting prevention, all contribute to the increasing use of plastic bags to cover large, sturdy and hard-to-steal containers for toys. With the plastic bags comes the threat of suffocation that the dry-cleaning industry is now fortunately well aware of. Such a danger arises when children quite normally consider and use the package as just as much of a plaything as the toy within. Any parent who has laid out a fair sum of money for a toy only to find his son merrily taking over as his prize possession the box it came in is a self-made expert on the unpredictability factor in children's preferences. And since this is so, one may well ask why toymakers don't simply stop using plastic bags for children's toys. For many of them persist in using the dangerous soft plastic, when hard plastic would be safer.

No one will quarrel with the toy industry's quite legitimate desire to reduce theft and damage and to increase the attractiveness of their product on the retail shelves. But replacing soft plastic bags with firmer plastic would promote all these ends and promote safety as well. For one thing, the firmer plastic usually has to be broken apart in order to remove the toy within; and so it presents a smaller set of surfaces and a correspondingly lesser danger of covering a child's nose and mouth and suffocating him. Nor will a firmer plastic bend easily enough to fit the contours of a child's face, and the suffocation danger is again reduced; whereas soft plastic (especially where there is static electricity) can fit a small face in a completely airtight way. Firmer plastic, however, costs more than soft plastic does; and since almost everyone else in the country must by now be aware of the dangers of soft plastic bags, the reasonable conclusion is that the toy industry also knows this, but prefers to keep costs low and to run the risk of an occasional dead child.

This conclusion is reinforced by the fact that many toymakers are in the habit of subcontracting out part of their work, including, at times, the packaging material and sometimes the packaging process itself. Anyone who deals professionally with plastics knows of the properties of soft plastic film. The Society of the Plastics Industry, Inc., has prepared a pamphlet for distribution through state and local health departments, the cover of which is shown in fig. 26, and which insists on page one that plastic film is "NOT A TOY." Well, page two of the same pamphlet states that plastic film is good for "toys," presumably as a wrapping material. (Fig. 27) If it is not a toy, and not to be used as one, then why in the name of human intelligence should it be used to wrap toys if it can kill? And note that page four of the same pamphlet warns not to leave the wrappers where small children can get to them. (Fig. 28) Who do the plastics industry and the Kentucky Department of Health (which publishes this particular pamphlet) think use toys?

The same kind of inattention to packaging problems is manifest in the industry's careless use of metal staples to close cardboard cartons. For example, archery sets by Kits, Inc., not only come in a plastic bag, but each set is also wrapped in a box sealed with heavy copper staples. It is true, of course, that most large cartons are sealed this way. But toymakers should know that toys ought to be exceptions to the rule. They wind up in the hands of children, and so do the boxes for the most part. Metal staples are dangerous and so they don't belong in boxes that children are likely to play with.

Other toys that come in boxes are sometimes wrapped in highly flammable materials such as excelsior, light tissue paper, or shredded newspaper. Until manufacturers stop—or are compelled to stop—introducing such fire hazards into the playroom, parents should give an especially thorough inspection to the packaging materials that their children play with.

One further problem with some toy packaging is that it is sometimes done not wisely but too well. For some toys are so securely wrapped that it is virtually impossible to inspect the product for safety and durability before purchase.

CAUTION!

Plastics Can Kill!

PLASTIC FILM IS NOT A TOY. IT CAN SUFFOCATE YOUR CHILD. IN RECENT MONTHS MORE THAN   CHILDREN HAVE BEEN KILLED BY PLASTIC

PLASTIC FILM IS GOOD FOR PACKAGING FRUITS AND VEGETABLES, CEREALS, CLOTHING, TOYS, CANDIES, BAKERY GOODS, HARDWARE AND SPORTING GOODS.

WHEN YOU TAKE THE PLASTIC WRAPPING OFF A PACKAGE, TEAR UP THE PLASTIC AND THROW IT AWAY. DON'T LEAVE IT WHERE SMALL CHILDREN CAN GET TO IT.

Fig. 26. "Plastic film is not a toy."

Fig. 27. "Plastic film is good for toys."

Fig. 28. "Don't leave plastic wrapping where small children can get to it."

Kentucky State Department of Health
620 South Third Street
Louisville 2, Kentucky

ILLUSTRATIONS COURTESY
THE SOCIETY OF THE PLASTICS INDUSTRY, INC.

PAM. AC-3 (6-59)

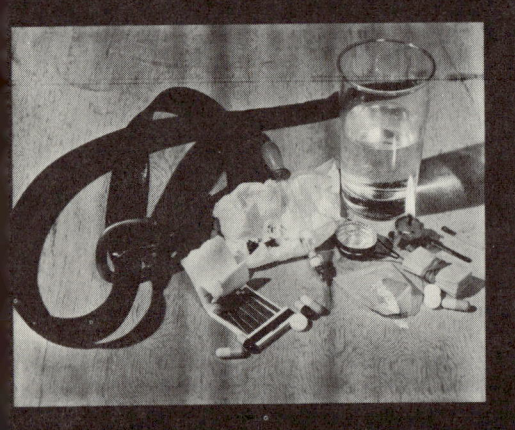

Fig. 29. The connection between childhood, toys and drugs pathetically depicted by a Drug Rehabilitation Center's poster.

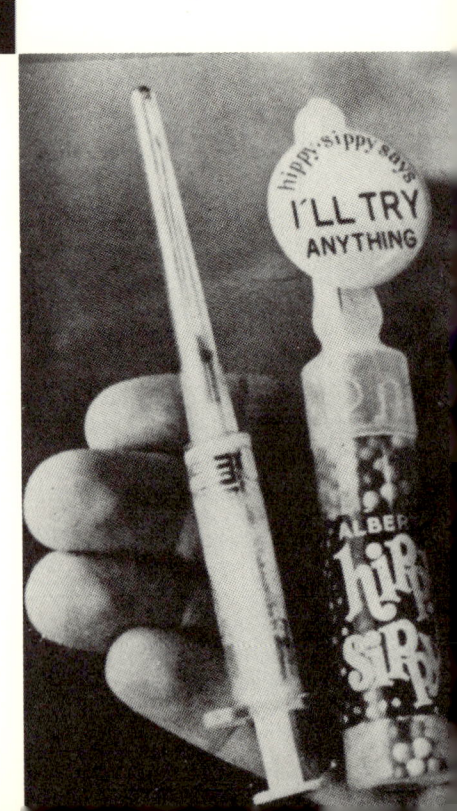

Fig. 30. "Trying anything" is hardly the message responsible adults have been trying to get across to America's youth.

(8) TOYS AND DISEASE

Most parents who worry about unsafe toys tend to concentrate on the possibilities of accidents—cuts, burns, blindings and the like. They should not overlook the possibility of disease as well.

Mothers are forever telling their toddlers not to put things in their mouths, but toddlers are forever tempted to put everything in their mouths, and mother's warnings are honored far more in the breach than in the observance. Furthermore, toys and children lead pretty intimate lives together; they sleep in the same bed, share the same bathwater, eat at the same table, and are constantly in each other's company, both indoors and out. Toys, like children, do get dirty, can pick up germs, and may communicate them. This is no fault of the toy industry, of course, but only a normal and natural fact of childhood existence.

Nevertheless, it seems fair to remark that toymakers should be careful not to increase the dangers of disease to the children who buy and use their products. Not long ago, Connecticut authorities in Hartford seized 337 toy ducklings that were carrying deadly salmonella bacilli. The toys were real ducklings that had been cleaned and stuffed; preliminary testing by health authorities demonstrated that seventy percent of them were contaminated. Salmonella can cause abdominal pains, vomiting, diarrhea, and death; and it is easily transferable from hand to mouth. It is a form of typhoid and can cause permanent ill effects.

This is no isolated example. Other stuffed animals—for instance, chickens (imported from Japan)—have been found to contain cotton contaminated with arsenic. Many liquid-filled teething rings harbor, as we noted earlier, coliform bacteria. One brand was found filled with polluted water from an Asiatic river. (If the importer was looking for a polluted river to sell, surely he needn't have traveled that far.) Even though coliform is not harmful, its presence usually indicates unsanitary and therefore unacceptable manufacturing conditions; for a harmful, even lethal, bacterium may just as easily have been present. And who will forget the frightening disclosure in the fall of 1968 that thousands of toys, rattles and children's jewelry items that had already been distributed contained deadly jequirity beans? Newspapers, radio and television stations joined in frantic pleas to people to destroy or return the items, as the beans were so poisonous that ingestion of just a single one could be fatal to a child.

Still, the greater part of the germs and health hazards connected with toys are not those built into the toys themselves; they are those that toys pick up ordinarily. Mothers wisely have a near-reflex habit of washing everything that children might put into their mouths. But what about toys that cannot be washed effectively, like the "Loonie" plastic drinking straws described earlier? Or how can one wash, without danger, a toy electrical appliance? Water and electricity don't mix, and the possibility that water might be left in some crevice in the back of the appliance with a resultant electrocution is a disturbing one. And what about toys that invite children to use them as eating or drinking utensils—water pistols, squirt guns, and the plastic hypodermic needles mentioned above? The dangers of harm to health from toys like these are often overlooked; they should not be underrated.

(9) PSYCHOLOGICALLY HARMFUL TOYS

We have, happily, a broader and fuller notion of health today than was prevalent a hundred years ago, and this contemporary understanding of health includes a deeper appreciation of mental fitness. Any review of the dangers that toys present to children has to include a discussion of the psychological dangers which certain classes of playthings present. Perhaps the most outrageous examples of a psychologically dangerous toy are the imitation hypodermic needles, large and small, which I condemned earlier for their faulty design and potential unsanitariness. These dangers are minor compared to the *psychological* harm they can do. (Fig. 29) The "Hippy-Sippy" comes with a button which reads: "Hippy-Sippy says I'LL TRY ANYTHING." Officials in several states have banned this toy because of the obvious boost it gives to experimentation with drugs. But what is incredible is that, in this age when twelve-year-olds are dying of heroin overdoses and eight-year-olds are already smoking marijuana, a toy manufacturer could fail to see the trouble with this kind of product *in advance* of putting it on sale. (Fig. 30)

Unlike the "Hippy-Sippy," the "Hypo-Squirt" is not the size of an actual syringe; it is about a foot long, and supposed to be used as a squirt gun. As an interesting sidelight, a salesman explained to me at the New York Toy Fair in March of 1969 that this product was developed as a switch away from guns, in order to counter criticisms coming from many quarters of the propriety of toys that make violence fun. From guns to drugs! This kind of clear thinking and intelligent premarketing analysis is the most damning evidence that we cannot expect voluntary safety standards from the toy industry itself to be effective and rational.

Another psychologically dangerous class of toys are those items which exploit the popularity of psychological jargon and which make light of mental illness. There is a wide variety of child-oriented puzzles and tests of skill and dexterity that—at least in their names—seem to threaten psychological harm to the youngster unable to succeed with them. Kohner Brothers, Inc., for example, makes a "Nervous Breakdown" series based on the obvious thesis that simple physical activity is made more difficult if performed when the hand-eye coordination is through a mirror. The Kohner product requires the child to roll steel balls into depressions in a plastic tray while watching their reflections in a mirror. Incidentally, this toy presents other harmful possibilities as well: the mirror is made of glass that could break and cut or be ingested; the compound used in making mirrors reflective is highly toxic and could be very harmful if introduced into the child's body either orally or through a wound.

The success of "Nervous Breakdown" and of the adult puzzles that were its predecessors, like "Instant Insanity," led, of course, to imitations. Two of these are "Neurotic Numbers" by Lakeside Toys, and "Frustration Ball" by Remco. "Neurotic Numbers" is a set of cubes with numbers on them, the goal being to arrange them so that each of the four long sides adds up to ten exactly. The advertising material for this game boasts that it can "almost cause a nervous breakdown." The Remco variety of "Nervous Breakdown"—the "Frustration Ball"—is a $6\frac{1}{4}$-inch-diameter plastic ball with eight numbered cups mounted inside. The object of the game is to put a loose steel ball into each cup in numerical order. The trade advertisement challenges children to "REMAIN SANE LONG ENOUGH TO DO IT" and adds, "Sounds easy, but wait 'til you try! You'll jiggle it and juggle it until your mind bends and your nerves crack." I readily grant that every child must learn to deal with competition and to overcome initial discouragements, but it is something else, I submit, to hand him a game that treats nervous and mental collapse as fun, however facetious this threat may be. Children, after all, are more impressionable than we sometimes think they are.

Proof of this impressionability is easy to find, and this brings up the question of psychological trauma from monster toys. Aurora Plastics Corp. has been making monster hobby kits, and their advertising intends them to be as frightening as possible. The effects of this kind of thing are illustrated by audience response to a commercial for the TV horror serial

Dark Shadows. It shows a monster smashing through a window and strangling a man—as a prelude to the real action of the show. Parents were so upset by this type of advertising and what it did to their children that these two (representative) letters appeared in the *Boston Globe*:

> This frightened my three-year-old so much that he talked about it many times at supper and kept checking his window when he went to bed, in fear a man was going to jump through and hurt him.

And,

> Ever since the commercial for this show first came on, my four-year-old won't go into a room alone—afraid that something [like a monster] might come crashing through the window.
>
> (*Boston Globe,* January 22, 1969)

Undaunted, Aurora marched on, and for the following season they placed an ad in the trade journal *Toy Trade News* which proclaimed: "AURORA HAPPILY ANNOUNCES EVEN MORE HORRIBLE MONSTERS" and went on to cite their sales record, achieved in spite of the fact that "back in 1962 when Aurora first introduced movie monsters, a lot of retailers were scared stiff." The ad, which takes up the entire back cover of the magazine, shows a Frankenstein walking out of the dark and grasping for the reader. Another of Aurora's favorites is "The Phantom of the Opera," a plastic monster that glows in the dark. It is advertised under the rubric "frightening lightning strikes" and comes in a box showing a shrieking phantom holding up a mask of a human head, with a brutalized victim imprisoned in a cage behind him.

Aurora is not alone in this field. Milton Bradley, America's second-largest toymaker (Mattel is the largest) sells "Milton the Monster," a game of chance associated with a cartoon show and supposedly for children aged five to twelve. The cover explains: "OBJECT: Be the first to get to Horror Hill" and shows a ghoul strangling a normal person while a living skeleton and another bystander look on, the skeleton dispassionately and the normal person in a state of shock and disbelief.

Consider the "fun" card my four-year-old daughter received in a prize package given to her for cooperating at a doctor's office. The card had escaped the attention of both the doctor and the lawyer-parent—but not of Joan, who wanted to know why the man in the picture seemed to be enjoying such a sad task. (Fig. 31)

It is not so much the nature of these games that is objectionable (the Milton the Monster game, for instance, is a fairly routine move-around-the-prescribed-routes item), but their high-pressure, scare-tactic advertising, aimed at the most susceptible of all people, little children. The insensitivity this involves is demonstrated, for instance, by the Mattel, Inc., —which makes a "Thingmaker" series designed to let kids produce their own ghoulish creatures. One Thingmaker comes in a box billing it as a "Fright Factory" and suggesting: "Be frightful! Scare 'em! Shock 'em! Thrill 'em! Teeth, scars, lips —and more—with Mattel's electric Thingmaker. Pull out your teeth!" Disfigurement can be *fun*.

Besides the obviously undesirable psychological overtones of this advertisement, one might also note that the Thingmaker is sold without any recommendation as to safe ages at which to use the technical equipment, although the November, 1968, issue of *Toys & Novelties* did give an indication that it was for children five through eight. The unit includes a heating plate that reaches temperatures of 440°F. and requires electrical current. The units and instructions *do* say, "Caution, Contact with heater plate may cause burns," but what five-year-old is going to read it? And despite the UL seal it carries and the implicit safety claim this makes, the five-year-old who *can* read might think that "Shock 'em!" is

Fig. 31. Doctor's gift of "fun" card to author's daughter.

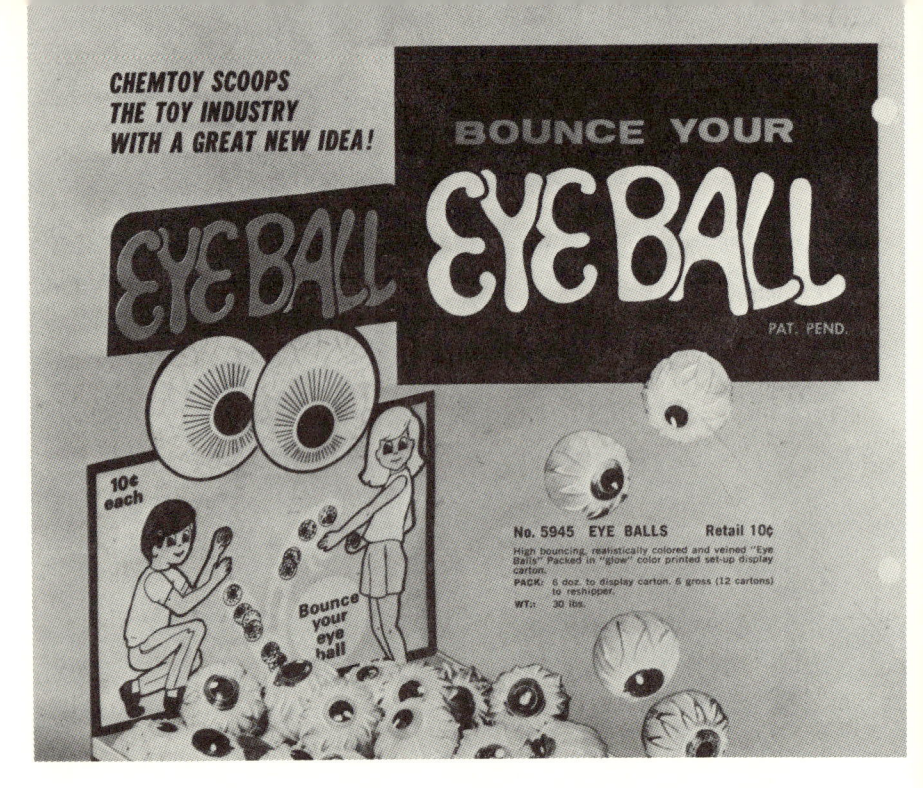

Fig. 32. "Great" new game for children—"Bounce Your Eyeball!"

Fig. 33. "People Pieces"—"trade 'em, collect 'em, transplant 'em."

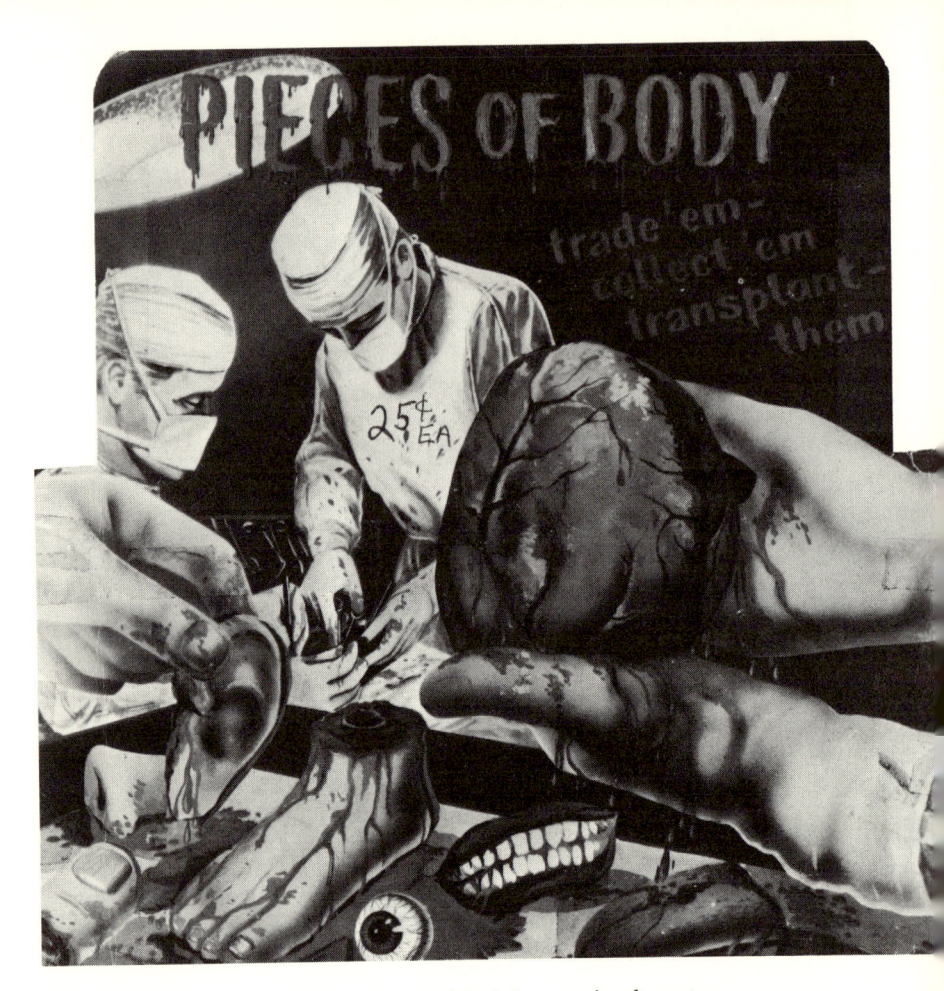

Fig. 34. "Pieces of Body"—sensational new toy.

an invitation to electrical, not visual, imposition on his playmates. Somewhere between the drawing board and the copywriter's desk, it seems, Mattel lost sight of some very fundamental safety notions, including the desirability of giving an accurate statement of what its product is supposed to do, and how.

In 1968 Chemtoy Corporation announced proudly that it had scooped the industry with a "great new idea"—namely, "Bounce your Eyeball!" That's right—for only ten cents you can buy a "high bouncing, realistically colored and veined 'Eyeball.'" (Fig. 32) If this isn't exciting enough, Chemtoy also has a "People Pieces" line—this promotion sells "colorful, realistic" hearts, noses, fingers, lips. It also includes an eyeball. The display package enables the child to pick out the parts he wants. And it even has educational phrases to help him with his selection. For example, the eyeball is given the caption, "an eye for an eye." What are they for? You could "transplant 'em!" as the Chemtoy ad suggests. You should not confuse the "People Pieces" with other, more useful products, such as educational anatomical models that the child can assemble. Chemtoy's line is precisely what they say it is: a "sensational new impulse toy." In case you are wondering if you are too late to get in on the fun, you can rest easy—"People Pieces" are part of their 1970 line also. (Fig. 33)

It appears the "People Pieces" idea is sufficiently appealing to be copied. Observe the even more gruesome variation below entitled "Pieces of Body" made in Hong Kong for the Traveler Trading Co., New York, N.Y. With respect to the "Pieces of Body" collection, a *Los Angeles Times Dispatch* (November 15, 1970) stated that a spokesman for the Toy Manufacturers Association described the toy as a "filthy piece of work." The spokesman was apparently commenting on the Hong Kong version of this obscene toy which was reportedly being distributed in Britain at the time. However, Chemtoy's "People Pieces" set was sold at both the 1968 and 1969 TMA

Toy Fair and was being widely distributed in this country at the very moment that the TMA expressed public revulsion about the import. (Fig. 34)

Other toys whose psychological value is dubious at best are those which exploit children's aggressive impulses by encouraging exploding, crashing, bashing. Milton Bradley announced one of the leaders in this category in the 1969 trade journals: the "Dynamite Shack"—"Explodes with fun and . . . everybody gets a bang out of it. . . . For ages 7 to 14. . . . Kids have to put dynamite sticks down the chimney before it blows up." And the familiar windup: "Dynamite Shack is completely safe, so it should prove a surefire hit with parents, too." The same company also makes "Bash," which is advertised for ages five to twelve and has as its wholesome object the hammering of body parts out from under a head. Both the cover picture and the actual toy show a man holding his own head, covered with lumps. The Louis Marx & Co., Inc., carries this one step farther with the "Socket-Mallet," which is a large and lightweight plastic device about two and a half feet long, described as "a kicky new toy to make your presence known." The mallet itself is soft and relatively danger-free, but one might still question the wisdom of encouraging children to club siblings and playmates over the head with *anything*. Children also ought to have healthy outlets for their aggressiveness, but one might ask whether this requires telling them, "See how much fun it is to clobber someone over the head," or, "See how great it is to smash your lumpy-headed toy apart." What happens when they lose the mallet but find their older brother's baseball bat or hockey stick?

For toys that may do the deepest psychological harm, however, all of these items have to take a back seat to playthings that glorify war and violence. This is the most hotly debated issue in the toy industry today, and the manufacturers are indeed beginning, slowly, to respond to parental pressures on this point.

Part of the hue and cry, we know, has arisen because of the rising rate of violence, foreign and domestic, in which America has become involved over the last decade, and in particular, because of the Southeast Asian War, which comes into our homes in color every evening. Critics of the toy industry charge that playing with guns and other violent toys is tied in with the disturbing growth of this national propensity to violence. There are highly qualified psychiatrists and psychologists who agree.

The industry responds to these allegations by bringing forth testimony from other psychiatrists and psychologists who point out that children have a need to find a reasonable outlet for their tensions and frustrations. No one denies this, and certainly it is better for a child to fantasize his violent impulses than to unleash them on his playmates. But the anti-war-toy sentiment is not quite that simple or that sentimental. The industry, nevertheless, persists in setting up arguments which no one makes and then in demolishing them. No one, for example, seriously contends that children who play with guns inevitably grow up into men and women of violence, or that children who do not play with guns invariably grow up into law-abiding citizens.

What is true, however, is that an early belief in violence as an acceptable means of relieving frustrations and tensions breeds an unspoken and unexamined later conviction that violent behavior is acceptable for adults as well. Surely one may legitimately wonder whether toy guns and other weapons have had any role to play in the emerging spectacle of "police riots" on one side of the law and armed "defense leagues" on the other, and in the public's apparently fatalistic acceptance of the violent and murderous nature of this polarization. One may legitimately wonder also about toy bombs and their psychological impression on children and whether that might be connected with the real bombs going off in densely populated urban centers. The all-too-easy acceptance of violence in our society—the quiet resignation to it, so long as it is not seen as an immediate and personal threat to each of us—is to me convincing proof of the extent to which we have all been conditioned over the years. Reverence for human dignity and human life is supposed to be one of the cornerstones of our American society. How is it, then, that it took so many of us so long to raise our voices against the wanton killing of civilians in Southeast Asia—no matter what the merits of the political struggle there?

Pope Paul VI recently felt strongly enough about the problem of violent playthings to address the following remarks to the European toy manufacturers:

> It is our duty to remind you [that] toys have a great educational importance: luxury toys root certain habits in the minds, weapons develop aggressiveness, other toys incite cruelty toward animals, and still others invite dangerous attitudes.
> *Boston Globe,* May 8, 1969

Thus there is a moral as well as a psychological objection to violent toys, and psychiatrists and educators are no less outspoken in their condemnation of today's toy weapons. Dr. Moisey Shopper, psychiatric consultant at the Cardinal Glennon Children's Memorial Hospital in St. Louis, says:

> Children of all cultures . . . like certain aggressively oriented toys. . . . I think, however, that when you get to the more sophisticated war materials, like hand grenades, machine guns, and camouflage outfits, that you are encouraging a pugnacious attitude. You are saying to the child, 'War is great—go to it.'

Author-psychiatrist Dr. Frederic Wertham says that war toys suggest that "murder is fun and war is pleasure," adding:

> The damage is not that children are being made belligerent and want to invade and bomb other nations. The harm done consists primarily in the fact that they unlearn respect for life and become conditioned to accept violence and war.

There is a partial truth, of course, in the toy manufacturer's answer that the climate of violence in the country accounts for the popularity of violent toys, and not the reverse. But it would be truer to say that the process is cyclical. Enormous pressure has been and is being brought to bear on stores and on manufacturers, by large and influential groups of private citizens, urging the cessation of both the manufacture and the sale of toy weapons. This would indicate that approval of war toys is not nearly as general or as genial as the industry would like to claim. Also, even if a national climate of acceptance for violence is somehow responsible for the market for toy weapons, this does not absolve the makers from a duty not to pander to and capitalize upon it. No one argues that a drug pusher is a wholly innocent third party providing a neutral service; so also, if the country is addicted to war and violence, we cannot rationally view the toy industry's role as simply one of catering impersonally to this addiction. The Pope's point that toymakers should be actively aware of their responsibilities is well taken.

Consider, for example, a product of the Andy Gard Corporation of Leetsdale, Pennsylvania: "The Andy Gard U.S. Army Tank & Jeep." One of a series of their war-toy products, all of which are reputedly "safe, unbreakable, educational, sanitary," it is recommended for children from one to ten. In bold script across the front of the carton is inscribed, "STAGE YOUR OWN ALL-OUT ATTACK" and the accompanying picture shows four children in the process of doing just that.

Besides the very doubtful educational benefits attained by staging all-out attacks, the claims of safety and sanitariness are equally questionable.

We saw earlier—under "defective design"—such weapons as the "Surface-to-Air Missile," "the Green Beret Pistol and Target Set" and the Marx "M-1 Rifle." As if the questionable psychological value of standard war toys like these were not enough, manufacturers have given wider scope to their entrepreneurial imaginations by branching out into other fields. For example, the A. J. Renzi Plastic Corporation sells an accessory to the ordinary garden hose that turns it into a "Super-Duper Outdoor Water Spray Gun"—a submachine gun of pink plastic that fits over the hose and fires away. It used to be fun enough to play with a hose and to squirt one another in relative innocence; one is forced to wonder whether converting the backyard hose into a weapon is really necessary.

One thing is very clear. The toy industry has invested enormous sums in developing and promoting these war and weapons products, and their sales appeal remains proportionately high. Because of this, we can be quite sure that any movement away from their manufacture and distribution will not be generated from within the industry itself. If there is such a move, it will be dictated not by conscience, but by economic pressure, legislative control, or the threat of legislative control.

We ought to be ashamed that while the President of the United States is commissioning federal investigations into the nature and roots of violence in our country, the toy industry continues to feed this violence—and denies all responsibility for what is happening, while making money from it. The industry willfully refuses to understand the inconsistency and absurdity of their arguments. Many toymen, for instance, are fond of saying that since guns kill people and automobiles kill people, then if the former are unsuitable as toys, surely we should ban toy autos as well. This argument blurs the obvious distinction between war and weapon toys and other playthings, including toy autos. Weapons are designed to wound and kill; autos and similar products are not. People may die in automobile accidents, but their death is not the chief function of the car. To kill with a car is to misuse the vehicle; to kill with a gun is to use it correctly.

The interplay of economics and weapons in the toy industry is subtle. One reason why some toy merchants defend certain kinds of toy weapons is that when the same item can be sold both as a toy and as a weapon, then its potential market is far larger. For instance, some parents think of and purchase the BB gun as a toy, whereas others view it as a genuine but somewhat safe weapon, a sporting instrument, an introductory firearm. Obscuring the distinction between toys and weapons keeps the market broader and allows the companies to blame accidents on people who ought to have known better (that is, who didn't understand the very distinction that the toymakers obscure).

Here are two examples with which to close this review of psychologically undesirable toys, examples that give additional force to the view that the industry cannot or will not understand that a toy that is not physically harmful may nevertheless be psychologically so.

First: although the United States Government and its Public Health Service have linked cigarette smoking to a variety of diseases, including lung cancer, emphysema, and heart disease, it is still possible to buy candy cigarettes as well as items such as the "Merry Play Lighter," made by the Merry Manufacturing Company. This "lighter" is only a battery-powered flashlight in the shape of a cigarette lighter, but the kit also includes a pack of candy cigarettes. The package reads, "Toy Lighter, Safe and Harmless," but one is tempted to add that perhaps it should also carry the warning that tobacco manufacturers are required to put on cigarette packages: "Cigarette smoking may be hazardous to your health." Also available for 39¢ is a package containing realistic replicas of all leading packs of American-brand cigarettes. The cigarettes are accompanied in the same package by a "free" plastic baseball. (Fig. 35) This ingenious combination was thought of by World Candies, Inc., of Brooklyn, New York.

And for the classic in play cigarettes, consider the item pictured in fig. 36, which comes in a plastic bag held together with a paper top in which there are drawings of a man with a butt hanging out of his mouth and—worse still—a lusty sadist reaching out with a lighted cigarette in his hand, about to burn the bare shoulder of a frightened woman!

Second: the automobile industry is pulling back, under heavy and well-earned criticism from Ralph Nader and others, from their heavy emphasis on "high performance" and "speed." Their recent promotional materials have begun to lay some emphasis on safety and convenience. The toy industry, which never seems to get the word, continues on the contrary to exploit the association between cars and high speed. Thus, at this writing, the "Hot Wheels" series is one of the nation's best-selling toys. One enterprising toyman (Lakeside Toys) has produced a "Crashmobile," which is supposed to fly into bits and pieces when slammed against an immovable object. Parents needn't worry about the short life of the vehicle, because the pieces can easily be put together again and the car recrashed; and on and on. While auto makers are toning down speed in an effort to avoid crashes, the toy merchants are touting it in an effort to produce them. (Figs. 37 and 38)

The combination of speed, death and ghoulishness is available in one package. The AMT Corporation markets the fast-selling "Graveyard Ghoul Duo," which consists of a "Bodysnatcher" hearse, which, according to the manufacturer, is "loaded with horsepower to make your last trip a fast one!"

Fig. 35. Play cigarettes and free toy baseball sold in same package.

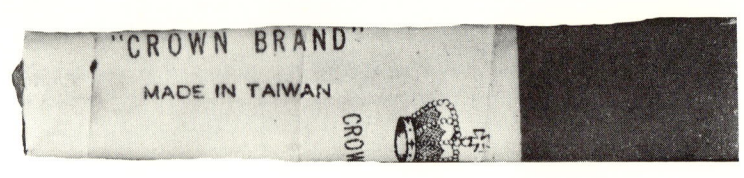

Fig. 36. For those children who might believe smoking alone is dull.

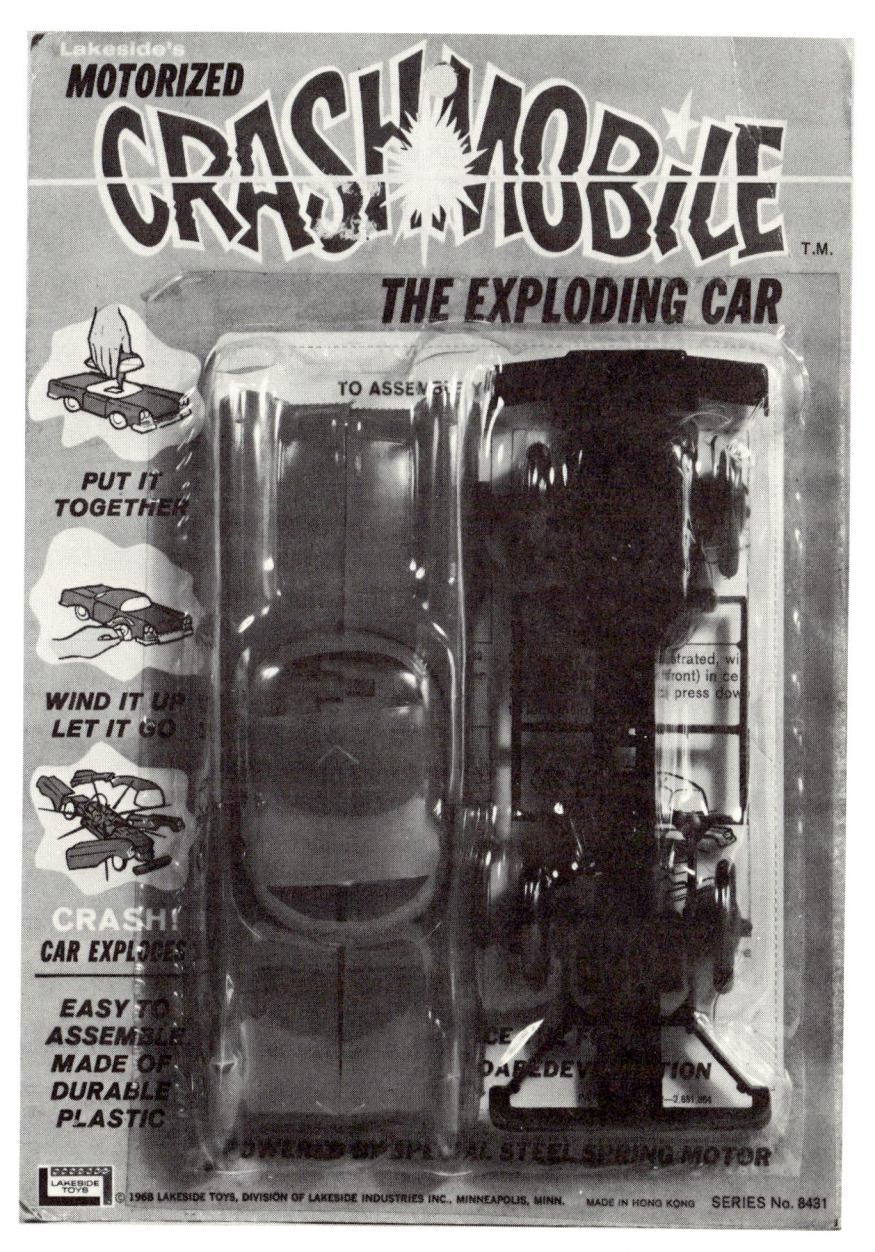

Fig. 37. Great fun! Create your own collision with the "exploding car."

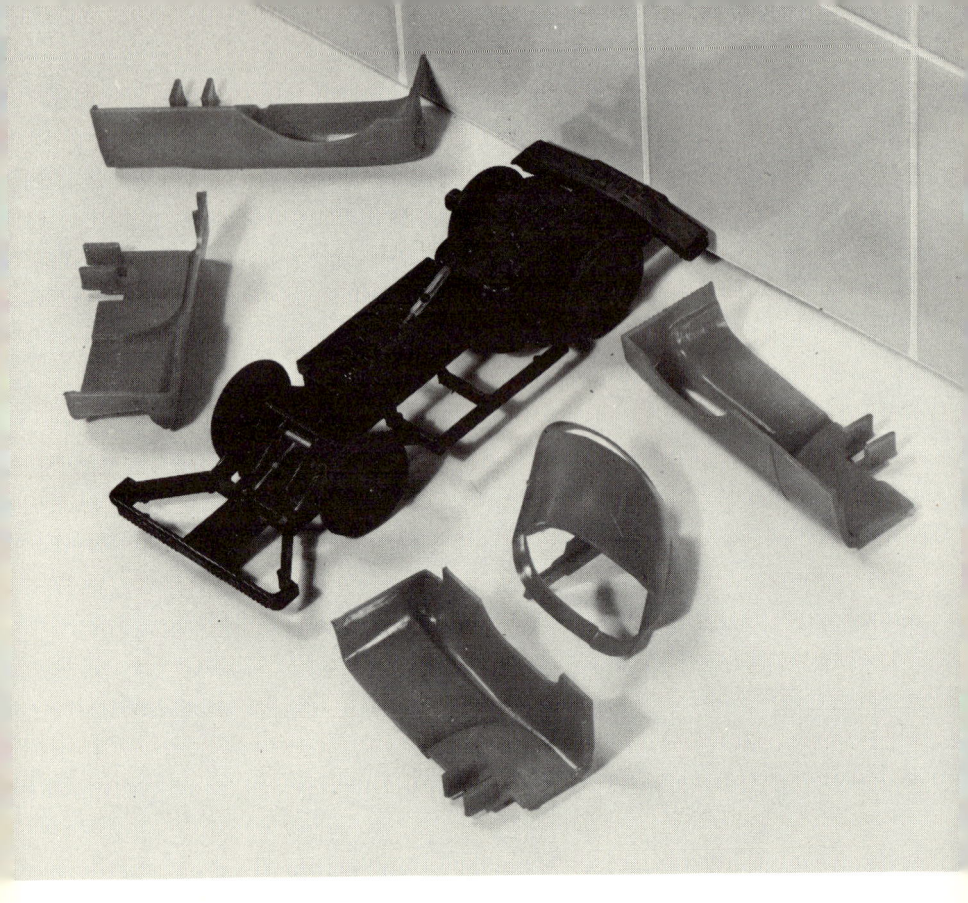

Fig. 38. The "exploding car" after a "fun" impact.

TOYS THAT DON'T CARE

Looking back over all the genuinely frightening possibilities for injury and even death that unsafe toys present, and reviewing the variety of ways in which these toys are dangerous, one primary fact stands out: Where there is a tension between sales and safety, or between "image" (the toymaker's) and injury (the toy user's), sales and image have far too often won out. In the author's view, and he thinks it is one which any parent would fully share, it is high time for firmer, stronger, and more effective regulation of the toy industry and of the hazards its products present. It matters not whether these hazards are present because of honest errors in design or in manufacturing, or because of psychological insensitivity, or through deliberate—if rationalized—deception through high-pressure sales techniques, inadequate labeling, and confusing or misleading packaging. The injuries are real. They can be prevented.

Most of us tend to hang on over the years to some childhood memento—a fading doll, a teddy bear now grown old and blind, the sole survivor of a fleet of trucks, a tiny rocking chair from some long-remembered dollhouse. We loved these things once and still do now, for the love and affection a child has for his toys is indeed one of the great love stories of mankind. We bring to our toys an innocence and an openness and fidelity that—in the best of us—anticipate and foreshadow more important and more lasting loyalties. Over and above the physical and psychological injury wrought by dangerous toys, there is a special wrong they do—a betrayal of the child by a toy that doesn't care. We, as parents and uncles and aunts and friends of the children of this generation, have a special duty to those children to insure that their fidelity is not betrayed. For in that betrayal by the toys we give them, lies a certain betrayal by ourselves as well.

3

Toy Industry Self-Regulation: The Fox Attempts to Guard the Henhouse

IN SPITE OF THE FACTS SET OUT IN CHAPTER TWO, THE TOY industry has consistently taken the position, articulated primarily through its trade association, the Toy Manufacturers of America, that strong legislative action to impose precise and safe standards on their products is both unnecessary and undesirable. They urge, instead, industry self-regulation—leaving it up to the toymakers themselves to police their industry for safety and for fair dealing. This chapter explores the notion of toy industry self-regulation: its operation in the past and its prospects for the future.

We may start with the historical fact that this country has never made any lasting progress in raising the standards of either safety or quality within any given industry simply by leaving it to the industry itself. Just the opposite has been true: In class after class of products and services, the fierceness of competition and the hunger for profit has tended to stimulate an interplay of intra-industrial forces that eventually leads to industry-wide abuses. The pattern has been that competition leads to abuses, legislation is enacted to correct the abuses, and this corrective function is assigned to a federal agency. Then, over the years, the agency itself becomes more and more "industry-oriented" and its protective functions less and less adequately carried out. The toy industry is still in the first stage of this process—little legislation and less protection—and we are only now beginning to recognize the widespread extent of the abuses. There is at present no single federal agency charged with the responsibility for curbing these abuses, and the only current force that curbs them—except the very limited remedies mentioned in the next chapter on legislation and the toymakers—is the pressure of public opinion and sporadic and wholly voluntary compliance by some manufacturers with certain trade association standards.

This state of affairs is intolerable. As the National Commission on Product Safety said in its final report to the President and to the United States Congress, "Self-regulation by trade associations and standards groups . . . is legally unenforceable and patently inadequate" (p. 2). This follows inevitably from the nature of voluntary regulation. For its very essence is that if you don't like it, you don't have to do it.

This weakness is dramatically illustrated by the story of the Ohio Art Company and the plastic caps. The story began in May, 1965, when the company headquarters at Bryan, Ohio, received a letter from the California State Fire Marshal's Office. The letter constituted official notice to Ohio Art that the plastic exploding caps they manufactured could not legally be sold in the State of California because of their inherently dangerous character.

The danger consists in the fact that the plastic casing—in place of the more usual covering material—substantially increases the possibility of incidental incendiary explosions. With this higher explosive potential, the caps come within the category of dangerous fireworks, which are banned by law in California.

Ohio Art turned for advice to the legal department of a trade association to which they belonged, the Toy Pistol, Holster, and Paper Cap Association. In their inquiry to the association, they asked the legal department whether there might be some way—as they put it—to "get around the copy of the law which you will note that the State Fire Marshal of California has sent to us." The company also told the association that they had been informed by the Massachusetts State Police that their caps were "illegal because they are made of plastic." (As a matter of fact, plastic caps are outlawed in several states, including the company's home, Ohio.)

By mid-1966, the relations between Ohio Art and the Toy Pistol, Holster, and Paper Cap Association had apparently deteriorated. In August, the association compiled a report, which noted that plastic caps were not approved for sale by the National Fire Protection Association. The Ohio Art Company intended to continue making and selling plastic caps, in spite of the fact that some states considered them inherently dangerous, and the company even wanted the association to push for repeal of the laws against them. Finally, matters reached an impasse. Thus, the report concluded:

> The Ohio Art Company has announced its intention of resigning from the Association for the year 1967 since we do not propose to include their program to amend laws to permit plastic caps as part of our legislative program. . . . It is our opinion that if they feel that the sale of toy plastic caps is their primary objective, then the company's continued membership is incompatible with our program.

Hence, when faced with the choice of abiding by the association's policies and standards or pulling out, Ohio Art pulled out; and, at this writing, they still make and sell plastic caps.

The voluntary nature of self-regulation is therefore unsatisfactory since it fails to protect toy buyers and consumers. Very few of us are going to ask the clerk in the toy store whether the toy we have just selected was made by a company belonging to a trade association; whether the association has a set of safety standards that its members agree to abide by; or whether the standards are sound and careful ones. And very few clerks will have any idea of the answers to these inquiries. Voluntary standards are unworkable because of the impossibility of checking on all of these matters, and because they tend to bring every manufacturer down to the level of the company with the lowest standards.

Another example of the inherent unsuitability of the voluntary approach may be found in the practices of the Toy Manufacturers of America at their annual Toy Fair. The TMA is the major toymakers' trade association, with about 300 corporate members, responsible for the production of between eighty-five and ninety percent of the toys manufactured in the United States, and for the distribution of perhaps half of the imported toys available in this country. There are between 900 and 1,000 domestic toy companies, and no one knows how many importers.* The fair is held in New York City each winter, usually toward the middle of March. It is the industry's most important trade fair and draws buyers from the entire nation as well as foreign visitors from many other countries. But it seems that no effort whatever is made to control the items offered at the fair, or to see that dangerous or even illegal toys are barred from using the TMA's facilities.

At the 1969 Toy Fair, for instance, I was able to order a gross of toy slingshots and to have them shipped directly to Massachusetts, despite the fact that under Massachusetts law, their sale or use is illegal there. At the same TMA Toy Fair, I saw inflammable playthings, dangerous bow-and-arrow sets with misleading instructions, dolls with long pins in their hair, various projectile toys with sharp points and edges, boomerangs, badly designed swings, and a good many other dangerous toys. I returned to the Toy Fair in 1970, and found things much the same. And there, incidentally, Ohio Art had

---

* Hearings before the Subcommittee on Commerce and Finance, Committee on Interstate and Foreign Commerce of the House of Representatives (91st Congress, First Session), May 22, 1969, p. 168.

plastic caps on display. Ironically, some of the packages of caps contained a warning not to hold the gun close to the face when firing the caps; yet other packages containing the same caps did not.

The point of this recital is that if self-regulation is not based upon high standards, or if the standards are not enforced, then it is useless or worse—worse, because it tends to lull the consumer into a false sense of security as to the safety of the products he is buying. If the Toy Manufacturers of America were really serious about toy safety, they would regulate the kinds of toys sold at their own fair. They do not.

The TMA has prepared a set of guidelines for toy safety issued in December, 1968. These, too, are instructive, for they bear out the point that the National Commission on Product Safety makes about industry-developed standards in its final report: "The need for a consensus commonly waters down a proposed standard until it is little more than an affirmation of the status quo" (p. 62). Here is the full text of the TMA guidelines, with a point-by-point commentary. The reader can judge for himself whether they constitute meaningful self-regulation by the toy industry.

Safety Guidelines for Toys, Games and Decorations

In recognition of our responsibility to maintain the high standard of safety in playthings that characterizes this industry, Toy Manufacturers of America, Inc., has prepared the following guidelines as an aid to manufacturers. They are in the form of a list, which it is hoped will be helpful in checking the safety of each product. It should not be assumed that these guidelines cover every law or standard that might be applied to playthings, and since they are concerned with safety at the manufacturing level, they do not include innumerable local and state laws and regulations regarding conditions of sale. These guidelines include safety features which it is important to check, where they apply and are appropriate, even though it would be impractical to attempt to incorporate them into laws or standards because of the phenomenal diversity of materials employed and playthings produced.

This preamble is especially interesting because it gives an insight into the toymaker's whole thinking process. First, it assumes that the status quo is already satisfactory: "to maintain the high standard of safety." Second, it speaks of complying with laws and standards and regulations. And this suggests that the guidelines are aimed more at keeping the manufacturer who observes them out of trouble than at keeping the toys themselves intrinsically safe. Third, it does not go into the problem of choosing between stricter and looser state laws—even if the laws themselves are used as an adequate basis (which, as the next chapter shows, they should not be)—and so avoids matters like the illegality of plastic caps or slingshots in some states. Fourth, it opens loopholes: "where they apply and are appropriate." And fifth, it concludes by denying the possibility of anything more carefully drawn or stricter in its application: "the phenomenal diversity of materials . . . and playthings."

Materials

1. Adhere to laws and standards already in existence (including the attached Federal Hazardous Substances Act) regarding flammability, toxicity, sensitivity, pressure generation through heat or other means.

All this says is "Do not break the laws." As a matter of fundamental citizenship, this would seem to be a rock-bottom minimum for all of us; but it is by no means taken for granted in the toy industry.

When a TMA spokesman appeared before the National Commission on Product Safety at its Boston hearings in December, 1968, he took issue with me on one of the several points I had made. I had brought to the hearing a toy play tunnel covered with cheap cloth so flammable that when I touched a match to a piece of it, I was forced at once to drop it because it burst into flames. In his testimony later that day, the TMA representative argued that my example was unfair, because the tunnel was already banned by the Federal Hazardous Substances Act and was thus illegal. But I saw the same tunnel on display at the 1969 Toy Fair in March, three months after the Boston hearings. By that time, the Food and Drug Administration had prohibited further distribution of these flammable tunnels, and yet I was able to order one at the Toy Fair and have it sent to me without any difficulty at all.

Furthermore, in June, 1969, Rappaport Brothers, Inc., went so far as to advertise that its play tunnels—which had in the interval been flameproofed—were *approved* by the FDA.* Yet there are no provisions under the Federal Hazardous Substances Act for "approval"—only for banning and seizure.

It seems to me, however, that the illegality of the tunnel is not the issue: The important thing is that it had been on sale in a major store and had been horribly dangerous. If it was illegal, then of course the manufacturer was even more irresponsible—if that is possible—in continuing to market it.

The point is that despite the minimal standard set forth in the TMA guideline—"don't break the law"—the illegal tunnels were being sold in stores and at the TMA's own trade fair. This is an accurate, if disturbing, measure of the TMA's zeal for toy safety.

    2. Adhere to various state laws regarding filling materials and fabrics suitable for stuffed toys.

Some countries—West Germany, for instance—hold that any toy capable of burning on its own is unsafe. American

* See Chapter Five.

toys, however, usually face much less stringent requirements, and it is quite possible for the stuffing and filling materials to be highly flammable and yet for the toy to have complied with state laws since the laws may only cover the exterior materials. But since any stuffed toy may be worked open through normal use by an active child, flammable *stuffing* is just as dangerous as flammable outer covering. The point is that the use of state laws as a guideline is minimalistic and unrealistic.

3. Test for strength of materials as protection against hazardous breaking or shattering.

How test? By what standards? What is "hazardous" breaking? Part Two of this book makes clear that there are hundreds of toys made of brittle plastic that are dangerously sharp when broken. This guideline, in addition to being wholly unspecific, is also largely unobserved.

Physical Properties

4. Check for roundness of edges and protusions, and smoothness of surfaces, except where the opposite qualities are essential characteristics of the plaything.

Failure to observe this guideline is the cause of very many toy injuries. There are dozens of examples of playthings that have unnecessarily sharp edges and dangerous protrusions. (See Part Two.) Furthermore, the "except . . ." clause opens a major loophole; for who is to say when the protrusion or sharp edge is "essential"? A scale model of a jet fighter plane, for instance, although intended for a toddler, might have a very sharp nose. Is the sharp nose "essential" if the model is to be a faithful copy of the original plane?

5. Limit extreme smallness of separate parts, or those easily removed and swallowed, in playthings for very young children.

This guideline, too, is still generally violated, and is in any case far too vague. How small is too small? Is it possible to give a minimum size for a separate part of a toy for the very young? If a guideline is to mean anything, it must be precisely and carefully drawn. Premium toys, such as the goodies in the crackerjack box, are frequent offenders, and I know of a case where a little girl choked to death on a doll's shoe.

6. Check electrical circuitry and parts to ensure safety in use and operation, as set forth in the Underwriters' Laboratories standards or their equivalent.

First of all, this guideline makes no distinction between the operating safety of the toy as an electrical device, and its suitability as a toy for a small child. Smart parents don't give their children real electric toasters or hair dryers to play with. And intelligent safety guidelines for the toy industry would put very strict limits on the voltage levels of those few toys for older children that might prudently use household current and yet still be suitable. The TMA guideline, however, simply avoids the problem of suitability and depends on the UL standard alone. But as we will see in Chapter Four, the UL seal is not an absolute guarantee of over-all safety.

Finishing

7. Adhere to existing standards, as set forth in the attached American Standards Association pamphlet Z66.1–1964, as to paints, enamels, lacquers, inks, and other coatings, regarding limitations on toxic materials.

The standards in the ASA pamphlet are designed to prevent fatal and less severe poisonings, but the level of toxicity which is forbidden is based on adult physiology. What may only mildly affect an adult may, of course, be much more harmful to a child. The guideline should draw up specific requirements aimed at *children's* safety, and it does not. (The British standards do.)

Packaging

8. Check packaging materials and fastenings as a guard against dangerously sharp edges and points.

This, too, is often overlooked by toy manufacturers, and is so general a rule as to be unhelpful to conscientious producers. What materials should be entirely avoided in packaging children's goods? What is the safest way of packaging them? What about the fact that children tend to play with the packages as well as the toys that come in them—are there any special dangers to be avoided?

9. Check for air vents in large plastic bags that are less than one mill in thickness.

Smaller plastic bags may still be large enough to fit over an infant's head or adhere to his face; they are equally dangerous. In any case, all plastic bags, large or small, should carry explicit warnings and instructions to parents in large, clear print. The guideline doesn't even mention a warning at all. Doubtless the manufacturers feel that warnings on the packages are psychologically unsettling to prospective buyers. The suffocation of their children is also psychologically unsettling, of course, and this guideline is no real help in preventing that.

Labeling and Description

10. Include adequate descriptive material with all playthings that are safe only in the hands of children of appropriate age or level of skill, or under certain prescribed play conditions.

This would be in general a great help to parents and children if it were universally observed. It is not, and the failure to provide this information often occurs with precisely those items that most require it—chemistry sets, electrical toys, and toy craft sets. (See Part Two for a number of examples of how poorly the industry carries out this recommendation.) Moreover, one fairly common practice is to keep the informational material inside the package, while putting enticing pictures that suggest that no special age or skill is needed on the promotional and packaging material. Consequently, the parent doesn't learn of the special precautions he should take until he has bought the toy, paid for it, taken it home, and opened it up. If at that point he withholds it from the youngster who originally wanted it, the child's ensuing disappointment is considerable, and the pressure to let him have the toy is often too much for the parent to withstand.

These, then, are the TMA guidelines. They are—excepting the weak and ineffective law reviewed in the next chapter—really the only regulation imposed on the toy industry on a broad scale. We should also recall at this point that—by its own estimate—the TMA only includes one of every three toy manufacturing companies in the United States, although they claim to be responsible for most of the domestic toy production and perhaps half of the imported toys sold here. This is hardly industry-wide coverage. A little TMA history may be in order here, to see just how vigorous the TMA has been in developing safety standards, and what real force they have. The following excerpts are from testimony before the Subcommittee on Commerce and Finance of the U.S. House of Representatives Committee on Interstate and Foreign Commerce, of the Ninety-first Congress. The Subcommittee was chaired by Rep. John E. Moss of California, and the hearings at which the following testimony was offered were on the Child Protection and Toy Safety Act of 1969. (This act was suggested to the Congress in an emergency Interim Report of the National Commission on Product Safety, based on the commission's investigation into dangerous toys.) Appearing for the Toy Manufacturers of America, Inc., were several leading toymakers, including Jerome M. Fryer of Gabriel Industries, Inc., and Aaron Locker, an attorney for the TMA. The hearings were held in Washington on May 22, 1969:

> Mr. LOCKER. [We] are presently developing standards with the Bureau of Standards on stuffed toys and dolls. We are presently developing a standard with the United States of America Standards Institute on home playground equipment and are about—
> Mr. MOSS. Let's deal with the Bureau of Standards. What operational method is being used with the Bureau of Standards for the development of these standards on stuffed toys and dolls?
> Mr. LOCKER. We are developing a product standard, sir, with the Department of Commerce, U.S. Bureau of Standards.
> Mr. MOSS. When did you start that?
> Mr. LOCKER. 1965.
> Mr. MOSS. That was the next effort at arriving at standards after the promulgation of the standards for a paint in 1955?
> Mr. LOCKER. That is true.
>
> * * * *
>
> Mr. MOSS. When was the safety standards drafting committee [of the TMA] established for the manufacturers of infants and preschool toys?
> Mr. LOCKER. Approximately nine months ago, sir.
> Mr. MOSS. And when was the group appointed for makers of costumes, playsuits, and disguises?
> Mr. LOCKER. Approximately five months ago, sir.
> Mr. MOSS. Other than these, the groups for proposing standards for the industry have yet to be appointed?
> Mr. LOCKER. The industry has been classified into approximately twenty categories and these groups are in the process of developing their standards now. Other than those I have mentioned, we do not have at present moment standards available for a standards institute, except for the

bodies or the groups that I have just enumerated. We expect to before the year is out.

Mr. MOSS. The toy association has drafted and approved general toy safety guidelines. These have been distributed throughout the industry. When were they drafted and distributed?

Mr. LOCKER. I believe in December of 1968.

* * * *

Mr. MOSS. When would it be proposed that the industry act upon them and what would be the effect of the adoption upon members of the industry group?

Mr. LOCKER. The industry group has already acted upon them in that they have been adopted and distributed. The effect is rather difficult to gauge.

We are a voluntary trade association. Admittedly we cannot enforce our standards, we can only distribute them, make the manufacturers and the industry aware of them, and urge them to live up to these standards.

Mr. MOSS. Could you require as a condition of membership that they adhere to the standards adopted by the industry?

Mr. LOCKER. I believe our bylaws do provide that power, but I think counsel everywhere are aware we could have antitrust problems in that connection. We could.

As I say, our bylaws do provide for discipline in the event of something like that. I might add this, we have not disciplined any member.

Mr. MOSS. Not minimizing what you have done, the fact is that in the period of fourteen years you have adopted one definitive standard on paints and commended the work to develop another on stuffed toys and dolls ten years later, and within the last year acted on two other groups and circulated toy safety guidelines within the industry, but you cannot now tell us how many members of the industry have agreed or will agree to adhere to the guidelines.

Mr. LOCKER. I believe all members have agreed to adhere to it.

Mr. MOSS. This would not be a matter of opinion, it would be a matter of fact. Have they agreed to adhere to it?

Mr. LOCKER. Specifically in writing, no, sir, if that is what you mean by "agreement." In the sense that the board of directors and the membership have approved the adoption of standards, they have agreed.

The effect of the adoption is something that I cannot gauge.

Mr. MOSS. Then there is no agreement. It is before each member and it is up to each member to determine whether or not he will adhere to the standards?

Mr. LOCKER. I believe that is so.

The demonstrated toy industry lethargy with respect to adopting adequate standards is particularly disturbing since it has been recognized by the industry for some time that standards are needed. In the Fall 1959 issue of the *Home Safety Review* the director of public relations for the TMA wrote, "The Association is well aware of the additional safety precautions necessary to protect youngsters."

For comparison, let us look quickly at what has been done in two other important industrial nations, each with a long and honorable history of intelligent and creative toymaking: Great Britain and West Germany.

The first and perhaps most important thing to notice about the British Code of Safety Requirements for Children's Toys and Playthings is that it was prepared by a Technical Committee of the British Standards Institute (BSI), which included representatives from a wide variety of governmental, commercial, and professional organizations—including the British Toy Manufacturers' Association, the British Medical Association, the Consumer Council, and the Royal Society for the Prevention of Accidents. Thus at the very outset, a diversity of interest and a range of expertise were available to the framers of the code. The TMA guidelines, on the other hand, were prepared by the Toy Manufacturers' Association alone, and thus suffer from the inevitable defects that result from inbred parentage.

The second thing to note about the British Code is its specificity. Thus in dealing with the safety standards for electrical toys, for example, the British Code has this to say:

> If a toy is fitted with an electrical motor, the operating voltage of the motor will not exceed 24 volts. If the current is taken from the mains [i.e., household current] either a transformer or a power unit shall be used.

Or, on wooden toys:

> All woodwork shall be smoothly finished on all edges, corners and surfaces. Screws shall be used in preference to nails and they shall be countersunk-head or raised countersunk-head screws properly countersunk, or round-head wood screws, as described in [British Standards 1210].

An elaborate testing procedure using special test equipment is prescribed for evaluating the hazard of removing the eyes from stuffed toys. Plastic toys must be designed to withstand reasonable usage if the plastic is likely to be sharp when broken. The materials used to fill rattles must be harmless if swallowed. Clockwork and similar mechanisms should ordinarily be enclosed so that the moving parts cannot be touched, and if this is impossible, then the mechanism must be "of a shape and size that will not allow a child's finger to become ensnared in it."

These standards were first published in 1961, and were revised in 1968. Further revisions and additions are contemplated, and the BSI continues research into the problems of toy safety. The regulations, which have the force of law, are issued under the authority of the Home Secretary, a member of the British Cabinet, and the enabling legislation that empowers the Home Secretary to issue the safety regulations also provides for a forceful and independent advocate to speak for the general public, the British Consumer Council.

The West German standards are not quite so specific as the British toy safety requirements, but they do make it clear that the toy manufacturer has a duty to the toy buyer to take into consideration the possibility of misuse of a plaything by a child too young to handle it or to appreciate the warnings that are associated with it. The West German standards assert that the decision to give what toy to which children properly belongs with the parents, and notes that the influence of salesmen in retail stores on safety advice "seems limited." But one of the better points made by the West German standards is that a toy should be made so that it is not likely to be dangerous *even if a defect develops through normal use*. Children's playthings and clothing must be so flameproof that they will not burn under direct flame, or, if they do, that they must stop burning as soon as the flame is withdrawn. Detailed requirements for water toys, including buoyancy and multiple air chambers specifications are prescribed.

In May, 1970, the Assembly of the European Toy Institute met in Amsterdam and approved some general toy safety standards drafted by a committee of that body. On the most important subject of the flammability of toys, the institute was unable to reach agreement on a standard. They stated:

> Safety requirements pertaining to the flammability of toys other than play-acting toys have not been specified because the committee was unable to obtain sufficient information on the risks involved [note they were careful not to deny that there are risks] and, furthermore, because the present state of standardization in the field of flammability does not enable one to refer to suitable definitions and test specifications.

The committee had available to it the West German standard referred to above, but apparently found it too restrictive. Incorporated into the general standards was a statement that clearly envisioned the sale of "highly inflammable" toys. The institute charitably concluded, "There must be a special warning concerning the conditions of use, which are particular to each highly inflammable toy."

Yet another example of what we can expect from the toy industry when left on its own.

To sum up the case against leaving toy safety to voluntary self-regulation by the industry, we need only mention several clear facts:

(1) The industry so far has shown no zeal for safety. The TMA guidelines are entirely inadequate and even they are not observed with any degree of consistency. The annual Toy Fair is a showcase, among other things, for dangerous toys.

(2) The competition in the toy industry is intense. This means that a company that voluntarily adopts higher safety standards will probably be at an economic disadvantage in comparison with its competitors. Thus economic pressure encourages manufacturers to settle for the minimum.

(3) Furthermore, the entire notion of voluntary regulation by trade association is intrinsically hollow. For as we have seen in the case of Ohio Art, a company that doesn't like the rules can simply quit the club; and as the TMA admits, they have never disciplined a member for failure to comply with their guidelines.

(4) When the manufacturers draw up the general standards, they inevitably do so from a one-sided perspective. There is no effective consumer advocate who can influence the guidelines, nor is there any effective independent, technical expertise invoked to hammer out specific details. What is codified is the status quo rather than the product of serious research and broadly based national experience.

(5) Finally, the voluntary standards are legally unenforceable. Anyone can go right on making dangerous toys in spite of them, so long as he doesn't feel compelled to stay in the TMA or a similar association.

For all these reasons, I concur entirely with the National

Commission on Product Safety that the problem is much too serious to be left to the goodwill of the toymakers. There are many well-intentioned toy manufacturers, but as a group, the toy trade associations simply lack the interest and the perspective to do the job that needs to be done.

Industry self-regulation, therefore, is unsatisfactory both in practice and in theory. To whom do we turn? The next chapters, which explore the activities of independent testing agencies and the present state of governmental involvement in toy safety, take up that question.

4

Watching the Watchmen: The Testing Agencies

IN THE LAST CHAPTER WE SAW HOW LITTLE THE INDUSTRY REGUlates itself and how ineffective the process of voluntary standardmaking is. The next chapter will explore the extent to which there in any official requirement of toy safety written into the laws of the United States or of the several states. But between self-regulation and compulsory standards under the laws, there is a middle position: use of a testing agency to provide independent evaluation of the quality and safety of customer products.

This chapter, therefore, looks at the impact of the testing agencies upon the manufacture and marketing of toys. The first and most important point to recognize is that like self-regulation by the manufacturer, safety control by compliance with a testing agency's standards is a voluntary matter; and thus it is often entirely ineffective as a safety stimulus.

The real function that most of the testing agencies serve—excepting the Consumers Union, and to a degree, the Underwriters' Laboratories—is entirely different. It is the function of inducing buyer confidence. This is a major factor in any industry, and the toy industry is no exception. This is why we find in the toy industry all the usual trappings which other businesses also use to ensure confidence: the confusing variety of seals of approval and of reassuring endorsements, put out, so we believe, by disinterested and reliable organizations. The reader who has gotten this far will probably express no surprise when he learns in this chapter that there is very little correlation between this confidence-inducing material and toy safety. But it is unfortunately true that many parents put an undue amount of reliance on these paid-for endorsements. For while the toy merchants themselves do little enough to keep harmful toys out of the open market, their third-party helpmates, unfortunately, do very little more. Even the admittedly useful agencies—the truly independent ones—are relatively helpless in preventing dangerous toys from reaching the marketplace.

The toy industry stands, at present, in an almost totally free position. In the absence of governmental premarket testing and control, a toymaker who wishes to deal with the problem of safety and quality standards has a range of options. The most common of these is the purchasing of the services of independent testing laboratories. Using them is a voluntary matter, and so is complying with their findings.

Thus, if a private testing agency does discover a danger associated with a toy, it is under no obligation to report this to any governmental authority. The toymaker who gets an unfavorable report from one laboratory may simply ship the toy off to a second tester, and so on until he finds one that will approve. And while this shopping around for approval is going on, the public will never hear of the reports of those agencies refusing to concur. This is simply a matter of economics for both the toymaker and the toy tester. The toymaker doesn't want the unfavorable publicity, and the toy tester doesn't want to lose the business by making the unfavorable reports public. No toy manufacturer would be likely to hire a private tester if the latter stipulated that the manufacturer would be bound by the tester's findings, and that in a case of refusal by the manufacturer, the tester could publish its findings anyway.

A second option available to toymakers is the development of a "house laboratory," a testing division of the toy company itself. Some manufacturers, and some retailers as well, elect to take this route. There is something a little devious about some types of house testing, for the manufacturers are occasionally satisfied with the illusion of independent testing created by setting up a subsidiary corporation, sometimes with a different name, which issues its seal or stamp of approval. This is, for all practical purposes, just an advertising tactic.

Playskool, Inc., for example, is fond of impressing their advertising with a circular seal that reads: "Approved—Tested by Playskool Research." This seal is prominently displayed on their standard hammer-and-nails set, which they recommend for children three to six years of age. The set includes real three-quarter-inch nails and a working hammer, which, in the case of the set I looked at, had a metal head loose enough to be a potential source of serious injury. One version of this set carried a notation that it is "educational" and "safe"; but how safe are a metal hammer and real nails in the hands of a three-year-old?

Enclosed in the hammer-and-nails set was some promotional material for another Playskool product, the "Tyke Bike," complete with "high-rising handlebars." Although the "Tyke Bike" is supposed to be for children who are learning to walk, it has been demonstrated to be unsafe. The plastic grips covering the handle tips are easily removed, or lost, and the bike's own design lends itself to accidents in which the toddler pitches forward against the uncovered handle bar tip, risking the loss of an eye.

The failure of many toy manufacturers to live up to their claims of safety and concern for the children who use their merchandise, and the minimal and often inadequate testing by the companies, which is proof of this failure, have led some parents to place increasing reliance on third-party seals of approval. This, too, can be a dangerous mistake. Even third-party seals, presumably awarded by disinterested groups, can

TOYS THAT DON'T CARE 97

be worthless and empty of any real meaning. More dangerously, some of them are open to easy exploitation by manufacturers in their advertising and promotional campaigns, and become in fact more an assertion of the maker's interests than of the consumer's. Furthermore, most of us are generally unaware of how few checks and controls the agencies have over the use of their seals by manufacturers.

Some of the experts called to testify before the National Commission on Product Safety, for instance, have argued that both the *Good Housekeeping* and *Parents' Magazine* seals of approval tend to be misleading and to lull the public into "a false sense of security." Both of these seals—the *Good Housekeeping* Consumers' Guaranty Seal and the *Parents' Magazine* Commendation Seal—illustrate the problems involved in the practice of third-party policing of toys and other consumer items. In 1961, the Federal Trade Commission required *Good Housekeeping* to rename its "Seal of Approval" a "Consumers' Guaranty Seal," in order to avoid misrepresentation of the seal's effective meaning; and the National Commission on Product Safety has said (Final Report, p. 66) of both the *Good Housekeeping* seal and its *Parents' Magazine* analogue, that:

> Certifications or seals . . . usually appear to the consumer to offer more than is actually stated. Most consumers regard the *Good Housekeeping* seal as a useful guidepost. They do not realize its limited scope. . . . The backing for the seal . . . by . . . *Parents' Magazine* is similar. *Parents' Magazine* does not represent that it is satisfied that products with its seal are good or that advertising claims are truthful. It restricts it guaranty to claims made within 30 days of purchase.

What do these seals really mean? How does a toymaker get one for his product? The answers to these questions are disturbing.

The first requisite for both the *Good Housekeeping* and *Parents' Magazine* seals is the purchase of advertising space in the respective magazines, for both these seals are only awarded to advertisers. This involves a minimum expenditure of several thousand dollars. The basic advertising order in *Good Housekeeping*, for instance, is a twelve-month contract for two-thirds of a page. The cost ranges from $14,545 (black and white) to $28,265 (color). The advertising director of *Parents' Magazine* explains that their minimum contract is "somewhat negotiable," but usually runs about $9,030 for two-thirds of a page in black and white.

Once the would-be advertiser has bought the space, his use of it and of the seal is affected by the acceptability of his advertising and of his product. The magazines ask him to submit a sample for testing, and the tests are conducted chiefly with the aim of seeing whether the product really is what the advertising claims. If the magazine feels that the product is fairly represented in the advertising, the ad is accepted and the seal awarded; the seal may then be used in connection with the product for the duration of the advertising contract.

Before discussing in greater detail the actual testing by the magazines or their hired agencies, it might be instructive to contrast the process thus far with what happens in the case of genuinely independent testing agencies, such as the nonprofit Consumers Union or Consumers' Research, Inc. Both of these organizations buy the products they are testing, in the normal retail way. The magazines, however, accept a sample sent in *by the manufacturer*. Both independent testing agencies give the product a thorough going-over, looking for *all* the relevant factors before deciding whether or not it is a good buy, particularly in comparison with competing products in the same field. The magazines, in contrast, merely test to see whether the product is what the advertising says it is: no more. That the usefulness of the magazine testing is limited follows from the fact that the manufacturer is likely to submit the very best sample of the brand, and will take care that the item he supplies will meet the tests. The magazine testing, however, is not comparative and does not go into such matters as durability, safety, suitability (unless the advertisement makes explicit claims in these areas).

Even with all these limitations, the testing process itself is still subject to a further criticism. *Good Housekeeping* speaks proudly of a testing force of more than one hundred people occupying a block-long floor in the Hearst Building in New York City. *Parents' Magazine*, on the other hand, uses various commercial testing laboratories. But although we may assume that the tests actually conducted for both magazines are thorough and exacting, neither magazine gives a graded quality rating for the various products submitted. An item is either acceptable or unacceptable. This, again, is very different from the practice of the independent, consumer-oriented testing services, which do provide quality ratings and comparative results among competing products, not merely on standards of safety and performance, but also on "quality per dollar," i.e., the relation of effective performance to dollar cost. The independent services report both the good and the bad features of the product tested, and offer an over-all and comparative judgment upon it. This, of course, is vastly more sophisticated and certainly more helpful than a mere "pass/fail" scorecard.

This is why the seals of both *Parents' Magazine* and *Good Housekeeping* are really not very helpful: They do not reflect or reveal crucial information on performance or safety or relative product value. Thus, for instance, we can come across items on the open market which display the *Parents' Magazine* seal and at the same time are labeled both as nontoxic and yet not for internal consumption (Kenner Products' "Lightning Bug Brand Glo-Juice").

Furthermore, *Parents' Magazine* does not let its readers know which products do not appear in its pages because they failed the tests and were found not to meet their own advertising claims. This would be a worthwhile service and would certainly increase circulation; but it might also create some problems in the advertising department, and as a practical matter, profit-making magazines like to avoid any kind of problem in that key department.

So what the seals of approval given by these two magazines come down to is simply a kind of minimum protection against deceptive advertising. It is noteworthy that we already have some *statutory* protection against fraudulent advertising, in the form of the Federal Trade Commission's (FTC) powers under existing laws, as well as the broad authority held by the Food and Drug Administration (FDA) and a proliferation of local and state false-advertising statutes. Both the federal agencies just mentioned can issue cease-and-desist orders against false-advertising claims, and can initiate prosecution against the companies that make them. And there are similar provisions in the laws of many states as well.

The remedy available to the consumer who feels that the product he bought was not what the advertising represented it to be is usually limited. What the seal promises is only a refund or replacement of the product. The *Good Housekeeping* seal expressly provides:

> If product or performance defective, *Good Housekeeping* guarantees replacement or refund to consumer.

Most consumers, however, don't realize how limited this kind of a guarantee really is. *Good Housekeeping* warrants only that the advertised items are "good ones and that the claims made for them in our magazine are truthful." If the product turns out to be defective in terms of its claims—if, for example, your son is electrocuted by a toy that is advertised as shockproof—then the magazine will let you choose between another toy or a refund of your money. Since the magazine makes no statement about the product except that it does what the advertising claims it does, the seal can also be misleading by omission: It fails to warn of dangers or inadequacies not mentioned in the advertising itself.

As an instance of this misleading by omission, consider the March, 1969, issue of *Good Housekeeping*, which carries a full-page advertisement for a certain dishwasher soap, including a picture of the box it comes in. The box as you buy it in the supermarket has a warning label on both the front and the back sides, cautioning that the soap can be harmful to human skin and eyes; the label was added after the Food and Drug Administration seized the soap eighteen months earlier for being "improperly labeled" in failing to provide such a warning. The advertisement in *Good Housekeeping*, which pictures the box, doesn't include the warning. Warnings of this kind are important, particularly so since children tend to play nearby when their mother is doing the wash and since they like to play with empty boxes, which usually do have a few flakes left in the bottom. The people at *Good Housekeeping* seem to have found no problem with this sort of advertising, since as far as they were concerned, the soap was good enough to meet the test of doing what the advertising said it would do. But, of course, the housewife who buys the soap because it is advertised in *Good Housekeeping* surely assumes that if there were any danger connected with it, *Good Housekeeping* would at least have warned her.

One would not wish to be too hard on *Good Housekeeping*, for the magazine's editorial staff has at times been alert to the need for educating parents about harmful toys. The December, 1969, issue included a report prepared by one of its staff dealing with the controversies over toy safety. The May, 1969, issue ran a short piece that set forth some guidelines for buying safe outdoor play equipment. Neither of these otherwise excellent presentations, however, named names of specific products found to be unsuitable.

In the same issue as the report on toy safety, *Good Housekeeping* carried a full-page ad for Fisher-Price toys. Although this ad contained a group picture of a number of toys in their product line, its over-all intention was "institutional," i.e., to promote the company itself in a general way. The copy asserted, among other things, that Fisher-Price toys are "Safer . . . [C]areful eyes make sure that every edge is smoothed down, every inch of color is fast, wheels . . . are firmly attached." But how does this general statement and the implied *Good Housekeeping* endorsement which goes with it cover such items as:

- the Fisher-Price musical lacing shoe toy which, as one parent complained to the National Commission on Product Safety, came apart so that "pieces of the broken musical mechanism found their way outside the toy and into the baby's bed."
- the Fisher-Price "Telephone Pull-Toy" about which another parent wrote that "if the wheel is taken off, which my three-year-old son did while the ten-month-old baby was [also] playing with it, [it leaves] a dangerous pointed spike."
- the Fisher-Price play xylophone in which the metal keys are attached with one-inch nails, which easily loosen through use and come readily out of the wooden frame. The wheels come off to expose a dangerous spike, and the base is secured with other sharp nails. This inexcusable contraption is advertised as suitable for children from one through six, and the package it comes in carries both the *Good Housekeeping* and the *Parents' Magazine* seals. (As a note on design, the author has seen other xylophones in which the keys were fixed to the frame with other materials than nails; and if nails have to be used, then why not screw-type nails, which would be harder to remove?) (Fig. 39)

Toys for children who aren't yet walking often wind up in cribs, and this opens up another danger in some of these Fisher-Price playthings. Several of them—aimed at children who are very young, even less than a year old—come equipped with tough plastic ropes. There are reported instances of infants managing to entangle themselves dangerously with ropes like these; it is a foreseeable hazard.

In the same issue of *Good Housekeeping*, then, we find a contradictory approach to toy safety. Editorially, the magazine states explicitly that it would disapprove of advertising for toys that "have rough or sharp edges or surfaces" or that are "for crib or toddler use [and have] attached small objects which can be swallowed or choked upon, such as loose nuts and bolts, removable eyes on stuffed toys or small projections which break off." And the magazine quotes from my testimony on durability before the National Commission on Product Safety: "Toys should be made sturdy enough to take wear and tear, and the seemingly brutal and unnatural use, to which children put them. If a toy cannot stand such wear, then it should not be manufactured." This editorial stand seems to me to be inconsistent with a blanket "institutional" advertisement including the specific Fisher-Price toys I have listed above. And in the promotional material that Fisher-Price puts in its toy packages, packages that carry the *Good Housekeeping* seal, we read that their playthings are:

> SAFETY FIRST Toys of flawless Western Pine, highest quality plastic materials, heavy steel parts. Finest nontoxic finishes, rounded corners and edges, safely concealed mechanisms. Playthings fashioned from materials appropriate to the toy's play-purpose . . . resulting in long-lasting toys that assure safe, happy play.

With this kind of promotion, plus the seal, it's easy to understand how buyers of Fisher-Price toys would tend to make no independent investigation of their own—which could be a dangerous form of overconfidence.

One final and relatively minor point that should be made about the *Good Housekeeping* seal is that, in practice, it comes into play only in extremely few cases. Although the magazine guarantees replacement or refund, they also require that every complaint be verified before reimbursement will be made. In 1968, they rejected eighty-five percent of the complaints received and a number of unhappy buyers discovered that the guarantee on, for instance, a household appliance did not cover the particular model in question.

The *Parents' Magazine* seal works much the same way, with a special fillip. Their basic policy is that they will refund the money or replace the product as the consumer wishes; if he doesn't pick one or the other within ninety days, then the magazine sends him the money. The *Parents' Magazine* seal (which is now a product-advertising "guarantee" rather than the "recommendation," which it used to be) is, they say, only granted to products "which are suitable for families with *children*." This should induce special confidence in the toy buyer who relies on *Parents' Magazine*'s good judgment and independence. But, the December, 1969, issue typically contains an ad by Kenner Products Company promoting "365-day toys." One of the playthings so described is the "Betty Crocker Easy-Bake Oven," which I mention in Part Two as potentially lethal because of its use of 110-volt household electrical current. The toy's advertising copy describes it as "safe" and bears the magazine's seal.

There is another problem connected with the *Parents' Magazine* seal. Habitual readers of the magazine will note that one of the regular advertisements therein is for the catalog put out by F.A.O. Schwarz, reputedly America's oldest and largest retail toy outlet. What the habitual reader is less likely to know or remember, however, is that *Parents' Magazine* owned the entire chain of F.A.O. Schwarz stores from 1963 to 1970.

The possibilities of self-deception by the magazine are obvious and enormous. While *Parents'* claims to be "devoted, as always, to the special needs of families with children," it is a matter of record that many inherently dangerous and poten-

Fig. 39. Toy xylophone put together with nails and spikes.

NOW...CHEMTOY LAUNCHES AN IMPORTANT NATIONAL PRE-SELLING CAMPAIGN!

featuring the PARENTS' MAGAZINE GUARANTEE SEAL on all these products:

- LIQUID BUBBLE TOYS ☐ JUMP ROPES ☐ MODELING DOUGH
- PLAY MONEY SETS ☐ SPRAY SNOW
- JAX'N BALL SETS ☐ PLAY PUTTY
- HARMONICAS ☐ FUN SETS
- EASTER EGG COLORS

REFUND OR REPLACEMENT GUARANTEED TO CONSUMER BY **PARENTS' MAGAZINE** IF PRODUCT OR PERFORMANCE IS DEFECTIVE & REPORTED WITHIN 30 DAYS OF PURCHASE

HERE IS HOW THIS PROGRAM WILL HELP ALL CHEMTOY DEALERS

1. National Ads in Parents' Magazine will pre-sell CHEMTOY TOYS to millions of youngsters and their parents.

2. Parents' Magazine Guarantee Seal printed on CHEMTOY packaging will create customer acceptance at Point-of-Purchase.

CHEMTOY PRODUCTS WILL NOW SELL EASIER, FASTER AND MORE PROFITABLY THAN EVER BEFORE

Fig. 40. Maximum use made of Parent's Seal of Approval in the 1970 Chemtoy wholesale fall catalog.

tially unsafe playthings are sold in F.A.O. Schwarz stores. Most of the dangerous toys that I exhibited in the course of my testimony before the National Commission on Product Safety, for instance, were collected in the course of one short shopping tour of F.A.O. Schwarz's Boston store. Some of the questions I would put to the magazine are these:
- Did *Parents' Magazine* test all of the toys sold by F.A.O. Schwarz?
- Did they let F.A.O. Schwarz sell toys that they would not advertise in the magazine because they were dangerous or flimsy?
- Do they make any effort to inform consumers of the toys they have rejected after testing?

These are the kinds of questions that child protection requires, and it is regrettable that the magazine has not yet seen fit to give them straightforward, factual answers.

One last problem concerning the use of seals of approval is the question of how the seal is used by the company to which it has been granted. For the manner in which some companies exploit the award of a seal does little for toy safety. As a glaring example of this, let me cite the way the Chemtoy Corporation used *Parents' Magazine* in its 1970 Fall Wholesale Catalog, which is sent out to toy shops across the nation and was distributed at the 1970 Toy Fair in New York City. Fig. 40 shows the catalog cover and the way in which the seal is splashed across it. Within the catalog of toys "from tots to teens" were, among others, the following:
- Several different types of slingshot.
- Varieties of peashooters, some "for safe fun."
- "People Pieces" (see page 67).
- Space-shooter disks described as "safe" and just as dangerous as the more expensive Ray Plastics, Inc., "Star Trek Gun" described in Chapter Two).
- Cap-crackers, which look like dynamite sticks and are as "safe as an ordinary cap."

- Double-action dart guns, which shoot two darts with rubber tips together.
- Crossbow apparatus designed to shoot rubber-tipped darts at high velocities.

I would suspect that the toys just listed would not be guaranteed by *Parents' Magazine*. But clearly the overabundant and overenthusiastic use by the manufacturer of the magazine's seal is an attempt to lend prestige to the company's entire line of playthings. This practice contributes to the assurance on the catalog cover that "Chemtoy products will now sell easier, faster and more profitably than ever before."

The same general criticisms of seals from magazines can fairly be applied as well to independent testing agencies that operate for profit. The agencies are paid by the manufacturers to test their products; their profits come from the manufacturers; the pressure, obviously, is in favor of the men who pay the pipers. The consumer tends to get shorter shrift.

Two of the most important of these agencies are the United States Testing Company, Inc., and its subsidiary, the Nationwide Consumer Testing Institute, Inc. (NCTI). The names themselves tend to be a giveaway, for they both are carefully framed to give an impression, in the former case, of some vague governmental connection and, in the latter case, of a fundamentally independent and consumer-oriented operation. Like the seals and testing operations of the magazines, both the USTC and the NCTI work actively to gain public acceptance —and to make a profit—through self-advertising by issuing seals.

The United States Testing Company, Inc. (USTC) is the world's largest profit-making independent testing laboratory. The USTC will undertake to test almost anything for an interested manufacturer, and many of those toys that are given premarket tests are examined by the USTC. The procedure in working with the USTC is this: A company that wants its product tested negotiates with the USTC until they establish a maximum testing-fee limit; then, within this limit, the testing agency carries on a battery of experiments designed to give a general picture of the total product. If the item in question passes the company's tests and meets its over-all standards, the USTC name may be used in advertising materials.

The NCTI, USTC's subsidiary, also tests many toys and playthings. (Part of its business derives from the fact that it is the major testing laboratory for *Parents' Magazine*.) One major difference between the USTC and the NCTI is that, unlike the former, the Institute issues a formal emblem of approval, the Quality Certified Seal. For a product to earn this stamp of recommendation, it must pass a two-phase series of tests. Phase One is a set of premarketing, laboratory-situation experiments; Phase Two is a "quality audit program," a periodic testing of the product as it appears on the open market for a period of one to two years (which varies according to the terms of the Institute's contract with the manufacturing company). If both these phases provide satisfactory results, the seal may then be used by the manufacturer for promotional purposes.

The apparent thoroughness of both these testing agencies looks reassuring at first glance, but in evaluating it, we must remember that both firms are oriented toward the manufacturer rather than the consumer. Basic to the entire scheme is the premise that a profit must be made by helping toymakers who are willing to pay for the testing services but are expecting, of course, to be able to use the agency's seal of approval or name in the promotional way. Both agencies therefore tend to emphasize to the manufacturer that their approval can be a major factor in buyer acceptance and in forming consumer habits. The NCTI will even assist the manufacturer in making the most effective possible use of the item in question. Neither agency exposes to the public the shortcomings and dangers of products that fail the tests. Neither, then, is really very helpful at all.

Other testing agencies, however, are useful, as well as independent and self-supporting. The best-known of these is the famous Underwriters' Laboratories (UL), the world's oldest and largest independent safety-testing service. Formed in 1894 to combat the problem of fire hazards caused by electrical devices, and renowned for its distinctive UL seal, the Underwriters' Laboratories association is nonprofit and self-sustaining and operates under the auspices of the National Board of Fire Underwriters.

Every conceivable kind of appliance, machine, or substance is tested by UL—including children's toys—which could, if badly made or if misused, become a safety hazard. Their work is not limited to the detection of electrical hazards, for which they are chiefly known, but extends also to inspection of burglary and signaling devices and alarms, fire prevention and control systems, and chemical, gas, and oil equipment. In each of these fields, the UL testing is entirely a voluntary matter on the part of the manufacturer. If he chooses to submit his product for testing, he must furnish the sample and pay all the costs incurred in examining it. The UL testing pattern concentrates on safety and not on performance and so the final judgment is not of comparative performance, but in terms of a passing or failing mark with respect to certain minimum safety requirements. Results of tests of products that pass the test are published annually; failures are not disclosed. In all of these respects, the UL shares the weaknesses of the agencies mentioned above, although its independence is without question.

Furthermore, until February, 1970, UL approval could have been misleadingly used by some manufacturers who were inclined to give the UL seal a weight and emphasis that it was never intended to have. For example, the UL seal attached to the cord of an electrical appliance or plaything meant that only the *cord* was safe, not that the entire item was harmless. The inner parts of the toy, the cord, and the plug may each have had its own test and approval (or failure). Now the UL only approves household products if the submitted sample is free of "all significant hazards."

Besides the fact that even the electrical approval by the UL is limited and this can be confusing, there is the further problem that some manufacturers let the seal stand for far too much. The UL seal is not a judgment that the item is suitable for children. (An electrical oven or a metal-casting set may be UL-approved, even though it reaches temperatures of between 600° and 800°F. But it is fully evident that items of this potential cannot safely be given to four-year-old children.) Manufacturers, nonetheless, are hardier souls than most of us, and some will continue to exploit our faith in the UL seal in order to sell their wares. It is common to find the UL seal on unsuitable and potentially dangerous electrical toys, prominently displayed next to an incantation about the toy's being "safe for play for little ones."

It can also be argued that the UL standards themselves are too relaxed with respect to electrical toys. The Metal Ware Corporation puts out an "Empire Little Lady Oven" that is UL-approved despite the fact that its sides heat up to 200°F., the top to over 300°F., and the inside to 660°F.! In response to an inquiry about this oven, the UL replied that if it were not able to get this hot it would not be able to perform as advertised and would thus be unfit for baking and cooking. It appears that they simply did not take up the question of whether such a toy were suitable for use by children.

A comparable case is that of the "Mirro Miniature Electric Corn Popper," which the maker sells as a toy but which UL studied as a full-fledged household appliance. The safety requirements, by the way, are less stringent for appliances, which are intended for adults, than for toys, which are for use by children. Both these electrical toys—and this is the point—are not really toys at all. UL is right in classifying the corn popper as an appliance; and since it is such, Mirro is wrong in selling it as a toy. The same holds for the miniature electrical oven.

But the use of the UL seal on the item lulls parents into thinking that the entire apparatus is foolproof, and when the product is sold for children, the parent naturally believes that since it has been approved by UL it must be safe for them.

As a general principle, toys that require household electrical current for their operation are inadvisable. Some of them, of course, are more dangerous than others. But all of them are potentially lethal, for electrical shock is potentially lethal. Some of them have hidden dangers, which not even UL approval guards against. Argo Industries Corporation makes a "Magic Cool Oven," with electrical coils like a real kitchen range; it sports on the package the familiar UL seal and is, we are told, "outside safe for little fingers to touch." The UL seal covered only the oven's electrical specifications, and certainly did not mean to imply that it was safe for kiddies to put their fingers in or on the oven.

Or consider the "Suzy Homemaker Super-Safety Oven" made by the Deluxe Topper Corporation and the Kenner Products Company's "Easy Bake Oven," both of which use light bulbs to supply the cooking heat. This practice is better in principle that that of using heating coils, but it carries still other dangers. Both ovens have some metal parts with sharp and potentially cutting edges. Both of them, moreover, present the possibility of seriously burning a child who removes or breaks the bulb and sticks his finger in the socket. The fact that there is a light bulb involved at all, with its fragility and the consequent danger of cuts and lacerations, makes both ovens unacceptable. Yet both carried the UL seal.

Electrical toys that may carry the UL seal have also presented other dangers which the UL testers did not deal with. Both the Mirro corn popper mentioned above and the "Chilton Corn Popper" are built in a way that permits water to enter the heater housings when they are washed or even wiped off with a wet rag or sponge. Water in these housings creates a shock hazard. Yet both carried the UL seal. Again, crumpled

TOYS THAT DON'T CARE

paper or cotton fabrics touched to the bottom of the Mirro corn popper glow red and char, a fire hazard for any household appliance, toy or not.

Moreover, the UL seal is not mandatory, for there is no requirement set either by the government or by the toy industry trade associations that it be sought and obtained for electrical toys. Whether or not a toy is submitted to the UL for testing is a decision resting entirely with the toymaker. If he does send the toy for investigation and it fails the tests, the UL will tell him so and tell him why. But what he does after that is his own business. No one steps in to tell him that he must not market the dangerous toy; and in cases where he suspects that it won't be approved, he probably won't even bother to have it tested at all. For instance, the "Rapco Metal-Casting Set" includes an electrical "furnace" that reaches temperatures of 800°F. inside; and when the pouring ladle is removed, the inside can be reached by hands or touched by children's clothing; even when the ladle is in place, the temperatures still reach 500 to 600°F. The toy carries no UL listing and is obviously dangerous, but there is no effective premarket regulation anywhere that can keep it off the market. The Federal Trade Commission has stated that twenty-four percent of the items submitted to UL for the first time failed to meet its standards, and that ninety-three percent of these are never corrected. Most of them are put on the market anyway.

Even more frightening than toys that lack the UL seal are those that have it but don't meet its requirements. Testimony was introduced before the National Commission on Product Safety concerning the "Suzy Homemaker Super Grill" which, on four samples tested, failed the UL strain-relief requirement. The grill nevertheless carries the UL seal. (Strain relief means that when a pull is exerted on the electrical cord, it cannot be fully transmitted to the electrical terminals on the toy itself. The appropriate UL requirement in this kind of toy is a strain-relief standard of thirty-five pounds of pull.)

Presumably the sample toy that the UL tested met the standard, but the toys bought on the open market did not. The UL sample, of course, came direct from the manufacturer, and was provided for the very purpose of meeting the tests UL imposes. In this case, there was a breakdown in UL field inspection. The consequences are that when a child pulls on the cord to unplug the toy, the inadequate strain-relief device might give way; the resultant strain disconnects the terminals, and the whole toy becomes electrically alive.

Just how misleading the UL seal can be is superbly illustrated by a report given to the National Commission on Product Safety by Stephen Bluestone of New York:

Purpose of Statement

My intention is to set forth a safety hazard analysis of two electrical toy heating mold units. The units, manufactured by different companies, are in a total of at least eleven different toy sets. One is the Thingmaker heating unit by Mattel, Inc., of Hawthorne, California. It is a part of such toys as Triple Thingmaker, Picadoos, Creepy Crawlers, Eeeks!, Creeple Peeple, and Zoofie Goofies. The other is a heating unit by the Topper Corp. of Elizabeth, New Jersey, and is included as a component in Rings 'n Things, Specs 'n Things, Bags 'n Things, Monster Makers, and Johnny Toymaker.

Mattel is commonly acknowledged to be the largest American toy company and Topper among the first five in size.

Appearance and Operation

Each unit is a rectangular metal box with an open top surrounded by a border. A removable lead mold rests on a ledge within the border. A distance beneath the top and directly below the mold is the heater plate, a flat rectangular surface with sides. The top perimeter of these four sides comprises the ledge upon which the mold rests. In other words, it is simply as if a flat mold was placed on top of a pan that was surrounded by a metal housing.

The procedure in operating all of the mold sets (all make solid plastic products) is to fill the cavities of the mold with liquid plastic and place it into the recessed top. The unit, activated by inserting the electric plug into an outlet, creates sufficient heat so that after about 20 minutes the molded plastic solidifies. Next, the hot mold is taken off the heating unit and plunged into cold water. The plastic is then removed from the mold in the expected shape of a flower, a monster, etc.

Thermal Hazard of Heater Plate

In order for the heating unit to perform its task of hardening the liquid plastic, it is necessary that the heater element achieve certain temperatures. Consumers Union, in the November, 1968, issue of *Consumer Reports* states that the Deluxe Topper Rings 'n Things "heater reached 550 degrees F. in recess where mold is placed . . ." and the Thingmaker, 440 degrees in the same place.

A metal surface that has attained a temperature of 550 degrees is capable of instantly igniting a match, scorching a piece of tissue paper in seconds, and causing serious and substantial burns to any part of the human body that comes in contact with it.

It is noteworthy to mention that *Toys & Novelties* magazine in a November, 1968, article entitled "Age Group Guide to Toys" indicated that both of the subject heating units were to be used by children aged five through eight.

The Topper heating unit was approximately three inches by six and one-half inches, in dimension. The Thingmaker is three and one-half by three. Both are totally open with no protective guard. There is no warning to a child how hot they get, nor is there any notice to a parent that these surfaces reach temperatures of 550 and 440 degrees, respectively. Nowhere in any advertising, on any package or on any instructions is there even mention of the fact that these heater plates get dangerously hot. There is to be seen, however, after deliberate and sharp-eyed search and, incidentally, after the sale has been made, a token message stamped into both metal plates. In tiny letters (Topper's are $\frac{1}{4}''$ and Thingmaker's letters are $\frac{1}{8}''$), the same color as the surrounding plate and in a most unalarming, matter-of-fact way is the phrase:

CAUTION—CONTACT WITH
HEATER PLATE MAY CAUSE
BURNS

May cause burns! Is there any doubt that if five- to eight-year-old fingers, not to mention anyone else's, touch this blazing hot surface, a burn will occur? The extent, severity and amount of pain cannot be speculated upon but what is certain is this: The injury received is unnecessary. It was awarded to a hapless child by a manufacturer who placed economy over safety.

It is painfully clear that many children for whom these toys are intended by the manufacturer cannot read that dim and obscure warning that is intended to save them from a severe burning. Children only start kindergarten at age five.

Thermal Hazard of Top Border and Sides

The function of the heating units is allegedly solely to harden the liquid plastic, thus requiring heat only beneath the mold. In fact, however, not only do the heating plate and mold heat up, but the top border and sides of the housing also get hot. With the Topper unit, the heat reaches the 200 to 225 degree level. What does 200 degrees feel like? Consumers Union stoically informs us that the sides heat up to 200 degrees. What this temperature means is left to the consumer parent to wonder about. To this observer, it is "very hot." You touch quickly and automatically you withdraw your hand quite aware of the fact that you came in contact with a surface hot enough to bring surprise, anger, and a low decibel stream of four-letter words.

Should a child suspect that the entire unit apart from the heating plate gets hot? Is he given any warning that the dull metal sides of his Topper unit reach temperatures of 200 to 225 degrees F.?

Yes, in letters $1/4$ inch in size and the same color as its background is the wording:

> CAUTION—CONTACT WITH MOLD
> OR ENCLOSURE MAY CAUSE BURNS

It is most difficult to read these words because the metal into which the "warning" is stamped is ribbed, further complicating the communicative properties of this message.

The Mattel Thingmaker unit also has a warning on the top border. It states in $1/8$ inch letters:

> CAUTION VERY WARM SURFACES

There appears to be no good reason why a child who is using either of these "toys" as a plaything, for enjoyment, should be forced to experience a burn or unpleasant heat exposure, especially from a remote, non-functional surface area. It is certainly foreseeable that a child of any age will accidently touch or intentionally grab these 160 to 225 degree sides and top border. Is it foreseeable that a younger brother or sister could most innocently and inquisitively enter upon the scene?

Underwriters' Laboratory Seal

Stamped into the metal on one side of both heating units is the UL seal. Seeing this seal gives one a feeling of confidence that the electrical product associated with it is safe. The trouble is that the UL approval only pertains to the electrical connections, circuitry, etc. It is not meant by Underwriters' Labs to be a guarantee that the product is safe. The value of the seal has been oversold. It is being abused by overzealous toy manufacturers who are interested in shrouding an electrical toy behind a veil of safety. Its approval has no relationship as to how a product will be used or misused. Its value here is a negative one, that of giving a false sense of security to the problem of open heater plates reaching 440 to over 550 degrees. Both cartons, Mattel and Topper, have the UL seal clearly and prominently printed on them.

Parental Supervision and Instructions

None of the observed television advertising for the heating unit products represents any parents or gives any indication that a parent or older person should be present to supervise.

Neither package makes any disclosures to the effect that supervision is necessary. Interestingly, the implication cannot be overlooked that presale safety information is lacking.

The Mattel package for "Creeple Peeple" even goes so far as to dissuade potential supervision by succinctly stating:

USES HOUSEHOLD CURRENT—SAFE

The intended meaning of this phrase is impossible to discern, considering the lethal properties of electric current; nevertheless, the message is positioned on the front label next to the UL seal of approval.

The Creeple Peeple instruction booklet has an introduction entitled "Dear Parent." It reads:

> By following the easy fully illustrated instructions your child can make Creeple Peeple as gifts, and for himself, with the *safe,* efficient Thingmaker. *It carries the UL listing Model No. 4477.* [author's italics]

A separate sheet found in the Topper package initially gives a ray of hope. In bold headlines, it opens:

IMPORTANT
Attention Parents
Please read before giving
this toy to your child.

After discussing the excitement that this toy will bring to a child, the "red flag" states:

We strongly recommend that you, the parent, supervise, or better yet, show your child how to make the first few toys. Instructions such as the time needed for molding, how important it is to wipe the mold dry and how to pour superplastic are simple and easy to follow but they are important for making good toys . . .

Nowhere does this "Important" advise the parent that he had better be sure his child is mature enough to handle this product. There is no implication that safety is a consideration. Nowhere is there even a reference to the barely visible burn cautions stamped in the heating chamber and on the top. Safety has been deftly skirted and has given way to such relative trivia as how to pour superplastic.

Similarly, the Mattel Creeple Peeple instructions are silent to the possible hazards inherent in its Thingmaker unit.

In short, the extreme temperatures produced by these toys is not one of the reasons why parents should supervise his child's playing with heat mold toys.

Turning on the Units

In neither is there an off-on switch. It is therefore necessary to plug in the electric cord each time it is to be used. This could involve continual encounters with live electricity, and although the Topper plug has a safety flange, many trips to the wall outlet doesn't appear to be a highly encourageable aspect of these toys.

* * * *

The negligence involved in putting toys like these on the market, with such poor design, such inadequate safety engineering, such inherently and searingly dangerous potential, such deceptive and almost nonexistent cautionary instructions and such misleading use of the UL seal, is reprehensible and should be criminal.

We may expect to see the testing agencies and "guarantee"

awarding magazines becoming much stricter with their industrial clients in the future. For there is developing in the law a theory that a testing agency which has approved an unsafe product has violated a legal duty to the consumer who buys the product on that agency's recommendation and is injured by it. A few more successful suits against the testers will doubtless encourage them to police their clients and to work vigorously to reduce abuses of their seals.

The abuse of endorsements is sometimes carried on wholesale instead of merely toy by toy. In some cases, a reassuring "recommendation" is available for an entire catalog of toys. The Jordan Marsh Company, which is a major department store concern with branches throughout New England and in Florida, mails out a toy catalog of "Discovery Playthings" to all its customers. The catalog recounts that the "Discovery Playthings" listed are inspected and approved by the Child Study Association of America (CSAA), Inc., "a national nonprofit agency founded in 1888." The CSAA in turn states in the catalog that the toys listed meet certain standards; they should be both "safe and durable. They should really work. They should challenge [the child's] creativity, encourage him to manipulate [the toys] in many ways."

With these laudable aims and standards in mind, how can one explain the inclusion in one issue of the catalog, studied by the author, of the following items:

- A crawl-in tunnel for ages three to nine, described as "a simple contrivance that endures through years of play because, like the best of play materials, it allows the child-mind to turn it to many purposes . . . even a young child . . . can . . . have it in or out of doors." This tunnel, and others like it, was found to be so dangerously and excessively flammable that the Federal Trade Commission seized and removed from the market 50,000 lest they get into American homes. And of course, the FTC had no way at all to get back the ones already sold and in use "in or out of doors."

- "Monkey Swing," for ages four to ten, which is the one described in Chapter Two as especially dangerous and unsuitable. The heavy seat swings in a 360° circle, as the catalog says, "up and down, by zigzag, sideways, dizzying round and round can be experienced on this one rope swing"—and it can crack the skull of a second child standing in its uncontrollable path.
- "Satellite Jump Shoes," for ages five and up, with which the child can play at being a "frog . . . a kangaroo, a mom mom." These shoes come with "rubber bumpers for the sake of the floors." The National Commission on Product Safety took a plainspoken view of this toy in its Interim Report; it is "inordinately dangerous" and can easily lead to "broken ankle bones and injuries to the feet and the legs . . . obviously dangerous for young children due to a lack of balance and ankle support."

So we can take the Child Study Association of America endorsement in this particular catalog for what it seems to be worth.

Finally, and fortunately, there *are* testing organizations that can be *truly* helpful to parents and others concerned about the safety quality of their children's toys. These are the nonprofit and consumer-financed agencies such as the Consumers Union and Consumers' Research, Inc.

Both Consumers Union and Consumers' Research are genuinely independent. Neither deals directly with manufacturers. Both publish their findings, pro *and* con, in monthly magazines. Consumers Union puts out *Consumer Reports;* Consumers' Research publishes a *Consumer Bulletin.* Neither magazine accepts any advertising whatsoever, and neither organization will permit its name to be used in any way connected with advertising or promotion. Consumers Union has even gone to court to keep manufacturers of products they rated highly from making use of the ratings.

The products that both organizations test and rate are

bought on the open market by their own shoppers. They will not accept samples supplied by the maker, as both *Good Housekeeping* and *Parents' Magazine* do, and as the UL also does. This means that Consumers Union and Consumers' Research reports—which, by the way, usually agree—are based on the same samples you or I might buy in our local store. As we have seen in the case of the UL-approved items mentioned earlier, these market items can differ significantly from manufacturer-supplied samples.

Consumers Union and Consumers' Research evaluations also go into the important matter of approximate cost and comparative quality among the competing products. Their samples are subjected to a broad range of tests, including laboratory experiments, controlled-use tests, and expert inspection. The nature and the findings of these tests are published, along with the organizations' over-all rating of each product. Both organizations make it clear that approval of one of the given manufacturer's products in no way implies approval of any of his other products. This sets them apart from the magazines, which engender confusion and ill will by belatedly explaining to dissatisfied consumers that the malfunctioning products they complained of were not covered by the seal because the seal only covered a specific model, a fact the consumer would not be likely to know.

There is really only one drawback to Consumers Union and Consumers' Research: they do not test *everything*. Because there are so many different products, their testing is highly selective. Their chief interests are in automobiles, appliances, and household items, and their opportunity to examine consumer products is necessarily limited. On the whole, they do not test toys in any genuinely systematic or full-scale way, and over the past few years, their comparative analysis of children's products has been largely confined to bicycles and chemistry sets. The November, 1968, issue of *Consumer Reports* did go deeply into electrical toys, but their annual product buying guide only evaluates bicycles and sleds. They do not provide comprehensive information on the vast majority of toys sold annually.

An over-all look at the testing agencies, whether governmental or private and for profit, or independent and not for profit, shows that there simply is no adequate premarket testing or general supervision of toys and playthings. The manufacture and sale of toys in America has reached colossal proportions, while premarket testing remains negligible. The assortment of agencies that do go into the problem are not —even collectively—in any way up to the task at hand, which is to ensure that dangerous toys are kept out of the channels of commerce.

The federal government lays most of its emphasis on parental education, and when it does deal with industry, it does so by suggesting voluntary guidelines. Concrete governmental action, as by the FTC, most often comes only *after* a hue and cry has been raised.

The seals of approval of both *Good Housekeeping* and *Parents' Magazine* are mere guarantees against fraudulent advertising, not positive assurances of product safety; and they are issued under conditions which, as we have seen, leave the field wide open for abuse. Economic necessity and manufacturer orientation keep both magazines from exposing the toys that fail, and furthermore, neither magazine is a consumer research agency—the seal is really only a promotional tool for the magazines, which encourages manufacturers to use them as vehicles for advertising purposes.

The profit-making testing agencies, like USTC and NCTI, are also industry-oriented and for the same reasons. Their revenue comes from the manufacturer, not from the consumer. They feel that exposure of failing products would be a violation of a "professional confidence" and they realize, too, that it would drive away potential customers. And a rejection by either agency (as by the magazines) in no way limits the manufacturer's right and opportunity to sell his dangerous toys.

Nonprofit agencies like the UL have been helpful, but even their tests are not compulsory nor is their approval required. Furthermore, their standards are occasionally too low or too little adapted to the fact that the items in question are for children. And the follow-up on approved products can at times be minimal. The cure is in compulsory testing.

Even the very best agencies, like the Consumers Union and Consumers' Research, which issue no seals and depend in no way on the voluntary compliance of the manufacturer who submits products, and which publish thoughtful and authoritative reports, are not enough. For their testing is necessarily limited; they can't take up everything, nor do they nor can they police the entire toy industry. They do provide a valuable and a necessary service; but it is a limited one, and it can at times make mistakes. They once approved a "Roly-Poly" musical doll—and retracted the approval when they found that it was easily breakable and had stiff and pointed metal spikes inside. I wish they would devote an entire issue to toys; it would be enormously instructive.

The situation is serious—700,000 toy injuries a year—and the public seems almost entirely unprotected from toy hazards. "There ought to be a law." There are a few, and what they add in the way of protection from dangerous toys is our next topic.

5

Governmental Action and Toy Safety

PERHAPS THE SINGLE MOST TELLING FACT ABOUT THE PRESENT state of federal consumer safety programs is this one: in its June, 1970, Final Report, the National Commission on Product Safety, established two and a half years earlier by act of Congress, told the President and the Congress that at least 350 major categories of products are "largely unregulated" with respect to their safety in the hands of American consumers (F.R., p. 89). Of these categories, twenty-five refer to toys of different kinds, and at least another thirty include articles that children usually own or play with.

Most parents, on the other hand, have the impression that, by and large, there are federal laws and governmental agencies that operate effectively to keep really dangerous playthings off the market. Because we have this impression, it operates as an unspoken assumption behind our purchasing and using habits, and we tend to believe as a matter of course that most things we buy for ourselves and our children are safe. The dangerous product, we expect, will be the exception, and not the rule. Nothing could be farther from the truth.

The fact of the matter is, as the NCPS puts it, that "federal authority to curb hazards in consumer products is virtually nonexistent" (F.R., p. 2). Because this is so, the present state of affairs is all the more dangerous, for we are even less inclined to take extra care if we assume that we are already protected; and since we are not protected, we lower our guard just when it should be highest.

The extent to which we are unprotected is spelled out by the Commission:

> Federal product safety legislation consists of a series of isolated acts treating specific hazards in narrow product categories. No Government agency possesses general authority to ban products which harbor unreasonable risks or to require that consumer products conform to minimum safety standards.
>
> Such limited Federal authority as does exist is scattered among many agencies. . . . Moreover, where it exists, Federal product safety regulation is burdened by unnecessary procedural obstacles, circumscribed investigative powers, inadequate and ill-fitting sanctions, bureaucratic lassitude, timid administration, bargain-basement budgets, distorted priorities, and misdirected technical resources.
>
> * * * *
>
> Federal law now provides no machinery to enjoin a manufacturer from marketing consumer products that are unreasonably dangerous. There is no way to compel the recall of such products for repair or replacement.
>
> No Federal law provides meaningful criminal penalties for manufacturers who knowingly or willfully market consumer products that create an unreasonable danger to life and health. (NCPS F.R., p. 2)

This is a stunning and comprehensive indictment. And it is a true one. As for the impact of state laws and state agencies, the Commission finds that they add up to a "hodgepodge of tragedy-inspired responses to challenges that cannot be met by restricted geographical entities" (F.R., p. 2) but require national and consistent action.

This chapter will explore these disquieting realities from the point of view of toy safety. As with consumer products generally, the responsibility for toy safety is distributed over too many separate agencies, is subject to intolerable and sometimes interminable delays, is circumscribed by narrow laws, and is—even where the laws do apply—fundamentally ineffective.

First as to the diffusion of authority on the federal level, no single federal agency is charged with over-all responsibility for supervising the safety or the quality of toys, although several different bureaus and offices do, as the NCPS notes, each have some share in the general federal effort to provide consumer protection. The number of different offices with general consumer protection responsibilities, either operational or educational, comes to about thirty-five. Very few of these agencies, however, actually deal with household products, and even fewer are involved with toys and other children's things. The reason for this is that a government agency can only deal with those things which the Congress has given it authority to regulate. And, in the case of toys, there are only two laws—both of them quite narrow ones—which confer congressional authority to supervise the marketing of dangerous or potentially dangerous toys.

Most of the federal agencies that aim to protect consumers are oriented more toward educational and informational services than to field operations and marketing control. Their efforts are directed largely toward warning, in general terms, of certain broad classes of hazard, rather than toward actively keeping these dangerous goods off the shelves and out of our homes.

Moreover, the federal presence in the consumer protection field is further weakened because most regulatory agencies tend, eventually, to become more and more industry-minded. They deal in their daily business with the representatives of manufacturers and marketers, not with the consumers. Their thinking and their policies are often shaped by the way in which the issues and problems are framed by the industries over which they have their limited authority. The agency's intellectual cross-pollination thus occurs within the narrow range of the major producers and trade associations operating in the field to which it is assigned. At best, this leads to a certain myopia; at worst, it leads to the situation about which independent consumer advocates are currently making more than justified complaint—the situation in which the agency is psychologically dominated by the industry, in which the tail is wagging the dog, in which we speak of an agency that, instead of being the captain, has become the captive.

Furthermore, most regulatory agencies suffer from a chronic insufficiency of funding, and within the agency itself, the consumer-safety programs very frequently receive only a low priority. The dimensions of this problem are summarized in the NCPS Final Report (p. 97):

> Federal safety programs to be effective require sufficient funding. When the original Federal Hazardous Substances Act was passed in 1960, and when the 1966 amendments added coverage of an estimated 1,000 new companies and tens of thousands of new products, the Food and Drug Administration requested no additional funds. Even with the 1969 amendments, FDA requested only an additional $500,000 for the first year of operation.
>
> The 1967 amendments to the Flammable Fabrics Act authorized $1,500,000 for the fiscal [year] 1969, but only $300,000 was appropriated. That amount went exclusively to the National Bureau of Standards, with none to the Department of Health, Education and Welfare, which shares jurisdiction for such investigations as would assist the promulgation of new standards.

* * *

Agencies with several and diverse programs to administer may be obliged to divert resources away from the protection of consumers, depending on the priority assigned. The Commissioner of FDA testified in 1969 that hazards associated with drugs were given first priority; food-related hazards were second; and product safety was third and last.

The budget for enforcement of the Federal Hazardous Substances Act increased less than 50 percent over 8 years, while FDA's total budget more than tripled. The act's share of the total FDA budget declined from 4.3 percent to 1.7 percent. Likewise, while FDA's staff tripled, the staff allocated to the act increased by only 5 percent. In the last two fiscal years, the program did not gain a position or a dollar.

The Hazardous Substances Division of the Office of Product Safety, consisting of only 21 persons as of January, 1970, has the burden of determining whether products covered by its enabling act (primarily chemical substances and toys) are hazardous. The laboratory staff, a director and four professionals, has facilities to conduct animal studies, chemical analyses, and flash-point tests. Most [of their] effort is directed to investigation of Flammable Fabrics Act cases to assist the development of standards. There is a 2-year backlog on referrals from field offices. [footnotes omitted]

Penny-pinching on this scale is a national scandal, and an affront to the Congress, which clearly wanted these agencies to be active in the protection of the American consumer. But even if all of these agencies had enough funds to do the job, it would still be badly done, for it is spread confusingly among a host of different offices. Where everyone is responsible, no one is; and "Let George do it" can as easily become the motto for bureaucracy as it can for anyone else.

Leaving aside for a moment the agencies involved in enforcing the laws that in their extremely limited way, deal with toy safety, let us consider the rest of the field.

There is a President's Committee on Consumer Interests, a President's Council on Consumer Affairs, and a President's Special Assistant for Consumer Affairs.

There is a Department of Commerce, which has under its

wing the National Bureau of Standards (NBS) and a Business and Defense Service Administration. The NBS develops testing methods, works out specifications, and set standards of performance for a wide range of products. But all of these are only *suggestions* to industry, and if and when they are adopted, by trade associations, for example, it is on a strictly voluntary basis. The Business and Defense Service Administration also prepares product standards and maintains a consumer information service. But its contributions to product safety are so negligible that it is not even mentioned in the NCPS Final Report.

The Department of Health, Education and Welfare includes the U.S. Public Health Service and the U.S. Office of Education. The latter includes safety-education programs within its activities, and the former, in addition to its responsibilities through the Food and Drug Administration (FDA) and the Bureau of Product Safety of the FDA, keeps statistics on product-related injuries and undertakes research studies in this area.

Even the Department of Agriculture is involved, through its Cooperative Extension Service, which publishes consumer-oriented bulletins, and other federal agencies with testing responsibilities and capacities (such as the General Services Administration, which buys for the government; and the Veterans Administration) are becoming aware of their responsibility to share the results of these tests with the general public.

But still, the problem of overlapping or mixed-up jurisdictional arrangements is a persistent and very difficult one. Again, to cite the conclusions of the NCPS:

> Division of the powers under one act among various agencies creates other enforcement difficulties. The Flammable Fabrics Act gives rulemaking authority to the Commerce Department, domestic enforcement to the [Federal Trade Commission—an independent agency], enforcement over imports to the Treasury Department [which operates the Customs

Bureau], and investigative duties both to Commerce and to Health, Education and Welfare. When extensive interagency liaison and cooperation are required, one agency sometimes forestalls actions by the others.

Such a division of duties also requires each agency to approach a different congressional sub-committee for funding under the act. In consequence, one agency may have insufficient funds to match the programs of the others. (F.R., p. 97)

Thus product-safety and toy-safety responsibilities are split among different and sometimes competing federal agencies and bureaus. The information-gathering process is fragmented, the educational effort is diffused, and the enforcement of the laws is parceled out. The net effect is that federal protection of the consumer is minimal. Because so many of us believe that there is much more of it than there really is, this current state of affairs is doubly dangerous, since it encourages us to assume a higher level of safety in the products we buy than may actually be there.

Before looking in greater detail at the federal laws that cover toys in particular, it might be well to take a passing glance at one other agency, which, although not exactly "federal," does have a certain governmental aura about it. This is the National Safety Council.

The National Safety Council (NSC) is a "quasi-governmental" agency, since it was founded by an act of Congress in order to be, chiefly, a nationwide safety information center. Its stated purposes under the statute are to promote safety in public as well as in private places and situations, to compile useful statistics, to publish helpful data on safety practices and procedures, and generally to stir up public interest in, and support for, accident prevention. The National Safety Council maintains the largest specialized safety library in the world, and is the largest source of statistical information on safety matters in the nation. As a nonprofit, noncommercial corporation under governmental auspices, it operates departments of public safety and public information, but is not engaged in the direct regulation of product design or manufacture. Its chief functions are educational, especially in the field of household product safety.

This emphasis on education seems to give the National Safety Council a certain cast of mind that some have characterized as "more business-oriented than consumer-oriented." These critics mean that NSC tends to assert that the greater proportion of toy-related injuries occur as a result of inadequate parental supervision rather than because of the inherent dangerousness or unsuitability of the toys produced by the industry. From the evidence adduced earlier in this book, no one could reasonably deny that a great many children's accidents and injuries are due to intrinsically unsafe toys and other children's products. And it is clear that this knowledge must have registered within the toy industry as well. Yet, given the dangers involved and the fact that the toymakers ought to know that children are often left to play without adequate supervision, the NSC emphasis on the parental responsibility seems misguided and unhelpful. For the more they stress the parent's fault in leaving the child to play with something dangerous, the more the toymakers will feel exonerated of responsibility for children's accidents, in spite of the fact that children could play safely under almost any circumstances if their toys were safe enough to begin with. The NSC is therefore quite mistaken in passing the buck from the manufacturers to the parents.

The extent to which the NSC does indeed pass the buck away from the makers of unsafe toys is well illustrated by the testimony of Morris Kaplan before the NCPS. Mr. Kaplan is the Technical Director of the Consumers Union, the private nonprofit testing agency. Speaking of the NSC's Committee on Toys, he told the Commission that the NSC has never looked into the Consumers Union findings,

... in spite of the fact that they indicate that they use all sources of input to find unsafe toys.... We have been publishing reports on toys for many, many years. In no instance am I aware of the National Safety Council's taking any action with regard to these published reports.

The picture is discouraging—overdiffused authority competing and understaffed, underfunded agencies, hundreds of classes of products totally unregulated by law, inadequate national information and education programs. While these are weaknesses that apply to consumer product safety across the board, it is particularly disturbing with respect to children's articles. Let us turn now to the specific federal laws covering toy safety.

There are two federal laws that deal with the manufacture and sale of children's products and playthings and which empower some governmental authority to oversee their safety. They are the Flammable Fabrics Act, originally passed in 1953, and the Hazardous Substances Act, originally passed in 1960. Neither is at all adequate.

The Flammable Fabrics Act was first enacted in response to a number of frightening incidents involving "torch sweaters," which burst into flame under the slightest provocation, often burning their wearers with extreme severity. In the original bill, precise standards were set out, and no descretion was left to the FTC, which was charged with the responsibility for the law's enforcement. Fourteen years passed before the act was amended, in 1967, to cover a wider range of items than the few enumerated in the original law, and to give some discretion in setting safety standards to the Department of Commerce. The present situation is that the standards are set by Commerce, although the act is administered and enforced by the FTC. And even though the power to set new and stricter standards was given to Commerce by the 1967 amendments, the first partial standards developed by the Department were not officially proposed until April, 1970. As for the activity of the FTC, the

NCPS reported that in the seventeen years between the original enactment of the law and 1970, the Commission acted only once to remove dangerously flammable articles from the market—several cases of silk scarves were seized in 1954. Only recently has the Commission stepped up its activity under the act. For example, in June, 1970, the FTC listed a few items as dangerously flammable, among them a 100 percent cotton organdy used to trim bassinets.

The fundamental purpose of the Flammable Fabrics Act is to keep out of the channels of interstate commerce those articles—chiefly clothing—which come under the act's general classifications and are found to be extremely flammable. In order to determine the fire-retardant or fire-resistant quality of articles covered by the act, the original statute referred to two specific trade standards, standards 191-33 and 191-53. But these standards were developed without the benefit of consumer spokesmen and chiefly in order to serve general industry specifications and requirements. Commercial Standard 191-33, for instance, which deals with clothing textiles, proposes the following test: a six-inch sample of the material being tested is to be held at a 45° angle from a flame for one second. If the material burns at a rate of five inches or less in three and one-half seconds, it passes the test and is not forbidden by law.

Such a test ignores the fact that children's nightgowns, for example, might well be exposed to flame for more than one second; or that a flame at several different angles may have an entirely different and more flammable effect upon the tested material; or that—especially with children—clothing cannot always be easily tossed off in a few seconds. Many children, of course, do not dress themselves at all, nor would they be capable of working their way out of a complex arrangement of buttons and clasps and pins.

A further problem with the Flammable Fabrics Act is that not only is the present standard for clothing textiles inadequate, but the act itself covers only an extremely limited range of items. Originally drafted to regulate only those fabrics used in ordinary items of clothing, it did not touch at all upon such important materials as infants' blankets and bedding. It specifically excludes interlinings. The fabrics used in stuffing dolls or toy animals are not covered by this act. As amended, it now confers upon the FTC the authority to include "interior furnishings," but as of this writing, no final regulations for these have yet been issued.

Moreover, even with the limited range of the act and the limited standards it sets, the FTC has not used it very enthusiastically. Although the Commission may seek injunctions to forbid the manufacture, transportation and sale within interstate commerce of any fabrics that violate the act, and although it may apply for court orders confiscating those fabrics which violate the act and are already in the channels of commerce, it has used its powers to seize, as we have noted, only once—and that was sixteen years ago. Thus the Flammable Fabrics Act, as it presently exists and is being used by the FTC, is only minimally effective. As a protection for children in particular, it is grossly inadequate.

It wasn't until June, 1970, that the Department of Commerce took its first steps toward setting up a separate flammability standard for children's underwear, dresses, and night clothing. At this writing, this belated effort is bogged down in the cumbersome procedures provided under the act for promulgating new and revised flammability standards.

The Hazardous Substances Act is little better. This law is molded by its history both in its range and in its effectiveness, for it was not originally intended to be a product-safety law at all, but rather a "truth in labeling" act. The original bill was entitled the "Hazardous Substances Labeling Act" and its provisions dealt with the necessity of ensuring that adequate warnings accompanied the distribution and sale in interstate commerce of consumer products that included materials which presented foreseeable and serious risks of danger to uninformed purchasers and users. The 1960 act defined a number of specified hazards and enumerated as "hazardous substances" those falling within the following classifications: "any substance or mixture of substances" that is "toxic" or "corrosive" or "an irritant" or "a strong sensitizer" or "flammable" or that "generates pressure through decomposition, heat or other means" and that might "cause substantial personal injury or substantial illness during or as a proximate result of any customary or reasonably foreseeable handling or use, including reasonably foreseeable ingestion by children."

The trouble here is that the act did nothing to prevent the marketing of most of these dangerous items, provided that the label carried adequate notice of the dangers involved. Moreover, it originally covered only those hazardous substances sold in containers—in cans, bottles or bags and the like. Thus it did not extend, for instance, to toys that involved these hazardous materials, since the toy was not the kind of "container" intended to fall within the scope of the act. A toy which included a corrosive substance, for example, would only be required to carry a warning label if the corrosive were "inside" the toy in the same kind of way that something might be inside a bottle or a bag. And clearly most toys are not "packages" or "containers" in this sense.

The act was amended in 1966 to eliminate this flaw by extending its provisions to cover, without the container requirement, "toys or other articles intended for use by children which *bear or contain* a hazardous substance" [emphasis supplied]. Even this revision, which was accomplished by the Child Protection Act of 1966, and which removed the word "Labeling" from the title of the act, did little to protect children from the most significant dangers found in toys.

The original Act also established a category of so-called "banned hazardous substances." These latter are materials so intrinsically dangerous to consumers that even proper labeling is not sufficient to diminish to a tolerable degree the very high risks they present. Such materials may be, upon order of the Secretary of the Department of Health, Education and Welfare, banned entirely from the channels of interstate commerce. The Secretary also has the power to seek court orders forbidding the interstate sale or transportation of inadequately or incorrectly labeled substances, as well as those which are banned completely. In those cases where the substance is likely to present an imminent danger to life or health, he may act at once to ban and confiscate the product, although his action may be reviewed, and, if unfounded, reversed by a federal court.

Some improvements in the Act have been generated by the efforts of the NCPS. In the course of examining the over-all safety record of children's things, the Commission held hearings in Boston in December, 1968. As a result of these hearings, which included a demonstration by the author of a number of particularly dangerous toys, the Commission concluded that temporary improvement in the Hazardous Substances Act was urgently required, and that the situation with respect to children's playthings and products was so intolerable that it would be irresponsible to wait for the Final Report of the NCPS with its recommendations, which was not due until the summer of 1970.

In February, 1969, therefore, the NCPS issued an Interim Report, limited to children's products, and recommending immediate adoption of several key amendments to the Hazardous Substances Act. These amendments were collected in the Child Protection and Toy Safety Act of 1969, which was presented to the Congress early in the spring of that year.

The situation prior to the passage of the 1969 amendments was indeed serious, for as the NCPS pointed out:

> . . . hazards associated with sharp or protruding edges, fragmentation, explosion, strangulation, suffocation, asphyx-

iation, electric shock and electrocution, heated surfaces and unextinguishable flames—and the untold aggravation, injury and death attributable thereto . . . in fact appear to predominate in the statistics associated with toy-related injuries. Yet the Hazardous Substances Act is silent as to these fundamental kinds of hazards (Interim Report, p. 3).

The amendments spelled out three additional classes of hazards—thermal, mechanical, and electrical—and added them to the list of hazards forbidden by law to be built into children's products. The Child Protection and Toy Safety Act was passed by the Senate on June 30 and by the House on September 4, 1969; it was put into its final shape by the joint conference committee of both houses in October, and signed into law by the President on November 6 of that year.

The 1969 amendments are an unquestionable improvement. It is interesting to note that the Toy Manufacturers of America, Inc., appeared before the House Subcommittee on Commerce and Finance of the Committee on Interstate and Foreign Commerce to debate the bill as presented to the Congress. The toymakers objected to giving the Secretary of HEW broad discretionary authority to determine which toys presented thermal, electrical or mechanical hazards as defined in the bill. They would have preferred to have exclusive and particular standards written into the law itself.

This, of course, would have repeated the mistake made with the original Flammable Fabrics Act, which instead of being the help it was supposed to be, became a hindrance because of its overnarrow draftsmanship. Happily, the toymakers' efforts to have the 1969 bill similarly hamstrung were unsuccessful.

As finally approved and signed into law, the definitions of the hazards covered by the amendments are quite adequate and do give HEW considerable discretion. Thus,

An article may be determined to present an electrical hazard if, in normal use or when subjected to reasonably foreseeable damage or abuse, its design or manufacture may cause personal injury or illness by electric shock.

An article may be determined to present a mechanical hazard if, in normal use or when subjected to reasonably foreseeable damage or abuse, its design or manufacture presents an unreasonable risk of personal injury or illness (1) from fracture, fragmentation, or disassembly of the article, (2) from propulsion of the article (or any part or accessory thereof), (3) from points or other protrusions, surfaces, edges, openings or closures, (4) from moving parts, (5) from lack or insufficiency of controls to reduce or stop motion, (6) as a result of self-adhering characteristics of the article, (7) because the article (or any part or accessory thereof) may be aspirated or ingested, (8) because of instability, or (9) because of any other aspect of the article's design or manufacture.

An article may be determined to present a thermal hazard if, in normal use or when subjected to reasonably foreseeable damage or abuse, its design or manufacture presents an unreasonable risk of personal injury or illness because of heat as from heated parts, substances or surfaces.

The determinations in question are to be made by the Secretary of Health, Education and Welfare, and if he does decide that an article presents one of the hazards enumerated in the act, he may, of course, seek court action enjoining its further manufacture and sale; and in the case of imminently dangerous items, he may act directly to ban them completely. Furthermore, since the definitions apply to "any toy or other article intended for use by children," the "reasonably foreseeable" test of normal use or predictable damage or abuse should be applied and interpreted in the light of what we know about the way children, and not adults, behave. This is all to the good.

However, it is still not enough. For we have seen how underfunded and understaffed the Food and Drug Administration's product safety facilities are. And so the practicalities of the matter are that despite the 1969 amendments, little will be done to keep dangerous toys out of our homes.

If the prediction—that little or nothing will be done—sounds overpessimistic, let me suggest that it is not unfounded in experience. The government has failed to remove, in a timely or effective manner, most hazardous toys from store shelves despite its authority to do so. The NCPS stated in its final report "that neither the interest created by congressional hearings nor passage of the Child Protection and Toy Safety Act has significantly reduced the hazards." The responsible agency generally states when pressed about this that, while Congress gave it the job to do, it did not grant them the necessary funds. While it is true that the agency has not received adequate funding for this task, it would appear to be a weak excuse for not ordering off the market, as *minimal* action, the dangerous toys exposed at hearings before the NCPS and incorporated pictorially in the Interim Report of the NCPS. The discouraging truth is that many of the dangerous toys which virtually gave birth to the so-called Child Protection and Toy Safety Act were being sold coast-to-coast months after the Act's passage.

As the NCPS noted in its Final Report:

> Dolls still have pins to hold their hair ribbons on, little girls can still bake their own cakes in their own electric ovens, a little boy can make a design with his glass screen Etch-A-Sketch toy—and run the risk of sketching a permanent scar design somewhere on his body . . .

There undoubtedly will be from time to time sporadic action by the government under the Act. For example, in November of 1970 the FDA proposed a regulation which would ban toys with parts which can inflict puncture wounds or that can be dislodged and then inhaled or swallowed. They also proposed to ban toy guns producing sound levels of 100 decibels or more. Under the Act the Agency could have declared that certain toys in those categories presented imminent hazards and thus could have banned their sale immediately. However, under the procedure followed by the Agency, industry had fifteen days in which to object to the proposed regulation. After the government considers these objections and enters an order, the manufacturers can still further delay the toys' removal by filing legal appeals. While all this goes on the toys which are dangerous continue to be sold. Those toys which were actually on the market being sold while the debate about their relative merits continued included some of the following: toy rattles containing dangerous spokes or wires; party noisemakers with parts that could be swallowed when dislodged by a child; dolls with components that could cause puncture wounds or lacerations; lawn darts, such as "Jarts"; toy guns producing sound at a level of 100 decibels or higher. Such belated and ineffectual action under the Toy Safety Act only buttresses the contention that stringent premarket controls are necessary if our children are to be adequately protected.

I have had an interesting and somewhat enlightening personal experience with the efficiency of the FDA in the matter of hazardous substances, and I would like to tell that story here.

When I testified at the Boston hearings of the NCPS, one of the things I brought along with me, as I have already mentioned, was a cloth play tunnel, several feet long, widely advertised and widely sold. The particular version I had was purchased in a leading Boston toy store, F.A.O. Schwarz. I demonstrated the flammability of this tunnel before the Commission. Here is a transcript of my demonstration:

> I would like to cut a piece out of this [tunnel], Mr. Chairman, and I would like to demonstrate that it is made out of the cheapest possible kind of cotton, and heaven for-

bid some child getting caught in this tunnel when it is ignited. . . .

Children have been known to play with matches. If this is in a backyard where there is a family barbecue or burning grass, there are many sources of ignition that could ignite this. I don't think it needs comment. [At this point I struck a match and touched it to the edge of the cloth.] That burns so fast that I couldn't drop it quick enough.

That doesn't even meet the standard of a civilized society, let alone a federal statute, and they are selling it for children.

Despite the publicity which the demonstration received, and despite the fact that the NCPS made particular mention of the tunnel in its Interim Report—even including a picture of one of the tunnels bursting into flame from a single small match—by early March, the FDA had still not acted. The hearings had been held in December, and the Interim Report of the NCPS was published in late February. In March, at the 1969 annual trade fair of the toy industry —sponsored by the Toy Manufacturers of America whose own spokesman had assured the NCPS that the tunnel was clearly illegal—as I indicated earlier—I was still able to find and to order the same tunnel from a booth staffed by a manufacturer's representative.

Finally, in late March of 1969, more than three months after the original demonstration and a full month after the NCPS Interim Report, the FDA declared the tunnels to be "banned hazardous substances" under the law, and sent telegrams so informing four companies engaged in their manufacture. The public was informed through an FDA press release, and recall of the tunnels—over 50,000 of them were still on the market—was left by the agency to the manufacturers.

This sort of administration of the law raises many questions. First of all, and most obviously, what about the delay? Why so long in acting? Secondly, what about the people who had already bought the tunnels? How would they be informed and protected? A press release from a federal agency gets some play, perhaps, across the nation in various news media. But what play it gets and to whose attention the vital information is called, depend in part on a host of "iffy" factors —including the amount of space left in a local newspaper after the advertising columns are filled; the amount of time left in a television news program after all the war reports are filed; and so on. Furthermore, aside from some spot checks in the field by the few FDA agents assigned to that sort of thing, what effective steps could and did the agency take to ensure that the manufacturers had indeed notified all their distributors at once, or that the distributors had immediately contacted the retailers? Was this done by telegram or by special-delivery letter, with a return receipt requested attached? But I do know that if an unscrupulous manufacturer wanted to sell "just a few more" of the dangerous flammable tunnels, all he would have had to do was to send a regular letter to the distributor, and have the distributor send a regular letter to the retailer; and by the time the correspondence had reached its ultimate destination, there would surely have been hundreds more of the hazardous tunnels in American homes.

This shows the great weakness of depending on recall or seizure as a means of controlling dangerous products. For we can never be sure of recalling *all* of them. It also illustrates another weakness of the present federal laws—the delays available to makers of dangerous things, delays either caused by protracted court battles over whether a particular item is or is not illegal, or by simple inertia on the part of the regulating agency itself. These two factors, the inadequacy of recall and the inevitability of delay, together make the strongest possible case for premarket testing. The opposite of premarket testing and safe control is a gambler's approach—wait until we find out that someone has been hurt, and then protect the rest of us. That amounts to giving the manufacturer one "free" accident at public expense!

There are two interesting footnotes to the play tunnel story, each of which gives some insight into the thought processes of, respectively, Rapco, Inc. (makers of one of the flammable models) and the FDA.

The Rapco story would be funny if it were not so sickening. Three months after the FDA order banning the Rapco tunnels from interstate commerce, the company—after making them "fire resistant," presumably by treating them with some flame-retardant solution—had them back on the market and advertised to the toy industry as *approved* by the Department of Health, Education and Welfare! This is nearly unbelievable arrogance, as the following corespondence makes clear:

June 18, 1969

J. K. Kirk
Associate Commissioner for Compliance
Food and Drug Administration
Department of Health, Education and Welfare
Washington, D. C. 20204

Dear Commissioner Kirk:

Thank you very much for your letter of April 28 and the enclosures pertaining to the banning of play tunnels.

The enclosed advertisement appeared in the June 1969 issue of Toys and Novelties, *a trade magazine of the toy industry. As you can see, the advertiser, Rapco, Inc., claims that its new play tunnels have the express approval of your department regarding fireproofing and warning labels.*

Would you please be so kind as to inform me of what this approval consists of? Could you possibly send me a copy of any order containing this approval, or copies of correspondence which effect it? Were the modified play tunnels and

their packaging submitted to your department prior to the running of this advertisement?
Thank you once again for your assistance.

> Sincerely yours,
>
> Edward M. Swartz

EMS/jdw

July 8, 1969

Swartz, Bonin, and Lemelman
Attorneys at Law
53 Beacon Street
Boston, Massachusetts 02108

Gentlemen:

Thank you for your letter of June 18, 1969, with the enclosed advertisement for Rapco Play Tunnels.

You will note from the material enclosed in our April 28 letter that there are no provisions for "approval" under the Federal Hazardous Substances Act. While we are always ready to offer our informal comments on the status of a firm's products under the law, this is merely our belief of the conclusion that would be reached by the Federal Court.

We object strenuously to any labeling or advertising which represents Governmental approval of products subject to this law and have so informed the firm.

Thank you again for your letter.

> Sincerely yours,
>
> T. E. Byers, Director
> Division of Case Guidance
> Bureau of Compliance

This gives us a very clear insight into the high standards of safety-consciousness and marketing integrity which the Rapco Company maintains.

It might be well to note that the fire "proofing" which some companies initially performed on such tunnels involved a simple treatment with a solution soluble in water. This would mean that if the tunnel were left out overnight, for instance, and it rained, the fireproofing could easily wash away. If the tunnel then dried in the morning's sun, as well it might, it would be every bit as flammable as it was before the treatment. I suggest that parents check into this before buying anything from the makers of toy tunnels again. Some in the toy industry have not learned the highly publicized lessons from the flammable tunnel exposé. Yet another version of the play tunnel has been marketed for 1970–1971. It is called "Traffic Jam" (Lakeside Industries) and is an eight-foot tunnel game which comes with the *Parents' Magazine* guarantee seal. The version examined by the author was appropriately fire-red. This incredible plaything is made of "heavy-duty polyethylene" which is flammable and which when it burns leaves a sticky-hot residue. In addition, the toy has a series of extremely small air holes which do not eradicate the possibility of suffocation, since a small child could easily become frightened and entangle himself in the unsupported plastic bag-like contraption. The back of the box contains the caption "Safety Tested." (Fig. 41)

As to the FDA, the anecdote is twofold. First, so far as I know and at this writing, the FDA has not investigated other play enclosures, such as backyard tents, some of which might be made out of similar fabrics as were the banned tunnels. Their bureaucratic attention was confined to the one item about which a public fuss had been made.

Secondly, the FDA, instead of explaining the intolerable delay in acting on the play tunnels, has given itself a large pat on the back. Nine months after the Boston hearings, the agency published a four-page color brochure, "Hidden Hazards in the Nursery," which showed impressive photographs of some of the dangerous toys brought into the NCPS hearings. The brochure states that "The National Commission on Product Safety and FDA's Office of Product

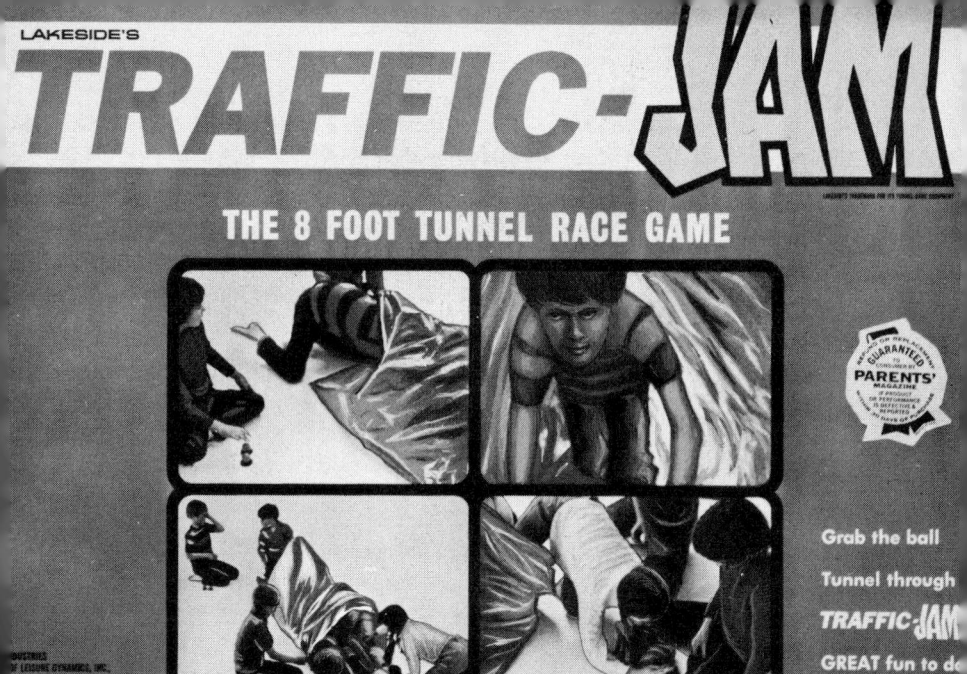

Fig. 41. Flammable "safety-tested" 1970–1971 play tunnel.

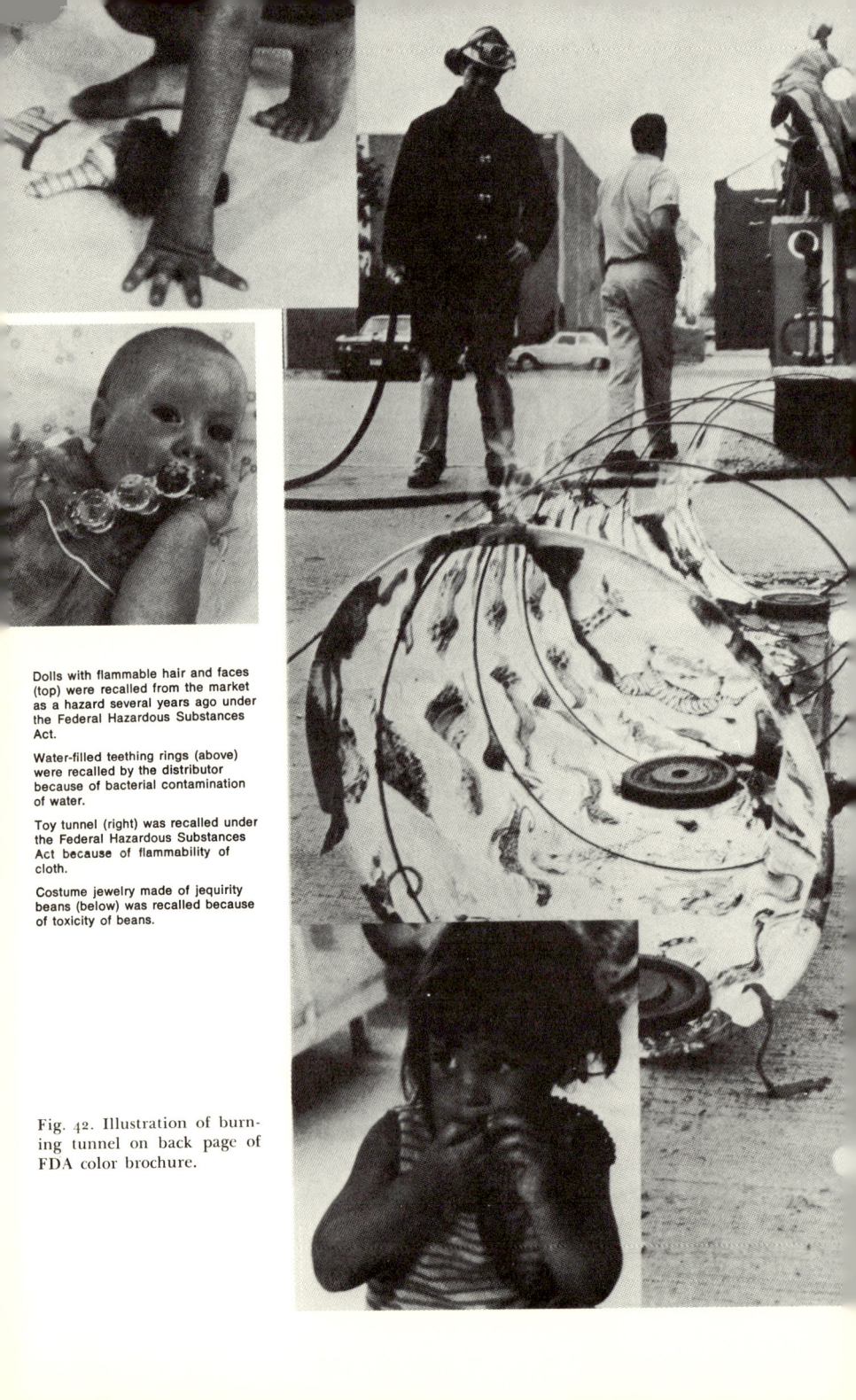

Dolls with flammable hair and faces (top) were recalled from the market as a hazard several years ago under the Federal Hazardous Substances Act.

Water-filled teething rings (above) were recalled by the distributor because of bacterial contamination of water.

Toy tunnel (right) was recalled under the Federal Hazardous Substances Act because of flammability of cloth.

Costume jewelry made of jequirity beans (below) was recalled because of toxicity of beans.

Fig. 42. Illustration of burning tunnel on back page of FDA color brochure.

Safety in recent months have pointed out some possible hazards present in what may appear to be harmless playthings." I am utterly at a loss as to what, if any, extent the FDA had a hand in discovering *or* in publicizing these dangers, although it was the FDA's, not the NCPS's, primary responsibility to do so. All of the items pictured in the brochure except one (a doll with a flammable face and hair) were introduced as exhibits at the NCPS Boston hearings. And yet the FDA leaves the impression that it has been actively engaged in ferreting out these "hidden hazards in the nursery"! The kicker comes on the back page, where a dramatic color photo of a burning play tunnel, with firefighters standing by, is offered for the reader's information and edification. (Fig. 42)

It seems to me that the substantial sum doubtless expended by the FDA on staging the color photos and on the printing and distribution of this pamphlet might have been better spent on putting a few more good men into the field to help out the overworked few already there.

Thus, reviewing the effectiveness of the federal government, its laws and agencies, in ensuring the safety of the toys we buy, we find that effectiveness is absolutely nominal. The burden falls heavily on parents and shoppers, and the fundamental problem of keeping dangerous playthings off the market is by and large avoided. But realistically, even if the average toy buyer did study all the safety education literature available, even if he did carefully inspect every toy coming into his home or about to be bought in a store, even if he did read all the labels, follow all the instructions, heed all the warnings, and notice all the fine print—and even if he had all of this cautionary material at his fingertips for every possible toy and could bring it into play while his six-year-old is pulling at his arm in the toy store or heading off to play with the neighbor's toys down the street—still, he would not be in a position to discover all of the dangers and hazards, nor to prevent all of the injuries that might be associated with the toys his children are playing with. None of us can become our own experts on toy safety. So what we now have in the line of national governmental effort is not enough. It is more a joke than an effort.

Fortunately, there is some hope on the horizon. The National Commission on Product Safety has drafted a comprehensive and generally superior program for congressional consideration: the Consumer Product Safety Act of 1970. This bill, which is the fruit of NCPS's lengthy and scholarly investigation of product safety in the United States at the present time, is an excellent one, although I would suggest that it is capable of further improvement.

The proposed act sets up a five-man, full-time Consumer Product Safety Commission, with broad regulatory authority and wide administrative discretion. The commission would be empowered to invite the formulation of product safety standards in almost every field (excepting only those already covered by some limited federal acts—such as the Motor Vehicle Safety Act and the Flammable Fabrics Act), and, if the industry involved could not or would not come up with genuinely acceptable norms, the commission could and would draft and promulgate its own standards. The commission would also have the power to seek injunctions against the marketing of consumer products that present an unreasonable risk to public health or safety and to wield a variety of enforcement measures against those who violate the official standards. In cases where it appears that a product is dangerous, but no current standards already apply to it, the commission could set emergency standards at once. In the case of all products whose noncompliance, whether with emergency or with long-standing safety requirements, is likely to present an imminent danger to health or public safety, the commission could ban the product in question at once, subject, of course, to later judicial review.

The commission would also have broad investigatory powers, and could require premarketing testing for safety by independent and technically qualified agencies. It would be authorized to exchange information with all other governmental agencies, and to report its findings, both good and bad, to the public on as wide and as frequent a basis as it wished. Violators—those manufacturers or others who do not obey the commission's safety standards—could be punished by fines or by criminal penalties, and parties injured by such products would have the right to sue in the federal courts for three times their actual damages.

Perhaps most importantly, there would be, separate from the commission although working closely with it, an independent Consumer Safety Advocate. He, too, would have broad investigatory powers, as well as the right to appear on behalf of the general public in any proceedings before the commission. He would be able to receive complaints from the public in order to bring them to the commission's attention for disposition, to evaluate proposed and current safety standards from the consumer's point of view, to have free access to all the commission's records, to appear before the commission in any of its proceedings. He would be able to make official suggestions for changes or modifications in existing commission regulations, orders, and standards, or to propose new ones, or to ask the commission to begin other proceedings, and to appeal to the federal courts any decision of the commission that he feels is not in the public interest. He is also authorized to speak freely and directly to the public and to issue official statements on any of these matters.

This is an excellent idea, one that has been advocated by a number of distinguished consumer spokesmen for some years —among them, of course, the deservedly respected Ralph Nader. I would add one or two suggestions, however, and they are these: The Consumer Safety Advocate must have an independent budget, not subject to the control of the commission. For him to do his job effectively, he must be able to develop his own staff, reporting to him personally, as well as to use the technical resources of the commission itself. Without some degree of financial independence, his functional independence will be greatly diminished. Secondly, he should be able to inspect products and manufacturers' establishments in the field, without waiting for the commission to agree to such a field investigation. Given this authority, he will be able to determine what, in his own informed judgment, may constitute a hazard that the commission should investigate; whereas if he and the commission both wait for information from third parties, then the hazard may not be noticed at all, or noticed only after it has already injured someone.

To my mind, the key sections of the proposed act are those which confer upon the commission the power to require premarket testing. As we have seen, recall is inadequate, and waiting for the first accident to happen before public and governmental attention is alerted is a stupid, if not an insane, procedure. The commission could quickly develop fundamental safety standards for the major product categories, including toys and children's things, and could, at least with toys—which are something of a special case both because of the consumers for whom they are intended and because of the circumstances in which they are purchased—formally require that every new item be check-rated for safety before being put on the market. As I read the NCPS bill, it does grant the proposed commission this power; and I would urge strenuously that it be granted by the Congress and used vigorously by the commission.

Premarket testing sounds complicated. Imagine all those federal toy inspectors touring the country fooling around with new designs for yo-yos! But it needn't be as complex as all that. The Toy Manufacturers of America claim to represent the major toymakers of the nation and they exhibit at their annual Toy Fair. Manufacturers meet retailers there, and the retailers place their orders—in March—for the months ahead, and particularly for the coming Christmas season. If an item gets little or no response from the retailers, the manufacturer knows this well in advance and cuts his production down substantially, or even discontinues the item altogether. The same could be done in the case of a toy that is rated unsafe. Since any intelligent manufacturer makes a prototype and a few trial models before going into large-scale production, all that premarket testing would mean is that these samples be shown not only to the potential retailers, but also to the Consumer Product Safety Commission. Assuming clear standards and an adequate staff, the toy in question could be approved, if safe, within a short time. If unsafe, the commission's technical experts could perhaps suggest modifications and changes that would bring the plaything within the compulsory specification. It might be a little more expensive for the manufacturer, and a little more expensive for the taxpayer, but—remembering those 700,000 toy injuries each year—the ultimate savings in medical costs and in human anguish would be unquestionably worth it.

The proposed Consumer Product Safety Act of 1970 is a lengthy and a complex piece of legislation, and it was first published by the NCPS only shortly before this book went to press. I do recommend it, generally, especially with the strengthening of the Consumer Safety Advocate's independence and investigatory powers that I have suggested, and with the understanding that, in the toy industry at least, quick development of strict standards and mandatory premarket testing of all children's things are absolutely necessary and should receive the highest priority.

We've seen how little the industry regulated itself, and

how little the federal government controls the industry—although this, at least, may change. What about state and local authorities?

Certainly there are opportunities for important toy safety legislation open to state and local authorities. The basic problem has to be solved on the federal level, since the toy business is a national industry and most of its products move in interstate commerce. But there is still room for the states to perform a useful function, however, for strict state laws may cover local dealers who might otherwise be unregulated, and they can also generate pressure for truly effective standards at the federal level.

Thus an adequate model-toy safety act should be enacted by all states. However, this approach has been largely ignored. State and local health and fire laws dealing with the sanitary aspects of products locally available or with their flammable characteristics can be modified to cover all possible children's articles. These laws should also be reviewed to ensure that their standards are adequate. Massachusetts and some other states have laws banning weapons such as slingshots, peashooters, and dart guns, restricting the sale and use of air rifles, and forbidding fireworks entirely. These are all very helpful and could be easily adopted in other jurisdictions. Statutes that prohibit fraudulent advertising should be applied to toy promoters, particularly with respect to safety claims; and where criminal penalties are provided for the violation of these laws, attorneys general and district attorneys should not hesitate to seek indictments and to prosecute offenders diligently.

We have perhaps grown too accustomed to waiting for our leadership to come from Washington. But there is no reason why it cannot begin at home. Still, given the insufficiency of most of the state and federal legislation presently on the books, it is not surprising that there are so many and such serious toy-related injuries each year. The next chapter explores what happens once the injury has occurred—what the parent of an injured child can do to gain some compensation for the pain and the suffering to which he and his child have been put and to regain financial losses.

6

Toys in the Courtroom

THE PRECEDING CHAPTERS HAVE EXPOSED THE INADEQUACY OF the major sources of protection against toy-related injuries. The industry itself is of little or no help, and its efforts toward safety and quality control have largely been ineffective and halfhearted. The private testing agencies are handicapped either by financial dependence upon the industry or by the sheer volume of consumer products, among which toys are only a relatively small class.

The government has essentially only one law that covers toys. The agencies that administer it are understaffed and underbudgeted, and their over-all impact is almost negligible. The states have only limited jurisdiction and limited capabilities. Given all of this, it is inevitable that there will continue to be thousands of cases every year in which children are unnecessarily injured by their playthings. Still, although this shameful state of affairs will certainly continue until we have strict premarketing control of toy safety by federal agencies armed with powerful laws and adequate funds, we are not bound merely to sit back and take it. Not at all.

In every aspect of consumer affairs, people are becoming more and more aware of the possibilities that the courts afford, both for recovering damages for harm already done, and for providing the publicity and the pressure upon manufacturers that will incline them to take greater care in the future. One important legal weapon within this arsenal is the products liability suit, a legal action brought against the maker or seller of a dangerous product in order to compel him to make good—as far as possible—the harm his hazardous goods have done.

It is well to stress again, of course, that the *prevention* of toy-related injuries is and ought to be the key to children's safety. Any discussion of the potentialities of lawsuits ought to begin from the stark fact that no amount of money can truly "pay for" intolerable pain, permanent injury or disfigurement, or the untimely death of a child.

Furthermore, products liability suits in particular are complex and difficult undertakings. They need not be, and I will make some suggestions later in this chapter as to how the law could be more finely honed to provide a better balance in the legal contest between consumer and manufacturer. Yet, as the National Commission on Product Safety reported to the Congress and the President:

> In the best of circumstances, a products case is still a bruising, frequently heartbreaking, always onerous undertaking for client and lawyer. (F.R., p. 73)

Nevertheless, once a tragedy has happened, there is some very real value in going to court in an attempt to secure just, full, and adequate compensation for the damage done. There are several reasons why.

The first of these, and the most philosophical, is that the legal process as a means of settling disputes is integral and essential to any civilized society. Under the law of the jungle, when one man harms another, the injured party seeks out his assailant and exacts what he considers a suitable revenge. This leads to chaos. Under the rule of law, however, society itself steps into the dispute, through its legal institutions, and defines the respective rights and duties of the parties—enforcing them, if necessary, with civil and criminal sanctions.

Secondly, and more pertinently from the point of view of the injured child or his parent, a successful lawsuit with a recovery of ample monetary damages can and does provide some real, if rough, compensation. Injuries are not simply tragedies; they often involve heavy financial burdens. A plaintiff who succeeds can often recover enough to pay his hospital and medical bills and other expenses connected with the injury, as well as compensation for the intangible but very real suffering and anguish he has undergone. It may even provide funds to make up for the loss of his future earning capacity. These are not in any sense the same as restoration of sight or health and integrity of limb and life, but they are important and necessary substitutes for these.

Thirdly, when a court steps in between two parties and decides that one of them has acted in a negligent, dangerous or unsuitable way that gives rise to a legal and enforceable liability to the injured person or persons, this has a useful deterrent effect—generally—on the rest of us. If I should read in the papers, for example, that a neighbor of mine has been ordered by a court to pay several thousands of dollars in damages to the family whose house was destroyed when his car—parked on a hill without the brakes' being set—rolled into their front room, then I would sit up and take notice. I would adjust my own conduct accordingly. I would set the brakes on my car whenever I park on a hill. Thus I have been given an example that has deterred me from harmful conduct. And this is all to the good for each of us.

The products liability suit, like any other lawsuit, serves all three of these functions, but with varying degrees of success. The first—the civilizing function—it performs well. As yet the author is unaware of any enraged parent attempting to exact an eye-for-an-eye settlement from an offending toymaker. The second—the compensating function—it performs only fairly well, for reasons we shall explore presently. The third—the deterring function—it performs quite poorly. The factors that lead to the limited deterrent success of products liability suits are many and complex. Among them, several stand out.

First of all, not every products liability suit is successful, and at times this lack of success may have had little or nothing to do with the actual merits of the case, for there are still in the law that governs these suits a number of technical obstacles operating to defeat otherwise sound claims and do so for reasons that are now leftovers from an earlier age. Thus a valid suit may still be lost; and a toy manufacturer is anything but deterred by a products liability suit he has won.

Secondly, lawsuits are usually limited to the two parties (the injured person, or plaintiff, and the defendant) involved and them alone; even a successful suit in one state might have come out differently, with a different plaintiff, in another. Thus, a claim based on a substantial injury might not deter a manufacturer from continuing to make a dangerous product, so long as these injuries are infrequent, or, if common, only infrequently severe. As a classic example of the limited effect of products liability suits, consider these two cases that dealt with poisonous firecrakers: *Victory Sparkler & Specialty Co. vs. Latimer* and *Victory Sparkler & Specialty Co. vs. Price.* In each case, the plaintiff's child swallowed one of the defendant company's "spit devil" firecrackers. The firecrackers contained yellow phosphorus, which is a lethal poison, and both children died from the effects of swallowing them. In the Price case, which was the first of the two, a Mississippi court found that neither the seller nor the manufacturer was liable for the youngster's death, on the grounds that swallowing the firecracker was not something either of them should have foreseen and provided against. In the Latimer case, some time later, a Missouri court took exactly the opposite view, holding that those who deal with child consumers have a duty to anticipate the ways in which children are likely to behave. Clearly the Price case, had it gone the other way, might have been a deterrent to the company, and had the company acted accordingly, the Latimer youngster would not have been killed by the poisonous toy. But Price was wrongly decided, and served as no deterrent at all. The possibility of error in the courts, or of inconsistently different jurisdictions, operates, therefore, to diminish the deterrent effect of products liability suits.

The economic advantage that manufacturers have over consumers is another factor that tends to diminish this deterrent effect. The defendant company has the financial and legal resources to deter and delay, before and during trial, and to take lengthy appeals afterward. While all of this is going on, the plaintiff consumer is running up the medical and other expenses that he has gone to court to recover in the first place. Eventually, the plaintiff may be completely worn down and will agree to a compromise settlement of his claim, taking less than its full value in exchange for immediate payment. Thus the legal action never comes to a definitive conclusion, and the deterrent effect of a conclusive lawsuit is again lost.

Also, to the extent that—for whatever reason—juries are sometimes reluctant to return full, fair, and adequate damages and occasionally tend to "compromise" or mitigate their awards, the deterrent effect is once again attenuated. A child who has been horribly burned and disfigured for life, for instance, should be given the fullest legitimate judgment possible, even if this means damages amounting to millions of dollars. Otherwise, justice is ill-served, and the lesser judgment, aside from being inadequate compensation, may in truth be insufficient to provide an impressive lesson to the makers of articles that can do such permanent and sickeningly unnecessary harm.

An additional factor cushioning a toymaker's liability for harm wrought by his defective products is insurance, which can afford him a buffer against uncertain future claims. If his business is large enough, he may prefer to self-insure in whole or in part, that is, to absorb damage payments within his business and pass them along to toy consumers, especially since such payments are deductible as ordinary and necessary business expenses under current tax law.* And whether he carries insurance or not, the toy manufacturer must be persuaded that he stands to lose a great deal from the continued production and marketing of a defective plaything (losses may also stem from weakened consumer confidence in his products, of course) before he will undertake a costly redesigning of the toy or expensive production-line changes.

For these reasons the National Commission on Product Safety reluctantly concluded that, given both the obstacles in the law itself and the limitations on deterrence under the present state of affairs:

> Despite its humanitarian adaptations to meet the challenge of product-caused injuries, the common law [the ordinary lawsuit] puts no reliable restraint upon product hazards. (F.R., p. 3)

Therefore, the third, or deterrent, function of the average products liability suit goes largely unfulfilled. Let us turn now to the second function, the compensatory effect such a suit has for the injured child or his parent.

It is important to appreciate that "the law" is not a static and ossified collection of doctrines buried away in impressive volumes that only lawyers read or even know about. "The law" is *not* something older judges have written down for younger judges to look up. In any given case, the nature of the law is much more complex and much more alive than that. And one of the most impressive demonstrations of the continued vigor of the law and its capacity to change with the times is in the very field of products liability.

As this process of evolution has been carried on over the

---

* See NCPS F.R., p. 74.

years, courts and legislatures have devised rules and principles to serve as guidelines for settling disputes. Sometimes it happens that different, even competing, principles seem to apply to cases that are roughly analogous. At this point, it is the duty of lawyers and judges to sort out the principles and—with the valuable and traditional assistance of a jury of men and women of common sense—to apply them to the actual situations that present themselves. These situations, like neckties, come in a dazzling, often bewildering variety.

In any specific instance, "the law" is the combination of these different principles as they are brought to bear upon the facts at hand through the competing efforts of the parties' lawyers, under the direction of the judge, and with the assistance of the jury. Hopefully, the result will be a resolution of the dispute that is logically consistent with previous decisions, well-adapted to the civilizing and deterring functions of the legal process, and, perhaps most importantly, well-suited to the requirements of justice in the case at bar.

The legal principles available in what we call the "common law" tradition, which we share with most other English-speaking nations, have been developed over the years, usually on a case-by-case basis, as the cases have arisen. Since we have no guarantee that the right case will come up at the right time—the time when the law is ripe for clarification or development—this leaves a measure of uncertainty and confusion in the law. From time to time, the courts are given positive guidance and clarification in their tasks by direct instruction from the people, through their elected legislators. This happens, for instance, when the Congress, or the legislature of one of the states, enacts a statute embodying a rule of law or of legal procedure, such as the Flammable Fabrics or Hazardous Substances Acts. Generally, however, this active intervention by the legislature is slow in coming and often does not materialize for a long period of time; and so the law is what it is largely through judicial development.

Probably the soundest lesson for a layman to draw from the foregoing sketch of the complex sources of our law is the inadvisability of relying on his own evaluation of his legal rights after his child has been injured by a toy. It is unwise for a parent to leap to the conclusion that there is no form of legal redress for his child's injuries, and that the costs of pain and suffering and medical bills must be borne within the family, for it might very well be that an attorney would conclude that the toy manufacturer has a clear duty to make good the loss. And only lawyers have the specialized training and necessary experience that equip them to put together all the pieces of the puzzle, both legal and factual, into a clear and convincing case.

Suits based on injuries caused by toys fall, as we have said, within the general category of "products liability" cases. This general category includes legal actions using any or all of three different but related theories, which will be outlined below. But first let us assume that there is an injury. At this point, of course, the child and his family want medical help and are not concerned about the possibilities of financial recovery. Later, flooded with relief (and sometimes also with feelings of guilt, which should be set aside because in ninety-nine percent of toy-related injuries, the toy is at fault and not the child or his parent) the parents often forget about or dismiss the possibility of bringing suit. This inertia is one significant reason why products liability suits have had so little impact on the manufacturers of dangerous products. As the NCPS remarked:

> Small wonder that some manufacturers do not even respond to letters claiming compensation for injuries: they know that more than two-thirds will never pursue the claim. A survey of 276 persons in Denver and Boston who had reported their injuries to Food and Drug Administration teams showed that only 4 percent contacted an attorney to investigate possible legal redress. (F.R., p. 74)

Assuming that the injured child and his parents have overcome this inertia and do contact an attorney, what are they in for? First of all, the correct court will have to be chosen, the proper defendants identified and brought—if possible—within the court's jurisdiction, the offending product clearly connected with the defendants, its dangerous qualities established, a suitable and appropriate theory of liability argued and proved, damages documented and expert testimony secured, technical defenses overcome, and a jury convinced not only of the defendant's responsibility for the injury, but also of the fairness of the amount of damages sought. After long delays caused by tactical maneuvering by the defense and by backlogs in the nation's courts (up to forty months in some jurisdictions!), a trial is held and a verdict handed down—let us assume—in favor of the plaintiff. The defense may appeal, which adds further delay; moreover, on appeal, a company that has been found liable in the lower court may obtain a reversal, resulting in a finding for the defendants, or win a new trial.

Because of the time and expense involved in carrying a products liability suit to a successful conclusion, several witnesses testified before the NCPA that "it hardly pays to press a defective product claim for less than $5,000 to $10,000. Consequently most injuries to consumers go uncompensated" (F.R., p. 74). Furthermore, the commission concluded:

> In the case of a narrow escape, the consumer has no legal right to go to court to seek an injunction against sale of the product [to others]. If the injury is slight and it does not pay to file a personal suit, even though thousands may have been injured by the same product, present law does not allow an attorney to file for damages payable to the public treasury in behalf of the whole class of consumers who were hurt. (F.R., p. 74)

Thus, when the injured consumer does consult an attorney, even though his original intention is to go through with the suit—because he is angry as well as injured—he may, when confronted with the realities of products liability cases, be discouraged from proceeding.

This is not to suggest that all such suits are doomed from the outset. Quite the contrary is true. The law is capable of providing justice to injured consumers, and the cards are by no means stacked against the little consumer and in favor of the large manufacturer or seller. But success in this field does require skill, persistence, and in part, perhaps, a little bit of luck.

Conduct by parents prior to their consulting a lawyer can adversely affect the outcome of their child's case. For it is unfortunately true that most of us initially respond to the presence of a product that has wounded us by throwing the blasted thing right out of the house. But to do that may be equivalent to letting go of the evidence we may need to prove that the product was indeed dangerous or defective. Or suppose that the product caused the injury by shattering or exploding. Saving the pieces may be crucial to the preparation and development of our case; and whether we do save them is, again, often just a matter of good fortune. Or again, some products liability cases are based on the theory that the article was dangerous because the directions and warnings were inadequate or misleading. But we may have thrown away the package on which the directions were written, or lost the instruction sheet. Fortunately, similar packages and instruction sheets can usually be found; but the original document is always the best evidence, and defense lawyers have been known to suggest to juries inferences that might be drawn from the fact that the originals were never produced in court.

Other fortuitous circumstances may also play a role in jury trials. Some people are naturally convincing and make good witnesses. Others are naturally nervous, or unattractive, or unpleasant to listen to. They make poor witnesses. We have no way of knowing just how these personal idiosyncracies—

which all of us have in one way or another—will and do affect the jury we are trying to convince. Two different people, one pleasant, the other not, may wind up with two different results in a jury trial, on the same evidence. This is a risk we run for the privilege of being able to invoke the common sense of ordinary people as an aid to the resolution of legal disputes. It is a very valuable privilege, and the risk is worth running; but still, it can occasionally lead to a miscarriage of justice.

Turning, now, to the general types of products liability suits, we have said that there are essentially three of them. The first is an action for negligence, based on the notion that certain persons, including those dealing in the manufacture and sale of consumer goods, owe a duty of reasonable carefulness to those whom they can intelligently expect to be affected by their activities. The second is an action for breach of warranty, which rests on the assumption that between buyer and seller there is an agreement like a contract, whereby the buyer pays for the goods and in return the seller hands them over with an express or implied promise that they will prove suitable for the uses to which they are intended to be put. The third, and newest type of suit is an action based on so-called "strict liability," which is a theory that—with respect to products that are unreasonably dangerous when put into the marketplace—the maker and anyone else who is in a position to be aware of the dangerous character of the item in question is to be held liable for the harm it causes whether or not the harm was a result of anyone's negligence.

All of these theories—the third is really a broad type of exception to the limiting possibilities of the first—have their own special rules and problems, and law libraries are filled with learned volumes detailing, defining, and explaining the decisions handed down in cases dealing with each of them. There is a whole specialized language proper to the framing and trial of the issues that such cases raise, and products liability is coming to be recognized as an important subspecialty within the legal profession.

Suppose that a mother picks up, let us say, a toy top for her young son at the corner drugstore. She brings it home, and opens it, and the first time he spins it, the top shatters and the spring mechanism flies off and hits him in the eye, causing an injury that is permanent and for which the medical and hospital costs are extensive.

She decides to sue, not only to recover compensation for the harm she has incurred, but also because she feels very strongly about the continued marketing of such a shoddy and dangerous product, especially since it is intended for children. Assuming that she has kept the pieces of the broken top, and that she can adequately establish that it was sold to her by the corner store, as well as the costs she has had to bear because of the injury to her son, what are her legal options and obstacles?

Probably the first question that has to be answered is, whom should she sue? This is not as clear-cut a matter as it might seem at first sight. Should she sue the drugstore, or the distributor of the toys, or the manufacturer? Or all of them? She may even wish to sue the magazine or testing agency that led her to believe the product that caused the injury was safe. Suits of this type are a developing trend in the law today. Perhaps the drugstore is uninsured and couldn't afford to pay the damages that she is seeking. Perhaps the toy came into the store in a package that the store personnel had no reason or opportunity to inspect. Perhaps the distributor is a dummy corporation for the manufacturer, with no real assets of its own. Perhaps the manufacturer got the plastic from a subcontractor and will claim that the shattering of the top was the latter's fault. Perhaps the circumstances are such that *all* of the parties alluded to should be sued or made defendants. A wrong choice *could* mean the loss of the whole case.

In a Kentucky case, the plaintiff sued the manufacturer of a baseball bat that shattered and wounded one of a group of ball-playing children. Then the court ruled that there was no proper relationship—no privity (see below)—between the injured boy and the manufacturer, and so no case. In a New Jersey case, the plaintiffs sued the retailer and the distributor, but not the manufacturer, in order to recover for injuries suffered by a fifteen-year-old who was hit in the eye when a plastic slingshot snapped. The court ruled that if the item broke because it was defectively designed or made, then the action should have been brought against the manufacturer, not the retailer or distributor, on the grounds that neither of the latter has a duty to inspect the items he offers for sale. These cases, and many others that could be cited, illustrate the importance of selecting the proper defendants—and it may occasionally be impossible to find one who is both likely to be found liable and financially equipped to pay the damages.

A second problem is more theoretical. What precisely do you claim is the principle of law that supports your case for damages? In some circumstances, you may wish to allege a breach of warranty, in others an act of negligence, in still others you may simply argue that the defendant is strictly liable for the injury caused by his dangerous or defective product, or it might be advantageous to proceed on all three theories. Which theory you choose is partly determined by the facts of the case, and sometimes also by rules of legal procedure (such as statutes of limitations—some types of lawsuits have to be brought within a certain time period after the injury or else they fail) or of legal substance (in some states, for example, it is almost impossible both to prove that the plaintiff has been entirely free of negligence on his own part and to establish that the defendant has been negligent on his; and without establishing both these points, no matter what the relative weight of the negligent conduct of each of the parties, the case will fail in these jurisdictions). In suits where you choose a breach of warranty theory, for example, it may be that the old requirement of "privity" still gets in the way. Privity is a notion developed out of the ancient legal regulations evolved to cover the interpretation and enforcement of contracts. Where a breach of warranty is charged, the plaintiff must be the one who was part of the original bargain in some states—that is, must be in privity with the defendant. Where this is absent, and privity is still required, the case will collapse.

Thus before you even get to bat in the courtroom, you may have been called out because you chose the wrong theory or the wrong defendant or the wrong combination of them.

Another way to lose is by choosing the wrong court. As Professor James says very well, "A manufacturer's liability . . . may not be worth very much to a consumer who must cross a continent to pursue it." (*Civil Procedure,* 1965, p. 648) In order to alleviate this hardship, a number of states have enacted laws that enable the courts to take jurisdiction of defendant companies in products liability suits even though the company has no assets or offices within the state in question. But there are limits to the effectiveness of these so-called "longarm" statutes and problems involved in the choice of a proper tribunal.

Suppose, for instance, that our hypothetical mother buys the top in Rhode Island and that the distributor is a Connecticut firm, while the manufacturer's business is conducted entirely within New York. She crosses the state line into Massachusetts, where she lives, and gives the toy to her son in Boston. Some states will allow her to obtain jurisdiction over the out-of-state defendant under such circumstances (Massachusetts, for example, will do so); others will not. The trend in the case law and statutes is toward permitting the suit in any state in which an activity took place that had some reasonable connection with the injury.

Quite apart from obtaining jurisdiction over the defendant, it may make a substantial difference which state's law is held to govern the suit, since a court in one state may, for some purposes, feel constrained to apply the substantive law of another state, and the law might vary between two states on a highly material point. Thus, some states do and others do not require that a plaintiff in a negligence case must be free from "contributory" negligence of his own. The matter is most complex, and the differences in law from state to state, both as to whether the courts will entertain the suit and as to how it may finally come out, are crucial ones. Intelligent selection of a forum, which could influence what law is applicable, is one of the lawyer's most vital and challenging decisions.

What kind of damages are compensable may also be a complex and hotly contested issue. The child blinded by the top in our example had a clearly defined injury to his eye. This is the damage he has suffered. But suppose, now, that his mother became ill from the shock of seeing him wounded. Would this be an injury for which the defendants could also be held responsible? The earlier law was clear that they could not, for several reasons, chief among them the doctrine that in a personal injury suit, there must be some physical (as opposed to psychological) "impact." More modern decisions do recognize the importance of psychological as well as physical trauma, but the question is far from settled and too often a plaintiff in the "wrong" state may be unable to recover.

Once the case is begun, the damages specified and within the reach and authority of the courts, the proper tribunal selected, the proper defendants brought in, and a proper theory of recovery argued, there may still remain several technical bars to compensation. Among them are the doctrines of privity, contributory negligence, third-party intervention (breaking the chain of causality), and others. Each of these defenses can be interposed in some states in order to defeat an otherwise proper claim. In toy-related accident cases, they are often unrealistic and mistaken relics of the common law of an earlier and vastly different era.

Let us look at privity, for instance, more closely. The privity requirement in an action for breach of warranty arises from a theory that there is something analogous to a contract in the sale of a product. The seller is supposed to have promised that the product for which he is being paid is fit and suitable for the uses to which it may reasonably be put. But lawsuits based on this theory must ordinarily be lawsuits between the same persons who were parties to the original contract. Thus, there are cases where children who have been given toys by friends or relatives have sometimes been excluded from recovery because courts have ruled that they were not in privity with the seller of the improper item. This restriction still persists, to a limited extent, in several states. It has been eased somewhat in others, but the extension even in many of these only covers members of the buyer's immediate family or guests in his home.

There are two ways in which the privity requirement operates to defeat the child plaintiff. First of all, it may exclude him from bringing suit at all, on the grounds that as one who has received the product as a gift he is not in any privity with the seller or the maker. This kind of theoretical approach argues that once the chain of privity is broken, it can never be repaired. A Florida court, faced with a situation where a boy (Smith) was injured by a slingshot sold by a retailer (Nussman) to a different boy, held in *Smith vs. Nussman* that the plaintiff Smith had no case against the retailer since the sale was not to him, but to the other youngster—hence a lack of privity. An earlier Illinois case, *Miller vs. Sears, Roebuck, & Co.*, dealt with a young boy who was badly burned when a "Ronson Repeater" spark gun ignited gasoline stored on the Miller family farm. Sears, Roebuck argued that since the boy himself had not bought the gun, there was a failure of privity. The court agreed and the case was lost.

Most courts have now given up the privity requirement in

cases where the lawsuit is based on a negligence theory. But many still hold to it in actions for breach of warranty. Beginning in the early 1960's, however, statutes began to be enacted in several states which operate to correct this flaw in the common law. In other states, the courts themselves have changed the rule. Laws and decisions have thus extended the notion of privity to members of the purchaser's immediate family, and to guests in his home, as we have noted. But this, of course, does not go far enough. It fails to protect, for instance, playmates using the defectively made or dangerously designed toys in the local schoolyard or park. Thus in many states, the law has still not provided for the obvious fact that children play with their toys, and with each other, throughout their neighborhoods. As an example of this, let us mention again the case of the broken baseball bat. The court there found that the privity requirement had not been met because the boy who was injured was not the owner of the bat, and because the accident took place outside of the home of the boy who did own it. But realistically, we may ask, how many children—especially in the city—own the kind of home that has a yard or a basement big enough to play baseball in?

There is a second way in which the privity requirement can defeat a plaintiff with an otherwise valid claim. This happens when the doctrine is so applied as to limit the possible defendants. Thus, under theories based, for instance, on breach of warranty—the contractual type of products liability suit—the plaintiff can only sue the one who immediately sold him the item, that is, the retail merchant. But in by far the majority of cases, the manufacturer is the real culprit, and is the only one with enough economic resources to pay appropriate damages; and yet the manufacturer may be completely insulated from a suit by strict privity requirements.

Insulation of this sort works as follows: the theory is that the plaintiff sues the retailer; the retailer, if he loses, may sue the distributor; the distributor, if he loses, may sue the maker.

The parties go successively up the chain until the one whose activity caused the injury is reached. But in states where there is a strict privity requirement, the plaintiff's only action may be against the retailer, and if the retailer can prove that the injury was not his fault—for example, where he argues successfully that he cannot be expected to inspect every prepackaged product that he places on his shelves—then the plaintiff's case falls apart. And unless the retailer loses, of course, he has no incentive whatsoever to sue the distributor or manufacturer.

In a case involving a toy top, an infant lost his sight when the defective plaything exploded. He sued the retailer but lost on the grounds that the latter could not fairly be expected to have claimed (warranted) that he guaranteed the top to be safe, since it came to his store already boxed. Since the defect in question was a hidden (or "latent" one)—the accident happened some three months after purchase—the court held that it was not the kind of thing that the retailer should have discovered or warned the buyer about, for he had no opportunity to notice the problem. And with the retailer let off, the manufacturer—the responsible party—escaped as well.

In another case, a New Jersey boy whose plastic slingshot broke off and stabbed him in the eye was denied recovery against the retailer and the distributor because the court held that neither of them had a duty to test the toy before selling it. Privity prevented a suit against the manufacturer directly, and the case was lost.

Examples like these show how the evolution of the law and its logic have not always worked out as effective protections for consumers in a product-dominated society. Nor has the law been always quick enough to adapt to changing circumstances and present-day economic realities. Thus in cases where a toy has been defectively manufactured, it can be critical whether or not it arrived in the retail outlet in a prepackaged condition. When it has arrived, the retailer's duty to inspect it is held by the courts to be slight or nonexistent. How can the storekeeper rip open every plastic package that comes into his shop? It is reasonable enough not to hold him to such an inspection, but this rule ought not to be coupled with a strict privity requirement which makes recovery impossible.

Privity requirements have their most stringent effect in suits in which the plaintiff alleges breach of warranty; they are no longer helpful to the defendant in negligence cases, and generally unavailable to the defense in actions where strict liability is charged. But both of these latter theories have their own traps for the unwary as well.

In ordinary negligence cases, for example, there are several obstacles to recovery that constantly reappear on the defendant's side. One of these is the doctrine that contributory negligence by the plaintiff is a bar to recovery, a doctrine still in force in many states. Allied to the notion of contributory negligence by the injured child is the concept of "imputed" negligence, by which the parent's carelessness is held against the child and serves to defeat his action against a maker or seller of defective or dangerous toys. Fortunately, imputed negligence is in force in only a very few states, and operates even in these only under quite limited circumstances. The theory of imputed negligence assumes that where a parental examination has or should have disclosed the dangerous characteristics of the plaything, the seller's or maker's responsibility comes to an end and the real cause of the injury to the child is the parent's failure to keep the toy away from him or at least to allow him to play with it only under rigorous supervision.

The same kind of reasoning is at work in the more general doctrine of contributory negligence. If someone else's negligent conduct causes me harm, I can recover damages only if my own conduct met the standards of reasonable care and did not "contribute" to the accident or injury. This sounds reasonable at first, but as it works out, it often leads to unfair and unsound results.

Conduct which might give rise to the defense of contributory negligence can be of two kinds, passive and active. The passive variety usually consists in a failure to discover, for instance, some dangerous characteristic of a product. In most cases, the failure to discover a dangerous defect will not constitute contributory negligence, since it will turn out that the child had no reason to suspect the fault, or to assume that the warnings and instructions that came with the toy were inadequate or misleading. Failure under these circumstances is reasonable, and so is not really negligence at all. Thus a teen-age girl in Hawaii was allowed to recover damages for injuries sustained when her hula skirt caught fire and caused burns over seventy-five percent of her body. The court found that she had no reason to know that the skirt was so dangerously flammable, and so was not negligent in wearing it near an open flame. Conduct which could give rise to the defense of active contributory negligence, on the other hand, arises when the plaintiff either does know the dangers involved in a product and persists in using it, or makes it unsafe himself by altering it, or by putting it to a use that is in itself abnormal and dangerous.

The impact of plaintiff's negligence differs, as we have said, from state to state. In some jurisdictions it constitutes an absolute bar, while in others it operates to reduce the damages allowable. In the second instance, the reduction is accomplished by establishing a ratio of comparative negligence. Hence, in an auto accident, driver A may be held eighty percent responsible, driver B only twenty percent responsible. B sues A and collects only eighty percent of his fair damages. This compares the relative negligence of plantiff and defendant and adjusts the result accordingly; and so it is called comparative, and not strictly contributory, negligence.

In a majority of states, a child is held to the standard of care of an ordinary child of the same age, experience, capacity, and discretion, and whether or not a child plaintiff was contributorily negligent is usually a question for the jury. However, in some of these as well as in some other states, the courts have rejected the application of the doctrine of contributory negligence to children of very tender years. And in some states, there is disagreement in the case law as to whether contributory negligence applies in suits based on breach of warranty or where the doctrine of strict liability (see below) is in force.

As we have said, imputed contributory negligence, or parental negligence, is also a doctrine on the wane. Massachusetts, for example, now has a statute expressly forbidding the application of this doctrine to young children. But this is not always true elsewhere. A six-year-old California boy looked down the barrel of his new dart gun in order to find out why the dart inside had broken while being fired. As he peered in, the parts that had been left behind came shooting out into his eye. The court allowed the jury to consider whether his mother had been contributorily negligent in allowing him to play without adequate supervision (and also whether he himself had been contributorily negligent by looking into the gun). Happily, the jury rejected both theories of contributory negligence and allowed him to recover. My research has not disclosed any cases dealing with toys where the end result of a personal injury case was that an injured child was denied recovery because of imputed or parental contributory negligence. But to the extent that this is at least theoretically still possible, legislation should be passed at once in order to correct the inequity.

More important than imputed negligence, and more potentially critical for the child-plaintiff, is the child's own contributory negligence in states where it still bars recovery. The fundamental problem is one of definition: What is a reasonable standard of care when the consumer is a child? Is it fair to hold a six-year-old to adult standards of behavior and prudence? And how can a child be held to a duty of obeying warnings and instructions that he well may be unable to read or understand? Should this kind of failure be enough to defeat his claims?

The doctrine of contributory negligence certainly does defeat otherwise sound claims, as in an early Montana case where a twelve-year-old was found contributorily negligent for setting off a firecracker in violation of a city ordinance. The court ruled that the seller was not responsible for the injury—permanently damaging the youngster's left hand—since it would not have occurred had not the lad lit the firecracker in violation of the ordinance. My view would be that the seller should be strictly responsible for any harms that develop from the use or abuse of articles generally recognized to be as dangerous as explosives, if put into the hands of children.

Akin to the problem of whether children should be expected to meet adult standards of carefulness is the question of foreseeability. Lawsuits based on negligent conduct with harmful results start from the premise that the duty of care involved is positive but not absolute. If I light a cigarette in New Hampshire and the not-quite-extinguished match burns a small hole in my sport jacket, and if months later I then lend the jacket to a friend who wears it to a hockey game, and if while at the game, the hole in the jacket catches the belt buckle of the man next to my friend as he leaps up to roar for the Boston Bruins, and if then the hockey neighbor, hooked to my friend, falls into his seat a little ineptly and crushes the hat of the man behind him, which has fallen onto the seat in the interim— no court in the world would say that I had a legal duty to the man who owned the hat not to run the risk of crushing it by being slightly careless with my matches several months and several hundred miles away. In other words, there is a limit, generally expressed as "foreseeability." You are only responsible for those things which you could reasonably be expected to foresee and to be able to prevent.

The usual test of foreseeability is the so-called "reasonable man" test. This means that it doesn't matter whether the specific injury that occurred was actually foreseen by the actor or not. What does matter is whether or not some harmful consequence from the conduct in question would be foreseeable by someone with a reasonable grasp on the basic circumstances and probabilities surrounding the activity in question. Thus in the case of a sparking toy gun, it would be reasonably foreseeable that live sparks could cause fires and possibly deaths, for we all know that these are quite possible consequences of such instrumentalities. But it is not necessary that we actually think of all the different ways in which these sparking accidents could happen—that we anticipate, for instance, the likelihood of a child taking one into a hospital to visit his new baby brother and igniting the contents of an oxygen tent in the process.

Some courts, however, confuse this test with a different but related line of thinking. The second line centers on the difference between normal use and abnormal use or abuse. Thus the argument is made that manufacturers and other products liability defendants should be held responsible only for accidents occurring while their product is being put to so-called normal usages. They should not be required to think up all of the potential ways in which their goods will be misused, nor to protect against these misuses. The argument concludes that products liability should therefore only extend to intended uses and not to abnormal uses of the items. But this is not entirely satisfactory, for it confuses what we intend with what we can reasonably anticipate.

Children are blessed with fertile and unconventional imaginations and with a high degree of inventiveness—especially those children who have not yet been regimented by conformist educational systems. Most toymakers design their products to appeal precisely to these characteristics of the child's personality. But because of this high degree of imagination, the youngster is far less likely to respect the distinction between "normal" and and "abnormal" use, and far less able to anticipate the dangers that the latter can lead to. Toys are given him to have fun with, and fun is "what you like to do," not what is "normal" or "abnormal" according to a manufacturer's fiat. Moreover, younger children ordinarily do not read, and those who do are often unable to grasp the full implications of the warnings or instructions that come with their toys. Even when they do understand them, they are likely to forget or ignore them, or even to experiment in order to find out whether the warnings are all that serious after all.

Thus children may take electrical toys into the bathtub, or take complex gadgets apart and swallow the parts, or do almost any other unexpected and sometimes dangerous thing. This is certainly foreseeable, even if not intended by the maker or seller of toys.

What is at issue, then, is how far a manufacturer of children's things must go to protect against these foreseeable, if "abnormal," variations on his intended themes. Should every toy be utterly childproof? Would this be economically feasible, or technically possible? Would childproof toys really sell at all? If we allow the manufacturer some latitude and refuse to hold him liable for everything bad that happens to people who play with toys, then how and where do we draw the line? Does a toymaker satisfy his responsibility by issuing warnings and providing instructions? If so, how clear must they be? What about foreseeable accidents that he does warn against, but which experience teaches us are likely to recur repeatedly? What about warnings that we know have little or no effect? What about toys that are inherently dangerous (like air rifles)?

There are no answers—no conclusive answers, at least—to these difficult and important questions. Thus, the foreseeability problem will continue to be a stumbling block for the plaintiffs in much of the future litigation over toy-related injuries. I would suggest, at least, that courts should recognize more fully than they have to date that children are not simply "small adults"—but rather that they have an entirely different psychological and practical capacity for dealing with the world in which we and they live. Since this is so, and we are aware of it, manufacturers who deal with children—who profit from them—should be held to the responsibility that comes with this knowledge and this duty to anticipate how children will deal with toys aimed at them and their special psychology.

The use of *adult* products by children is, in this respect, a somewhat different problem, since adult products are *not* explicitly directed at children. The manufacturers and sellers might, in such cases, have much more reason to claim that the use or abuse of their products by children was genuinely unforeseeable.

This claim, however, does not always succeed. In the case of *Hardman vs. Helene Curtis Industries, Inc.*, a six-year-old Illinois girl sprayed her hair and her dress with her mother's hair conditioner, "Lanolin Discovery." Later, while she was carrying a candle, the hair and the dress both caught fire and she was badly burned. The court ruled that the manufacturer *was* negligent in this instance, since it had carried out no flammability tests on the product, had put no cautionary instructions on the hair spray, and should have foreseen that a child might very possibly be using the conditioner. But a directly contrary result was reached in Missouri, in the case of *Lawson vs. Benjamin Ansehl Co.*, in which a five-year-old boy's clothing caught fire after he had sprayed himself with very flammable fingernail polish and touched his clothing with a lighted match. Here the court maintained that *so* irrational a use of fingernail polish could not reasonably have been foreseen, and that under the circumstances, the manufacturer could not be held liable.

Decisions like this tend, unhappily, to overlook the necessity of protecting children, in some cases, against themselves. In the spark-gun case which I discussed earlier when talking about privity, for instance, the court held that such a toy was not inherently dangerous and that in any case, no manufacturer could be expected to anticipate that some child might use it around a tank of gasoline. The two firecracker cases involving the poisonous "spit devil," which at least two different children swallowed, also point to how contradictions can occur in the case law. In the Price case, the court held that this kind of swallowing could not be reasonably foreseen. In the Latimer case, a different court arrived at the opposite conclusion. The "spit devil" was small, shaped like a lozenge, and came wrapped, without a warning, in plain red tissue paper. The Latimer court argued that in making and selling products for consumption by children, there must be a reasonable anticipation of how they behave; and the decision further hinted that because of the lack of warning on the individual item—there were warnings on the box sent to the retailer from which he sold the firecrackers one by one—the manufacturer might be at fault in addition to whoever sold them to the child.

The latter seems to me to be the reasonable and civilized approach, by which courts do make allowances for the fact that children require special handling. People who deal with the public for profit ought to be held to a higher degree of care when they promote and sell products that are likely to be bought for and given to children. If a toy is unsuitable for some uses to which a child might foreseeably put it, then it is probably entirely unsuitable for a child. The burden of providing against the harm and the injuries that can flow from this unsuitability ought to rest on the one who is in a position to take proper precautionary measures in the first place.

There are still other ways in which plaintiffs in toy-related products liability suits are blocked from recovery by legal theories which sometimes miss the point. Let us assume that, up to now, all the proper elements of a good case have been established. There was a compensable injury, the suit has been brought against defendants reasonably related to the injury, and there does seem to have been some negligence either in the manufacture, marketing, or sale of the toy in question, negligence such that a reasonable man might foresee such an injury as its result. This, we anticipate, will suffice, given proper and adequate proof. Not so.

Let's return to our original example—the toy top that a mother bought at the corner drug store. We've seen that there must be some negligence (otherwise the top would not have flown apart as it did), and that there is a proper relationship, at least between the child and the manufacturer and probably also with the retail store. There is a real injury, and we will assume that we are in a court that has no difficulty exercising its jurisdiction over the case and the parties thereto. We still have to show that there was a fairly direct connection between the negligence we have charged and the injury we claim resulted. The negligence, in the language of the law, must have been the "proximate" cause of the injury.

The notions of proximate cause, and, closely related to it, that of intervening cause, are concepts that continue to create problems for lawyers, clients, judges, and legal scholars. In a generalized way, we may say that the concepts are elementary: Where negligence is alleged as the cause of an injury, the causation charged must be fairly well connected with that harm which is said to be its effect. There are two ways in which this causal chain can fail. The first failure is due to "remoteness"—the cause is too far removed from the effect to be reasonably said to have brought the effect about. As philosophers from Plato on down have been well aware, in one sense there is some causal connection between every event in the universe and every other event in the universe. Obviously, the law does not, and cannot, begin to investigate or to undertake to hold men responsible on the basis of chains of causation that are exceedingly tenuous. For example, no court is going to say that a child who was struck by lightning will be able to recover damages from his mother and father, since, had they not conceived him, he would not have been harmed.

TOYS THAT DON'T CARE

Thus, the law speaks of "proximity" and "remoteness" and requires that the causal connection between negligence and injury in a lawsuit be not remote but proximate. But it is sometimes hard to say what proximity is. And disentangling the various factors that contribute to an injury is often very difficult and very subtle. The following three cases make this clear.

A five-year-old Wisconsin boy aimed a toy airplane, powered by a rubber band, in the general direction of his six-year-old sister. He was showing her how it worked. It worked well enough to hit the girl in the eye and to blind her in that eye. The court, in dealing with the question of causation, held that the toy in itself was not negligently designed, nor was it naturally dangerous—hence, no harmful act at those stages "caused" the injury. The real cause, the court asserted, was the improper use by the five-year-old. Thus there was no recovery against the manufacturer, nor against the retailer for selling the item (*Strahendorf vs. Walgreen Co.*)

This is a good example of how courts tend to confuse proximity in time with proximity in causality. The two are sometimes quite different. I would, of course, agree that the event that was closest in *time* to the injury was the firing of the airplane by the younger brother. But the *direct* cause of the injury in an effective (although not a temporal) sense, was the fact that the so-called plaything was designed with a metal-weighted nose and was capable of speeds up to 22 m.p.h. My conclusion would have been that giving something like this to a child—or selling it to adults but for use by children—is an activity that certainly could be foreseen to cause harm; and that it is like setting in operation a chain of events that leads almost inevitably to tragedy. The use by the five-year-old was the *occasion,* but not, in the realistic sense, the basic *cause* of his sister's blindness.

In another case, a California court offered an elaborate commentary on civilization's long experience with bows and arrows but went on to say that in the particular situation at hand, the proximate cause of the accident—in which a ten-year-old boy hit his four-year-old brother with an arrow, which knocked out his eye—was *only* the activity of the elder brother, and not, for instance, the failure of the manufacturer to provide an adequate warning of the dangers involved in bows and arrows.

Similarly, six-year-old Dale Pitts, in Illinois, was playing in the garage of the parents of his friend Lonnie Phillips. Lonnie threw a dart that had been bought at the local grocery store run by the Basiles. The dart veered off to the right and struck Dale in one eye, permanently impairing his vision. In the case of *Pitts vs. Basile,* the court ruled that regardless of the manufacturer's failure to provide suitable and sufficient warnings and directions on the package (which, as a matter of fact, implied that the darts were suitable for quite young children), the cause—the proximate cause—of the accident was Lonnie Phillips' inability to throw the dart "correctly" along a straight horizontal plane. But it seems to me that this again confuses occasion with causation, and that the real cause of the accident was the nature of the toy when put into the hands of children, whose lack of expertise is surely and unavoidably present and foreseeably so.

These three cases raise the issue of proximity in terms of how directly negligence is related to the accident. There is also a second way in which the problem of proximity arises, and this is the matter of the "intervening cause."

A cause is proximate if its connection with the harm resulting from it is sufficiently direct. But for a cause to be the cause of the harm, or at least a cause for which recovery is possible in a court of law, there must also be an absence of other causes that affect the chain of causation by "stepping in" or "intervening." Sometimes this is just a matter of description. The same act, for instance, deliberately sharpening the point of a toy arrow, could be held to be the proximate cause (as opposed to the manufacture of the arrow with a wooden and already sharp tip) or an intervening cause; it could also fit the category of "contributory negligence." Each of these notions was developed in order to serve the basic need of the law for fairness—the need to do as much justice as possible. But when we are in the realm of toy-related injuries and the conduct of children, the three concepts turn out, as we have seen, to be ill-adapted both to the demands of logic and the requirements of justice. Not always—but often enough to suggest the need for further change and evolution in these legal doctrines.

Up to now, we have been talking chiefly about suits based either on negligence or on breach of warranty. There also exists in the eyes of the law a different sort of wrongful conduct, the kind associated with the doctrine of so-called "strict liability." What the doctrine means is this: A manufacturer who makes a product intended for sale is held to a duty to make the product in such a way that it is not unreasonably dangerous to those who might foreseeably come in contact with it. If it turns out to have been unreasonably dangerous, then the plaintiff's case may be established without having to demonstrate negligence in production.

This rule of law has been well received and is now in force in many jurisdictions. But a problem arises in its application, for it must still be shown that the plaintiff sustained injury from a product which was in fact defective. In the sense in which the term is used in strict products liability cases, a "defect" may be regarded as an unreasonably dangerous condition in the product in question. We are perhaps accustomed to think of a defect in the rather narrow sense of a flaw in an article's production or manufacture, a breakdown in the execution of its design. Before the era of mass production, we might have expressed the notion by saying that the item's workmanship was faulty. But a glance back over the categories of unsafe and unsuitable toys in Chapter Two will demonstrate that there are *many* forms of defects, some of which have not as yet come to the attention of the courts. Quite apart from any flaw in the production process, necessary warnings may be omitted, improper instructions provided, or misleading advertising materials disseminated in connection with the product. The basic design of the toy may be unsafe; the article may be inherently dangerous or dangerous in the hands of children too young to appreciate its hazards; the item may be likely to break or fall apart, creating hazards in the pieces or materials; the item may be too readily adaptable to imaginative but dangerous misuses; it may be unsafely packaged; the article may provide a medium in which dangerous bacteria can thrive; its psychological effects may be damaging.

In suits involving injurious playthings, the law could run into difficulties over the basic question of what is, and what is not, a "defective" toy. Confusion could arise from the fact that things that are potentially dangerous, but harmless if used properly, are not in adult cases considered "unreasonably dangerous." The point is that an adult can reasonably be expected to use a thing for its normal purpose and with care. Anything that is used by an adult for its normal purpose, with due care, and that *does* cause an accident, might well be unreasonably dangerous. But this approach could overlook the situation in which children find themselves. For a child, an air rifle is unreasonably dangerous, as is any kind of projectile toy. Manufacturers have, ordinarily, no qualms about who buys these projectile toys. As a matter of fact, they often attempt to induce sales even to the quite young, by their aggressive marketing and promotional practices. The sounder view, then, would seem to be that the manufacturer should be charged with knowledge of the audience his product commands. Thus, he should be held responsible for placing an unreasonably dangerous instrumentality in the hands of children. This is a more *functional* than theoretical approach, for it looks both to the character of the product *and* to the character of the consumer. And when the combination of these adds up to danger, then the maker who urges sales under these dangerous circumstances should be held liable. Courts in future years will have an increasing opportunity to impose just such a standard. This will help to ensure that products liability suits will act as a deterrent to the manufacturers of dangerous toys.

Another burden that usually falls on the plaintiff in products liability cases is that of proving that there was no way in which some third party could have tampered with the product, or that if such an opportunity did exist, no one did in fact so tamper. It is surely possible that a product that left a manufacturer in sound condition may have caused an accident simply because someone else tampered with it. But sometimes the requirement of proving that the product has not been interfered with has been carried to absurd lengths. Possibly one of the most discouraging of these cases is a California decision, *Hartsook vs. Owl Drug Co.* Here, a mother bought a plastic "Blo-Yr-Top" after asking the drugstore clerk whether it was safe and receiving an affirmative reply. She took it home in her grocery bag, underneath some other items. The top exploded on its first use by her child, who lost an eye. At the trial, the drug company argued that since the top had been carried home under the other goods in the bag, the Hartsooks could not legally establish that the defect existed when the top was bought. It could, the defense argued, have been damaged as a result of being under the other things. The court fell for this argument and denied recovery.

Naturally, one would like to know whether a top so fragile and so apparently susceptible to the slightest pressure could really be a toy that was free from defect. The *Hartsook* decision is a clear example of how the logic of the law sometimes loses touch with reality. One of the basic elements in any realistic understanding of children and the things they use is that sturdiness is a fundamental prerequisite of safety. Children play hard. Their toys are unavoidably subject to heavy wear and tear. Toys are put to novel, often very strenuous uses. Accordingly, a toy that cannot stand up against this kind of ordinary play by normal children is not suitable for children at all. To market such an item with the claim that it is suitable for children is simply wrong. This is equally true where the defect involves the often deceptive and usually inadequate promotional and cautionary material that accompanies the average toy.

It is stupid and naive to think that children will be or can be confined in their creative play activities by the notions a toymaker may deem appropriate or which his legal staff may urge him to specify in lengthy directions aimed at children who can't read. Toymakers expend great quantities of inventiveness and energy in thinking up new toys; surely they ought to foresee the uses to which their present products can be put, and make them safe for such uses.

Children are not adults—that is a theme which runs throughout this book—and they should not be held to adult standards of care or predictability. In by far the greater number of toy-injury incidents, the child himself is not at "fault" for doing what comes naturally to him. People who make fortunes selling toys to kids ought to take along with their profits their fair share of responsibility for child safety. This can be accomplished through the efforts of innovative and realistic judges or, if this fails, by determined parents who alert their elected representatives to the urgency of the problem and the necessity for special statutory provisions for lawsuits by injured youngsters. But the growth of the law and in particular a more realistic approach to such matters as contributory negligence, proximate cause, absence of intervening cause, burdens of proof, questions of privity, and definitions of unreasonably dangerous products, in those cases where children are seeking redress for their injuries, is by no means the end of the matter.

This cursory review of the law and of some cases exemplifying the points I have wished to make about law reform has presented a view of the present status of children's injuries that may suffer from a double distortion. The first distortion stems from the fact that the number of reported cases is not truly illustrative of the number of injuries occurring from toys. For one thing, too many parents tend to assume that either they or their child must have been at fault; they accept the accident more or less fatalistically, and never think of blaming the toy or of bringing suit. But they often should do both. For another thing, many of the injuries—cuts, scratches, and so on—are not grave. The child recovers easily enough, and there is no medical expense to speak of. So there is no fuss made over the incident. I would suggest that for both of these reasons, we really have no valid statistical mode of recording how many or what kinds of injuries to children are caused by defective toys.

The second distortion arises because a great many of the cases that do get into court, especially those cases where the product is clearly dangerous or the manufacturer's negligence is plain, are not finally decided by the courts. They are settled out of court. Other cases which *are* decided and in which the child plaintiff does receive a fair award of damages are never appealed. These cases do not make their way into the law reports, which chiefly concern cases that have been appealed and that involved some knotty point of law. And the existing system of law reports and reference manuals provides no special category for products liability decisions involving toys, so that even many of these decisions may go unnoticed. The many decisions I have personally studied often pertain to accidents in which loss of sight or severe burns were sustained. Many of these are especially tragic, because the report shows that the injured child has lost his case. And the tragedy is compounded by the realization that adequate safety measures and stiffer federal controls could have prevented many of these injuries.

The point of this chapter, then, is this: Given the state of the law and the complexities and difficulties facing plaintiffs in products liability suits based on injuries to children caused by their toys or playthings, we are in urgent need of the continued growth of the law itself in certain areas and, where necessary, of strong preventive legislation. The reform of the law should be in the direction of increased attention to the special circumstances and capacities of children and thus toward extracting a higher duty of care on the part of toy merchants as the standards in these cases. The legislation should be strict, enforceable, and clear. Voluntary control by the industry, and informal control by private testing agencies and consumer services, and the present state and federal legislation are, as we have seen, insufficient.

The solution is really twofold: education for safety and legislation for safety. The next chapter raises the fundamental question anyone about to buy a manufactured plaything ought to ask: "Is this toy necessary?"

7

Is This Toy Necessary?

THE PREVIOUS CHAPTERS HAVE ALL DEALT, IN ONE WAY OR ANother, with the question of safety quite directly—the dangers to be found in toys, the regulatory procedures that do or ought to exist within the toy industry, the role of private testing agencies and of government in ensuring children's freedom from toy-related injuries. The second part of the book will go into greater detail concerning toys to avoid or discard, again, chiefly for reasons of safety.

It seems wise to broaden our perspective a little, at this point, and to observe that we are not all that dependent on toy manufacturers for our children's amusement and delight. This chapter, accordingly, suggests an alternative to storebought toys, with some reasons why a homemade plaything can have certain very definite advantages.

The idea of returning to the homemade variety of toy, which was the standard kind during the early days of the Republic, is not as rustic or as involved as it sounds. We tend today to be swallowed up in an affluent society where conspicuous consumption of mass-produced goods is the ideal. But there is no intrinsic reason why we have to pass these habits on to our children, nor why they should be so easily and so early initiated into the assumption that style, vogue, and planned obsolescence are better characteristics of consumer products than quality, durability, and appropriateness.

The lust for the newest model, which keeps the great automobile companies and appliance manufacturers going, is not unknown to the American toy industry, either. As we noted in Chapter One, the toymakers are every bit as up-to-date and every bit as marketing-conscious as we might expect the people in a $3 billion industry to be. Thus there is a constant rush to develop new and different items, as well as to offer an annual set of "improvements" on old familiar staples like dolls and guns and trains and planes. A world-famous illustration of the "series" principle in toymaking—which is a variation on the "improvement" theme—is the redoubtable "Barbie Doll" and her collection of friends, all produced by Mattel (although Hasbro's "G.I. Joe" series has been a close competitor). Hasbro has read the signs of the times and is now pushing "Major Matt Mason," space commander, who requires, besides the companionship of his friends, innumerable varieties of auxiliary equipment (life support systems and the like), space stations, and so on. One of the notable characteristics of all the series dolls is that they do not go it alone; no one will ever accuse them of being unsociable. "Billy Blastoff" (Eldon Industries) and "Johnny Astro" (Topper Corporation) are also on the horizon.

The series toy is a good example of one of the reasons why homemade toys may be on the whole a preferable alternative to store-bought playthings. For the series toy tends to operate in just the reverse of the way a genuinely valuable plaything should. The best toy, of course, is the one that continually gives the child room to interact with it, to engage his imagination, to develop his skills, to enlarge his own mental and creative horizons. But the series toy is, in effect, a single item with a specialized and limited play range. The more the parent buys to add to the collection within the series, the more limited the play range becomes.

Limiting a child's play range is not a good practice, for as Dr. Allan Fromme has pointed out, children do not satisfy themselves with only a few play ideas—although we adults often do. A man might take up golf or fishing and stick to it over the years, quite content without a wider variety of leisure activities. Children, on the other hand are, as Dr. Fromme reminds us, "naturally variable and fickle." Thus,

> [t]hey have a shorter attention span and, although their interests are every bit as deep and genuine as ours, they are relatively short-lived. Do not, therefore, spend too much money on any toy because, in all probability, its history will be short-lived. (*ABC of Child Care,* p. 305)

This is very sound advice, since the sums of money involved in the commitment to a series toy can become quite considerable over several months or a year or two. The basic principle behind the series toy is the same one that motivated the old Saturday afternoon thriller serials in the movie houses—keep 'em always on the hook.

A second objection raised by many physicians and child psychologists against store-bought toys—not only series toys—is that very often they are inappropriate, as well as disappointing. Dr. Joel Alpert, Chief of Pediatrics at the Children's Hospital Medical Center in Boston, has complained that "the trouble with too many store-bought toys is that they are so complicated, expensive, break too easily, and do not challenge a child's ingenuity." Therefore, he adds, "they often leave both the parent and child unhappy." (*Today's Health,* July, 1968, pp. 27–28) Mrs. Harriet H. Gibney, Director of Health Education at the same medical center, speaks in almost identical terms: "Our doctors became increasingly concerned about the many expensive, complicated, inappropriate, and easily broken toys which [well-meaning] families—often under the pressure of TV advertising—were buying for their children."

The basic flaw with complicated and "sophisticated" toys is that they tend to dominate, rather than to ornament, the child's play. Toys should be auxiliaries to play, and not its sum and substance. We in this country—under the pressures of the hard sell and our consumer-oriented society—seem to have reversed these priorities. We tend to think that play means toys and vice versa. But this is not at all true, and we ought to become, both for our own sakes, and especially for our children's, much less dependent on the idea that play is "with things" and that the "things" have to be expensive and come from a store.

Another danger connected with store-bought toys is that of overdoing it. Because the store-bought toy may be too specialized and hence quickly boring to the child, parents are tempted to escalate their buying efforts, bringing home toy after toy in order to amuse the child. But if the toys are *all* specialized, then boredom will set in just as quickly each time, and the basic function of the playthings—the stimulation of the youngster's imagination and the engagement of his active skills—will still be lost in the parade of new and different toys.

Moreover, there is a much more serious danger in certain patterns of toy overbuying, and that is the danger that both parent and child will confuse the giving of things with the giving of love. It is too well known in psychiatric circles to require any documentation that one very common parental failing is to identify love with goods and services. Affluent parents who are simply "bothered" by their children may feel that it is sufficient to give them new toys constantly—this keeps the kids amused, they reason, and so out of their hair. But keeping your kids out of your hair is admitting (if you do it regularly and as a matter of principle) that you don't really care for them as persons. A poorer family may buy bundles of toys for the opposite reason—as overcompensation for other economic deprivations, or for having to be so often out working that the child is too frequently left alone.

Whether the motivation behind it is healthy and just misguided or more symptomatic of psychological confusion and thus more dangerous, it is not good for a child to be given too many toys. For one thing, the sheer diversity and number of them tend to overwhelm him. It isn't so much "his" play world anymore, as it is his toys' world. Furthermore, the toys may be so specialized that, as we have noted, they limit rather than extend his creative involvement in his own play.

But play should be active. Children are naturally innovative and imaginative. They enjoy developing their own styles and habits of play; they like trying on different roles and imagining various situations and circumstances. Even those activities that seem to us routine, like keeping house or going to work, have an attraction for a child, and when his play is fundamentally uncluttered with complicated toys, he is that much freer to involve himself in the play world in which he learns so much.

For toys and play have a very important function in the process of growing up. They are one of the ways in which a child discovers *himself*. Toys that help him do this, that provide the *occasion* for his own discoveries, must therefore be the kind of playthings that leave him opportunity to experiment. Toys that can't or don't do this become either boring or oppressive, and some authorities have expressed concern that the combination of nonparticipatory toys with overdependence on passive watching of television programs is robbing the child of vitally necessary experiences of growth, initiative, and activity.

Too many toys can stunt the child's human growth by confronting him with a play world in which every conceivable situation is already programmed. A sensory overload of playthings tends to induce a kind of passivity in the child. This passivity is not entirely healthy, for we know from psychology that a fully human person needs reasonable outlets for his energies and even his aggressions. A passive childhood may lead to an explosive adulthood. And this is no minor problem in America today, where the left accuses the right of being militaristic and violence-prone, and the right defines the left in terms of bloody and frenetic revolutionary activity. The thing we need least is a next generation of passive-aggressive personalities.

Escapism is another danger with store-bought toys—not the escapism of the healthy child in which he weaves rich and creative fantasies, but the escapism of the materially avaricious, through which the child absorbs a set of socially questionable values in his play and later on lets them mold his future life. Little girls who get overly dependent on elaborate dolls and on the jet-set affluence of their playthings, may grow up to think that good clothes, a $60,000 house, and a husband with a five- or even six-figure income are the things really worth having in life. (As a matter of fact, a recent survey of teen-age girls revealed that they did indeed want to be living in $60,000 homes by the time they reached middle-age, and that they did expect their husbands to be earning high five-figure incomes.) Other questionable attitudes are fostered by playthings such as war toys, the notorious "Hippy-Sippy" pseudo-hypodermic needle, and toys like "Bash," where the object is to pound in the other fellow's skull.

A desirable toy, therefore, should be simple enough to involve the child actively in his own play, should not bore or overwhelm him, and should let him develop his personality without twisting it. I think that the homemade toys are hard to beat in offering these qualities with little effort and at a very low cost. They can be both psychologically better and physically safer, as the parent has a good opportunity to inspect them carefully before giving them to the child. I can't imagine a mother's giving her daughter a long hatpin to play with, although long pins have been found in store-bought dolls. Nor would a parent consciously give her youngster anything that had an obvious potential for transmitting or for carrying disease, yet we have seen how store-bought items often do have just this risk. Nor are homemade toys dangerous if disassembled. Most of them are so simple that there is nothing to disassemble at all, and in any case, the process of taking apart a homemade toy does not ordinarily involve dealing with complex motors or electrical circuits. A parent who has helped a child make a homemade rattle, for instance, will know what is inside it; and this will not be a poisonous jequirity bean.

Another advantage of homemade toys is that they are very versatile. They can be adapted to different children of different ages, and to different moods and whims of the same child. Don't be fooled by the notion that you have to spend a lot of money and depend upon a trained psychologist on the staff of a toy manufacturing concern to find a toy which will be "educational" for your child. In a real sense, all toys and all experiences are educational, and the issue is only one of degree. A child is far more likely to get something valuable out of his toys if he can get involved with them, discover new ways in which to use them, bring them into his play with other children, and explore their possibilities with his own, and not someone else's, imagination.

Doctor Lidia Dawes, a distinguished child psychiatrist and former Chief of Child Psychiatry at the Beth Israel Hospital in Boston, prefers simple, homemade toys for just these reasons. She says that:

> Toys should be simple to let a child use the full range of his imagination. Household items are particularly good because they allow his imagination to roam. At one moment, a pot lid can be a boat wheel or a doll's cradle. At the next moment, it can be used just as Mother uses it. An oatmeal box can be a drum, a king's throne, or a doll wagon. Afterward, a child can imitate his mother by pretending to cook his cereal. (*Today's Health,* July, 1968, p. 28)

Doctor Dawes also points out how homemade toys can be genuinely educational:

> The nice thing about these simple toys is that they offer so many different kinds of play, can be pulled and pushed

around, can give a child pleasure in motion. They can be used to build castles or tunnels, and provide a youngster [with] a chance to learn about construction and destruction. In play, a child learns to build, to plan, to learn, and to share—all invaluable in later life. (Ibid., p. 28)

After all, a large empty cardboard box used indoors can be anything a child wants it to be—a rocket ship, a medieval palace, a cavalry outpost, a jungle hut. Some thoughtful manufacturers have even put directions explaining how to make such playhouses on the packing cartons of their stoves, refrigerators, and other appliances. (You might drop down to your local appliance store and verify this for yourself.)

I can't see that there is any special educational or creative value in a commercially produced playhouse (which, by the way, is usually *either* a stockade *or* a castle, but rarely both—another instance of specialization limiting the child's play range.) Store-bought dollhouses, for example, are usually very carefully detailed and rarely give the child enough room to play with the doll family. As E. M. Matterson said, they leave "little scope for the imagination and no room at all for elbows."

But a dollhouse made at home from boxes and things can be tailored and changed and adapted to what your little girl wants and needs right now as well as in three weeks or six months. Likewise, a boat made from a milk carton will provide hours of happy sailing.

In the same way, a plastic rattle is a plastic rattle, and it would be hard to find a four-year-old who gets much of a bang out of one. Children, after all, are very age-conscious, and no self-respecting four-year-old will be caught playing with baby things. But if you enlist the same four-year-old in a project to build a noisemaker, and describe it to him (or let him describe it) as an Indian instrument for a rain dance, or a medieval musical instrument, or whatever you and he can contrive, you will probably have a successful toy. Furthermore, he will have gained the sense of satisfaction that comes from helping to make something, and this is no mean achievement, either.

Thus, homemade toys are able to involve a child in useful and self-satisfying activities by bringing him right into their very conception. This is valuable in itself even if the homemade toy is tossed out at the end of a rainy afternoon. Take a look at the toys your children leave alone after only a brief while. The chances are they are toys that were designed to be watched, not used.

When children tinker with their toys, this is not just an aimless fooling around, but an intensely fascinating and important process of discovery for the child. Complex toys have only limited educational and play value if they cannot be messed with at least a little bit. A child learns bit by bit, by experimenting, interfering, testing, imagining, pretending. Complex toys tend to place limits on all of these activities, and so homemade toys—which give greater scope for tinkering, for role-playing, for fantasy—are preferable. Moreover, homemade toys usually develop out of ordinary materials, and this helps to integrate the child's world into the parental world of which he is and ought to be a part. Just notice how so many children love to try on Mommy's shoes or Daddy's hat, for instance.

This contribution that toys make to the child's developing sense of identity is an important one: and, as we have seen, homemade toys do this especially well for two reasons. The first is the open-ended capability of most homemade toys to involve the child in active and imaginative play; while the second is the opportunity they afford to work the everyday world into the play world and vice versa. A child with some anger or fear or mystery that has been bothering or puzzling him is often able to externalize it through play and fantasy —and in the process, to learn how to handle it in an integrated and psychologically helpful and healthy way. Again, homemade toys are often better for this purpose, because they give him free rein to do so.

Improvisation—which means ease and speed in toymaking—is another special virtue of homemade toys. They can be put together at a moment's notice, in order to meet your child's immediate needs. "There's nothing to do" is a universal children's complaint, and if a parent's only response is another trip to the toy store, then his child is being spoiled with too many trips and the parent is spending far too much money. The toymakers, of course, are trying to get you into just that habit, but don't let them. It's not worth it, either to you or to your child.

The Children's Hospital Medical Center in Boston has published a really superb little book called, *What to Do When "There's Nothing to Do,"* a sort of do-it-yourself manual for parents on how to put together simple homemade toys and develop interesting play ideas. The main idea behind the book is that it is entirely unnecessary for mothers to keep hopping down to the toy store every time the children are bored or restless. The book includes, in addition to a number of quickly set up "instant" toys, many fascinating ideas for longer-range projects as well.

Another factor that inclines me to favor homemade toys is that they are more likely to appeal to the child as an individual. They can be tailored for him right now, as he is. Store-bought toys that children ignore are not only a waste of money, but also an unsatisfactory experience for parent and child alike. The child may feel, and sometimes he is correct, that he is being bought off or shut up by being supplied with an object rather than with personal parental concern. Homemade toys, on the other hand, usually involve both parent and child in the selection and the organization of play materials; and this is reassuring and consoling to the youngster.

One other failing of complex and expensive store-bought

toys is that the parent is sometimes prone to pick out the ones that satisfy his needs and not the child's. We are all familiar with the enthusiastic father who plays with his six-month-old baby's new electric train all Christmas Eve. With homemade toys, there is little danger that parents will be acting out their own fantasies instead of, or in competition with, their children's.

Finally, many store-bought toys can be used for play by only one child at a time. This leads to exclusiveness in play, to fights, and to a general social self-centeredness on the part of the child. But playing around the house with ordinary things arranged to provide interesting and amusing situations and circumstances, opens up possibilities for co-operative play, for sharing, for interaction. This gives a formidable advantage to the homemade toy, for, after all, the relations that matter most in this world are the relations we have with people, not those we have with things. So the more a toy helps a child to relate to his playmates, the better it is for him and for his parents.

In the past, the homemade toy was the rule, not the exception as it is today. If all of us who share a common concern about our children's physical and psychological health and growth would give some thought to a return to genuinely creative, and safe play, we might see again a renaissance of the home as the primary source of play materials. So the next time you are about to buy a toy on impulse, ask yourself, "Is this toy really necessary, or could I do better myself at home?"

Part 2

8

Shopper's Guide: Toys to Avoid or Discard

THE FIRST PART OF THIS BOOK HAS SHOWN THAT TOYS CAN BE dangerous and that existing governmental safety programs and laws provide insufficient protection. We know also that the industry has been lethargic in exacting voluntary cooperation and in setting adequate safety standards. We have seen that testing agencies cannot possibly handle the problems involved in inspecting every toy, and that some of them do not perform examinations thorough enough or strenuous enough to reveal the inherent dangers in the toys on the market today. And we have discovered that when toy injuries do occur, turning to the courts for compensation is often beset with difficulty.

What, then, do we do? Do we give up on toys entirely, at least until there is strong safety legislation on the books? For one thing, a world in which no accidents could ever happen would doubtless be an intolerable world. For another thing, we do want our children to enjoy the fun of toys: to expand their imagination and develop their creativity and to discover themselves through interaction with a world that is delightful—and safe. The purpose of this second part is to contribute toward a balanced approach to toys by providing a kind of buyer's guide to a selection of toys I have found to be especially dangerous. Shopping for toys that are safe is not impossible. It does, however, demand some thought.

Toys are massively over-promoted and every high-pressure technique that has ever been developed throughout the history of marketing is used in one way or another to push them. The first line of defense is a firm buyer resistance. Don't buy toys on impulse alone—or on a child's demand alone. It may be safer and wiser to turn to simpler play materials and to let a child develop their possibilities himself. When it does come to store-bought toys, take your time, follow your common sense, and look out for the following things especially.

It's an old and useful adage in the newspaper business that the man who hollers loudest in denial is usually admitting something. The same thing is true in toy advertising. All too often, the toys that make the most noise about safety are the most treacherous. Beware of items labeled "nontoxic" or "harmless" or "nonflammable"—ask why it is so important to the manufacturer to stress these features. By whose standards are they safe? What tests have been conducted? What do they mean by nontoxic? Remember also that seals of approval from *Good Housekeeping* or *Parents' Magazine* are only money-back guarantees. They are not assurances of safety (or of quality). As we saw, all that the *Good Housekeeping* seal really promises is that if your child is poisoned, lacerated, or electrocuted by a toy, the manufacturer has agreed to give you your money back if the toy didn't work properly. Until the federal government cracks down on the exaggerated claims of toymakers and retailers, and requires premarket testing according to strict and vigorously enforced specifications, there will continue to be little if any connection between the claims of safety and the real harmful potential of many toys.

Nevertheless, once the underbrush of advertising hocus-pocus has been cleared away, safe toys *can* be found. Annual toy sales run to at least eight million separate units, and millions more are always in the works. With this number to choose from—plus those which you can make at home—no one has to settle for shoddy, defective, or dangerous playthings. The more that we toy buyers exercise our power of selection in choosing what we will and what we will not buy for our children, the more the manufacturers will be forced by economic reality—the law of supply and demand—to produce toys that are sturdy and well made, properly designed, and reasonably safe for children.

The following pages list some classes and examples of toys that I personally have seen and usually purchased, in a variety of places. I have visited the annual toy fairs and premium shows where the manufacturers display their wares to buyers for retail stores. I have shopped for toys in supermarkets and drugstores, in and through mail-order catalogs, discount houses, department stores and shops that specialize in toys and children's things. The list below covers toys available in past seasons, as well as in some future ones, and many of them may have already found their way into your homes. If so, get rid of them.

Categorizing toys with any semblance of order and logical precision is probably an impossible task. The industry itself has problems in this area. What I have done here is to set up a number of fairly common headings, which correspond to the ways in which we toy shoppers tend to group playthings in our own minds and also roughly to the ways in which toy merchants categorize toys on their retail counters. I have arranged these headings in alphabetical order. In many cases, I have referred to a toy by its trade name; in other instances, where the trade name was unavailable to me or where there are several versions of the same item, I have simply given an adequate description of the type of toy and the danger it presents. Many of these toys have been mentioned earlier in this book as examples of one or another kind of danger or defect, but I have thought it worthwhile to pull all these examples together here, in order to provide a kind of shopping manual for toy buyers, as well as a guide for parents with already well-established toy collections.

This is by no means an exhaustive list. I have had no research staff out scouring the toylands of America for obvious or hidden dangers. I am absolutely convinced that there exist toys not on this list which are also dangerous and that some toys I might personally consider safe have hidden defects that I am in no position to know about (although a manufacturer might be). I have set out some general priorities after the catalogued items and these may be of some help. A number of mothers and fathers did write to the commission, and their letters were very helpful indeed. Since no single agency now handles these problems, let me urge you to report any dangerous toys you happen to discover to your attorney in order that he may report it to the proper agency. The urgency of the problem of dangerous toys demands a concerted effort from everyone involved; and since everyone either has or knows some children, then it should be obvious that *all* of us are involved and so obligated to join in this national effort.

I will be happy if this book can prevent even one unnecessary death or injury. The toy industry is fond of repeating that even one such injury to a child is one too many. I agree, and offer this buyers' guide as a starting place from which to begin to reduce the number and extent of these unnecessary burnings, blindings, maimings, and deaths.

A Buyers' Guide to Toyland

1. Babies' Playthings

Marketing dangerous toys for infants altogether too young to defend themselves seems to me to be utterly reprehensible, and I consider that failing to test and examine them for safety amounts in many cases to very serious negligence.

Some of the products mentioned below *are* this dangerous, and are sold for babes in arms, in spite of that.

a. *Beads.* Under no circumstances should these be given to infants. Babies will put anything at all into their mouths, and even though the beads may be nontoxic (not all of them are), that does not mean that a baby may not choke on them.

b. *Blocks.* Two special hazards: the paint may be (but rarely is) toxic and even "nontoxic" paint may make a child sick (see Chapter Four). Also, the blocks may have sharp, instead of rounded, corners. Watch out here, too, for size: they ought to be big enough not to be swallowed accidentally.

c. *Crib toys.* Are they flammable? Can they catch and carry germs? Can they be swallowed? The Sanitoy "Hour Glass Action Toy" is filled with baby oil and small bits of colored plastic. The rattle purportedly contains only "pure harmless baby oil" but the package doesn't say why the "pure" oil is a seamy yellow color. And if the thing should break, of course, the baby would be tempted to put the plastic pieces in his mouth. The Baby Playthings "Little Angel Swing Me Suction Toy" (#A27) by Childhood Interests/Alan Jay-Clarolyte, is a swing toy with small bells, intended to be hung over the crib. The one I am familiar with was badly made and one of the bells, small enough to be swallowed or choked upon, came off the cord. The "Musical Lacing Shoe" by Fisher-Price Toys was the subject of a letter to the National Commission on Product Safety, in which the writer complained, "Pieces of the broken musical mechanism found their way outside the toy and into the baby's bed." For example, the Winnie-the-Pooh crib mobile has brackets which can be readily fractured by infants, leaving potentially dangerous jagged edges and points. In general, crib *and* bathtub toys may often have small parts that fall off and which may pose threats of choking, toxicity, and disease transmission. Many squeeze toys for babies have squeakers which may be swallowed, for example, "Dizzy Doodle Doll," by Parksmith Corp., New York

City, and "Kooky Eyes Squeaker Toy," by Azrak Hemway Corp.

d. *Cribs and playpens.* We usually feel that our children are safest when in their cribs or playpens. But even these present numerous dangers. Some such "refuges" have sharp edges, exposed nails and fasteners, or toxic finishes. Others are shoddily made or poorly designed. Still others come with flammable bedding or with cushions that are not waterproof and which eventually begin to fall apart—exposing potentially harmful stuffing that a baby might put into his mouth —after being washed. Some cribs and playpens have been known to collapse and cause serious injury to the baby inside; others have been so badly designed that a child can get his head or fingers caught in the slats or mesh. If the slats are too wide apart (more than three and a quarter inches), a baby will be able to fit all of his body through—except his head. This can be fatal. Figures presented to the National Commission on Product Safety indicate that perhaps 200 children a year are strangled in this way as they squirm through the too widely spaced slats and suspend themselves by their heads. For the same reasons, cribs with horizontal slats should be avoided altogether.

In more recent years, cribs—such as the "Kiddie Koop," by the Pride-Trimble Corp.—have tops that can be snapped down. When a child stands up inside the crib, he can push the top partially open, and then stick his head out through the opening. With the head out, the top then closes down again on his neck, and the more he pushes to get free, the tighter the grip on his throat. Despite the fact that the manufacturers were notified of such deaths, and the widespread publicity which attended them, the Pride-Trimble "Kiddie Koops" were being sold in a substantially unimproved design last spring and may still be on the market today.

e. *Rattle toys.* Again, the basic principle here is that any baby toy with small parts inside it should be carefully examined. If the toy is brittle or fragile, it may break and the parts may fall out. This creates an obvious swallowing hazard. Some rattles—like the Star Manufacturing Co.'s "Star Baby Toys" rattle, the Childhood Interests/Alan Jay-Clarolyte "Little Angel" rattle, and the World Toy House, Inc., "Nursery Land, Best for Baby" rattle—are made of very brittle plastic. They shatter easily, and the sharp and jagged edges of the broken shells are dangerous. So are the contents—the "Star" and "Nursery Land" rattles contain stones; the "Little Angel" rattle, beads.

Musical rattles also pose a threat to children's safety. One such threat is the "Toddlers' Toys Musical Chime Rattle" (#350) by the Stahlwood Toy Mfg. Co., which has a flimsy top and a cardboard body attached to a polyethylene handle. Our sample came apart when it was unwrapped, disclosing a set of sharp wires inside, which constituted the musical "mechanism." The packaging pronounces this rattle to be "safe—sanitary—nontoxic."

f. *Baby harnesses.* These swinging harnesses are fast becoming very popular. The idea is to hang them up in the house—over the door jamb, for instance—and put the baby in them so that he can bounce up and down, "safely" and to his heart's content. Several parents, however, have called some of the dangers associated with these items to the attention of the National Commission on Product Safety. One such harness, the Cosco "Tiny Tot Exerciser," has been mentioned in particular for the following reasons:

- When the baby swings, he sometimes gets into a side-to-side pattern and bangs against the doorway; there is no crossbar to prevent this.
- The baby's face can get caught in the suspension ropes.
- Upon occasion, the metal supporting bar has snapped back in the face of a mother disengaging her child from the harness.

- The suspension springs have been known to break, dropping the baby onto the floor.

g. *Teething rings.* These and various pacifiers come in a plethora of sizes, shapes, and designs. They may be designed so as to provide a comfortable home for germs, or have sharp edges, toxic finishes, and the kind of brittle material construction that can shatter and cut. One should be able to sterilize a proper teething ring in boiling water without its falling apart. Babies will naturally chew the paint from any surface on any of these items, so those in which the color is molded in and not painted on are preferable. Some teething rings have been filled with unsanitary solutions; the best course to take is to get one that is solid and not likely to be chewed or broken open.

h. *Tops.* Usually tops are not given to infants, but to older children. But sometimes they wind up in the crib as well. The thing to watch on most tops is the base: Is it rounded or plastic, or does it merely have an easily removable cover fitted over the nail-like spike at the bottom on which the top is supposed to turn? (Fig. 43)

2. *Candy "Toys"*

We have seen in Chapter Two how toys may look like edible things but be dangerous if eaten, or may look like something else but be intended as food or candy. As if this were not confusing enough, there are articles, such as candy cigarettes, which are edible and look like things that adults not only do *not eat* but that they are constantly being told (by the U.S. Public Health Service, for instance) are generally bad for their health and longevity. Conditioning a young child to like cigarettes, whether candy or not, is a classic example of the total indifference to consumer health and welfare that characterizes some merchants.

Fig. 43. Top showing spiked base and generally flimsy construction.

Fig. 44. Colorful and decorative flammable plastic cooking crystals to be baked in toy oven.

Consider these two products from Mattel, Inc.: the "Thingmaker" series and the "Gobble-de-spooks." The "Thingmaker" includes some stuff called "Plastigoop" which a youngster is supposed to use to make plastic insects, monsters, and such with a dangerous electric toy mold. The "Incredible Edibles" are also insects, monsters, ghosts, bats, and so on, and are also made with a dangerous electric mold—but these are for eating. Thus, the same company makes two nearly identical products, with the essential point of difference being that the one type is plastic and inedible, while the other is a form of candy. Now imagine a preschooler who sees the plastic ones lying around the house, and who has previously seen his brothers and sisters eating the candy versions.

Mattel is not the only toymaker involved in this kind of confusing duplication. Remco puts out a "Silly Soapmaker," which is a set of molds for small pieces of soap that children are supposed to make. Wham-O markets a "Shrink Machine," which produces similar micro-toys that are equally inedible. And on the other side of the coin, we have sets manufacturing artificial, miniature "playfoods" that look like real comestibles. Thus, the Norstar Corporation imports an entire series of "Play Food" and Amsco Industries, Inc. sells the "Little Miss Playfood" series.

Then we have items like the "Plastic Cooking Crystals Makit and Bakit" kit, which the Quincrafts Corp. sells. The general appearance and packaging of these crystals closely resembles the different kinds of sugars sold as toppings for cake or ice cream. But the Plastic Cooking Crystals are not sugar, but plastic, and are not for putting on cakes, but for making plastic toys and for executing your own plastic art work. Not only are they inedible, but they emit fumes when heated and are flammable, as the directions note in an astoundingly self-contradictory statement: " 'Makit and Bakit' may be used in Childrens [sic] Electric Ovens with Great

Success" in bold letters, and following this, "Plastic is flammable . . . do not place near flame or broiler, but it is as safe in an oven as a cake." [!] (Fig. 44)

3. Catapult Toys

I have put these into a separate category because all the members of this varied class share common dangers. Catapult toys are usually associated with something warlike—such as fighter planes or parachuting units—and almost all of them consist of a two-part set of slingshot and projectile. The latter, of course, is a threat to anyone it hits, particularly in the eye, and some of the outfits have poorly designed or badly made slingshot components that may backfire into the face of the child at the controls. For example:

- The "Arrowcopter" (Basic Products Development Co., Inc.) gives complete launching directions, which specify that the "position shown is essential for a successful launch" but which do not make clear that incorrect firing will send the copter back into the child's face.
- The "Blue Angel Stunt Plane" (Pactra, Inc.) has a weighted nose, which sometimes flies off the plane when it is fired.
- "The Incredible Bird of Paradise" (#4313, B. Shackman & Co.) has a *steel* nose with a sharp and only thinly covered point to it. Incredibly dangerous.

Similar defects in design can be found in the "Mission-X Top Secret Plane" (#747, Stevens Manufacturing Co.); the "Sky Diver" (#623, M. Shimmer Sons, Inc.); the "Sling Launch Skydiver and Paratrooper" (#599) and the "Target Catapult" (#590, both Chemical Sundries Co.).

4. Chemistry Sets

No one is against "educational toys" or against the thesis that certain types of empirical "work" are educational. But injuries to children, even in the name of science, can be avoided. Still, there are chemistry sets being produced for quite young children in which poisonous chemicals are included and which do not provide adequate instructions. As a general rule, no young child should be given a chemistry set, and sets made available to older children should be stored well out of the reach of the younger ones. Parents should personally study the directions, warnings, and contents before buying any chemistry sets. Children should be carefully instructed in the techniques and anticipated results of the experiments. Sets or experiments that claim to make "food" when in fact the product is inedible, or that package dangerous chemicals in the same way as they do harmless ones, should be avoided entirely. If a child is unable or unlikely to follow the manufacturer's directions and your own, do not buy the set—even if you intend (and you should) to supervise his every use of it. Make certain that none of the chemical or experimental products are flammable in any dangerous degree, or at all explosive, or capable of producing noxious fumes and gases.

Eye protectors should be provided with chemistry sets. This will bring the toy manufacturers in line with accepted practices in a substantial number of industrial and school laboratories. In Ohio, for example, eye protection is required in all school and college laboratories.

Five companies share most of the chemistry set business in the United States today. They are the A. C. Gilbert Co. (which has now been merged into Gabriel Industries but continues to produce the famous Gilbert Chemistry Sets); Chemcraft, a division of Lionel-Porter; Physio-Chem Corp., makers of "Homelab"; Remco Industries, Inc.; and Skil-Craft Playthings, Inc. *Consumer Reports* magazine (see the CU 1970 *Buying Guide*) provided for me the basis for the following commentary, which I have supplemented with my own research:

- A. C. Gilbert. The instructions were poorly organized

and some of the experiments were dangerous. One experiment, for example, claimed to make "raspberry jello" but neglected to make clear that the product that resulted was neither gelatin nor edible. Another involved heating a can with water in it, but did not emphasize the necessity of leaving the cap off until the heating process was completed. Heating a sealed can of water could lead to a dangerous explosion. Larger sets include alcohol lamps that would leak onto clothes or work surfaces, and so be prone to easy ignition by the lamp itself or a stray spark.

- Chemcraft Chemistry Sets. These also include potentially dangerous alcohol lamps in some sets. Some space-conscious models contain rockets powered by baking soda, which fire away when the inner pressure builds up sufficiently. An impatient or a curious child might be tempted to look inside to find the cause for the delay, and lose an eye in the process. One experiment called for the use of dry ice to freeze grapes, but failed to warn against touching either the dry ice or the grapes (while still in the solution) with the naked finger.

- "Homelab Chem-Sets." These have been found "not acceptable" by *Consumer Reports,* for such failures as omission of adequate safety warnings. The magazine also noted that some sets "completely ignored certain important regulations under the Federal Hazardous Substances Act." More recent models, such as the "Discovery Set" series, have improved upon some of the inadequacies of earlier versions.

- Remco "Chemistry Science Kit" (#410). Despite printed warnings that certain chemicals in the set are poisonous and "not to be used by children except under adult supervision," the instruction booklet contained pictures of children holding dangerous chemicals near their faces and mouths almost as if eating or drinking them. The advertising on the box promotes the set as an "educational toy" but it is not, nor is it suitable for young children, despite the illustrations in the booklet. Many of the chemicals are poorly labeled, and

some are wrapped like candy even though they are poisonous.
• Skil-Craft. Some of these sets have the same kind of baking-soda rockets as the Chemcraft units—and the same drawbacks. Certain experiments are entitled "Making Cherry Jelly," "Making Milk," and "Wine from Water," and they nowhere make clear that the end products are inedible. Some of the boxes are so built that they spill their contents out as they are opened, and the "Chemistry Lab Set (#500)" in general encourages a more or less "hocus-pocus" attitude toward experimentation and a substitution of home chemicals for items required for, but not included in, the set.

5. Clothes, Clothing, and Burns

Perhaps the most painful—and most disfiguring—of all possible injuries is a burn. Physicians at the Shriners Burns Institute estimate that burns are the largest single category of accidents to children. Still, needlessly and tragically, we adults continue to invite these disasters by making available to our youngsters, and by allowing the law to permit, excessively flammable playthings and clothing.

The statistics available present sufficient evidence of widespread and gruesome tragedy. For example, the National Fire Protection Association reports that clothing accounts for over 2,000 fire deaths annually. A large percentage of these victims are children. Yet, despite the work of one or two organizations in attempting to keep track of these injuries, they have gone largely unpublicized and inadequately catalogued. This, perhaps, is one reason why what little federal and state legislation there is on this matter is so pathetically inadequate.

The bare statistics do not tell the whole story. The author presently represents several children with devastating and overwhelming burn injuries. Most of their injuries involve large portions of the victim's body, months and even years of hospitalization, with repeated surgical grafting and reconstructive procedures. Permanent cosmetic deformities are the rule, human features may be completely destroyed, and functional disabilities frequently result from tissue destruction and scar-tissue formation. Burn injuries are particularly tragic because of their disastrous effect on the whole person. The severely burned often are doomed to live in a hell not of their own making. The psychological effects are even more devastating and incalculable on burned children, who must attempt to grow and mature psychologically and emotionally despite grotesque deformities.

Consider the following illustrative cases from the author's recent experience.

Case 1: A sister and brother, aged one and two, respectively, were on a comforter containing a synthetic fiberfill. This caught fire, and melted into a hot napalmlike substance which clung to the exposed hands and faces of these children. The remainder of their bodies were covered by clothing that shielded them from contact with the molten comforter. One child has lost fingers on both hands. The other has lost the use of both hands. Both children suffered extensive and irreparable facial deformity. It should be noted that at the time of this accident and at the time the comforter was manufactured, there existed a family of modacrylic synthetic fibers that are naturally flame resistant and do not melt—two properties that would have entirely prevented the tragic consequences. (Fig. 45)

Case 2: A three-year-old girl came in contact with a source of ignition while wearing a cotton flannelette nightgown that was not treated with any flame-retardant chemicals. The nightgown caught fire and burned so rapidly that the child's entire body was enveloped in flames. The nightgown was designed so that it could only be removed by pulling it over the head, and was unsafe in that the child could not quickly remove it under emergency conditions. She suffered third-degree burns of her chest, back, breasts, legs, face, neck and arms, including disfigurement of her lips, chin and neck, and especially severe scar contractures and fusions involving her neck and arms. She has required five hospitalizations for plastic reconstructive surgery in the past two years, and further surgical procedures are planned. The medical bills alone amount to over $30,000.

The above are only two of many burn cases of which I am personally aware, but they are graphic illustrations of the seriousness of the problem generally. It should be pointed out that in Great Britain, since 1964, it has been illegal to sell any flammable nightgowns and pajamas for children.

As I have stressed in Chapter Five, the Federal Flammable Fabrics Act sounds fine in theory, with its penalties for the manufacture, shipment, and sale in interstate commerce of dangerously flammable articles of wearing apparel, but in practice it is little more than an unfunny joke. For the standards of flammability it uses are really quite inadequate to protect children—and adults—from the dangers it aims to forestall.

These burn hazards occur particularly in children's clothing, which is notorious for being produced as cheaply as possible. Halloween and other costumes of extremely flammable cloth are still readily available; blankets, nightgowns, and children's sleeping bags can easily be purchased which may burst into flame upon exposure to a source of ignition. Yet the federal act does not even cover blankets! The additions to the Hazardous Substances Act by the Child Protection and Toy Safety Act of 1969 do indeed empower the Secretary of Health, Education and Welfare to ban the sale of children's articles that are dangerously flammable, but as we have noted, this has not proved to be an adequate response to the problem.

Flammability in children's and in adult's clothing and other articles made of cloth or of synthetic fabrics is a function of two variables: the nature of the fabric itself, and the effectiveness of the flameproofing techniques, if any, applied to that fabric. Among natural fibers, cotton burns the fastest and wool the slowest. Some so-called fireproofing consists really in flame retardation—that is, the material is treated in a solution that slows down the speed at which the garment will go up in flames at least enough to bring it within the commercial standards embodied in the federal legislation. But even though use of such techniques may indeed reduce the likelihood of a flash fire in your youngster's pajamas, it may also be the case that repeated washing will flush the flame retardant out of the garment entirely.

As for synthetic fabrics, most of them are not extremely flammable, but some are. Their greater danger potential, as we have seen in Case 1, lies in the fact that most of them will melt if exposed to sufficient heat, and this melting process leaves a sticky, gummy residue that causes burns at least as severe as those suffered from exposure to an open flame. The residue itself, moreover, may be quite flammable. This makes certain synthetic fibers, such as Kodel, totally unsuitable for use as a filling for comforters and quilts or children's sleeping bags—assuming it is enclosed in a shell or covering that is flammable. Not all synthetics are dangerous. The same company that markets Kodel also markets a synthetic called Verel, which does not melt and which does not support flame.

Industry has generally chosen to ignore the dangers of fabrics or fiberfills, such as Kodel, despite the fact that safety literature has contained warnings of the hazard. The Spring 1965 issue of *Family Safety* contained an article which stated:

> Synthetics also have a burning characteristic that can be more horrible than the flame itself. The synthetic fiber when burning softens to a sticky tar or melts into a bubbling-hot liquid that rolls down the skin like molten lava, burning deeply into the flesh long after the flames have gone out. Doctors consider these burns from synthetic materials the most difficult to treat.

No federal statute or regulation deals with the serious hazard presented by these molten materials. Therefore, a really thorough check should always be made before you buy anything for your child that could present a danger if it were ignited. The safest practice is to ask the store to demonstrate to you the fire-resistant quality of the article, by exposing a sample piece of the fabric to an open flame, for instance. Be careful as you do this, of course, and watch to see that it does not burst into flame or burn with extreme rapidity or melt into a gummy, adhesive tar. Also inquire, and satisfy yourself, as to the certainty that the flameproofing will not lose its effectiveness even after repeated washings.

If you are reluctant to demand the sort of demonstration referred to, but are nonetheless convinced that flame-retardant garments are needed, and perhaps worth some additional expense, then at the very minimum I strongly urge that you shop carefully to find for your children garments that are flame-retardant. You might experience difficulty since such garments are not, as yet, generally available. The fact is, however, that if enough of us shoppers ask for them, we will create a demand that manufacturers will be compelled to recognize.

The importance of this kind of hard-nosed buying cannot be overstated, for the problem of excess flammability is nationwide. During the year, I had occasion to check the leading department stores in several major cities around the country. In only a few of them (Sears, Roebuck; J. C. Penney) did I find any children's clothing for sale which claimed to be truly flame-retardant. And this was in spite of the fact that a New York fabric maker has claimed to have developed a successfully flame-retardant cotton flannel for use in children's wearing apparel that reportedly does not support fire even when directly subjected to flame.

A recent National Fire Protection Association survey of fatal clothing fires revealed that almost three times as many of these deaths occurred in the population under five years old than in any other segment of the population between five and sixty. Children have a natural curiosity about fire that is as old as man himself. They must be protected from the effects of this curiosity, and since a child cannot be expected to forego clothing and bedding, this protection must obviously come from adults and be carried out through constant vigilance and through active and effective and tough legislation.

Many courts and juries have been cognizant of the insufficiency of federal legislation in this area. They have found that compliance with the Act, which the industry should know to be inadequate, is not a defense to a products liability action. An item of clothing or other article that meets these minimal governmental standards may still be considered negligently designed and manufactured or an unreasonably dangerous product.

At present, however, the commercial pressure to keep on producing cheap and dangerous children's articles remains strong. Cost, fashion, fit, comfort, and attractiveness are all factors the consumer naturally considers in any clothing purchase. Few think of or examine the fire risks. Since the merchants sell what they think the public wants, the public must arouse itself to these dangers to their children and bring concerted counterpressure to bear on both sellers and manufacturers. And if the manufacturers themselves were to devote a small portion of their profits to researching flameproofing and to educating the public about the dangers now to be found in their products, the number of children burned could be significantly reduced. If other countries can do this —and they have, as Chapter Three points out—then it is hard to understand why we have not yet gotten around to making truly safe garments for our children.

6. Dolls and Stuffed Animals

Dolls, through the ages, have always held a special place in the affections of young—and older—children. Even adults continue to collect them. Among toys, they are classics, as old

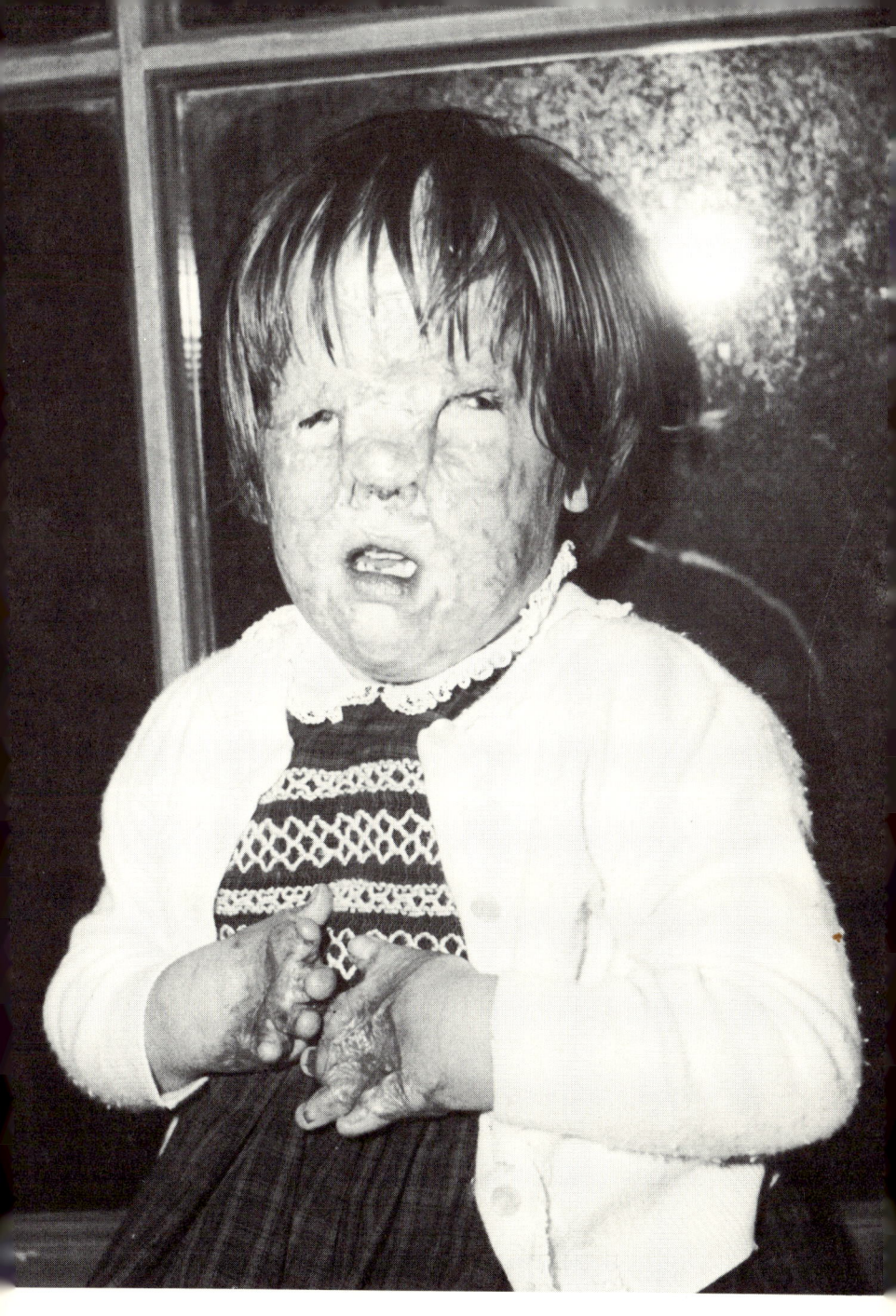

Fig. 45. Child permanently disfigured by "comforter" which is excessively flammable and which while burning melts into a hot, molten-lava type of residue.

Fig. 46. Doll accompanied by small, swallowable nipple and sharp hairpin.

Fig. 47. Doll with easily removable head and arms leaving exposed sharp wires.

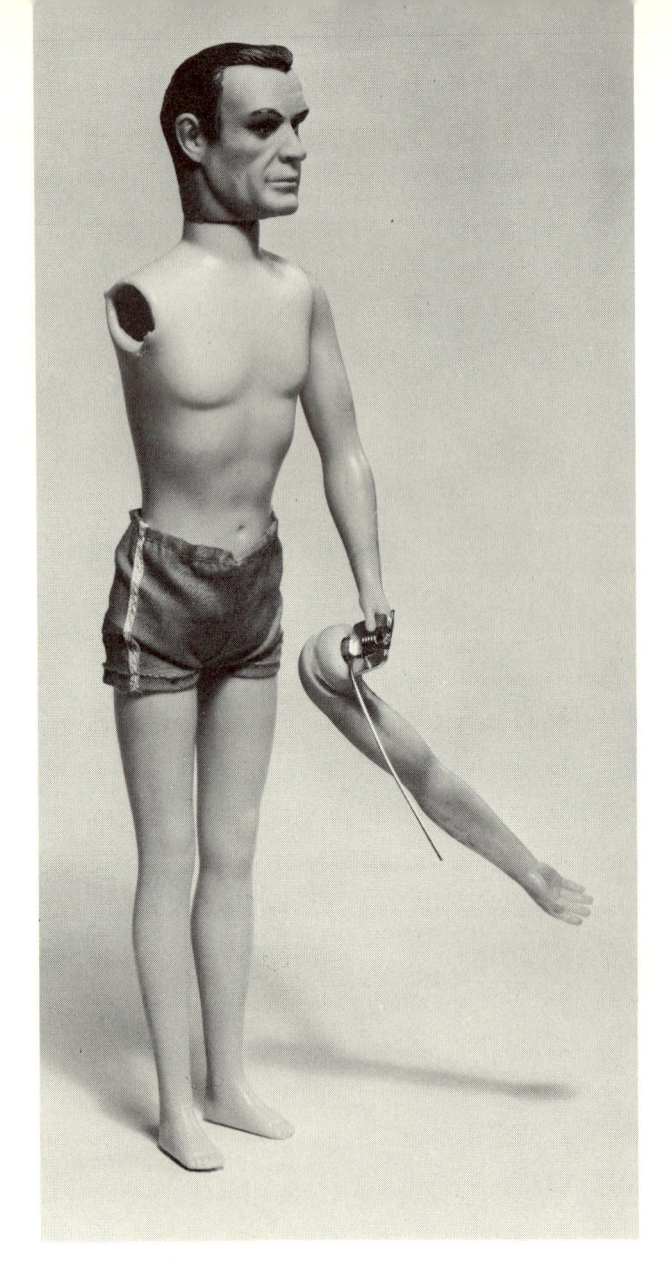

Fig. 48. Ideal Toy Corp. doll with sharp, readily exposed mechanism in arm.

as civilization. This venerable tradition has not deterred toymakers from cashing in on dolls by redesigning them for cost and not quality control. As a result, many dolls are dangerous, especially in the following ways:

- Flammability. This can extend to a doll's hair, clothing, body and stuffing. Stay away from these: "The Genuine Wishnik" (Uneeda Doll Co., Inc.); "The Hippie Doll" (Gregor, Inc.); "Honey" doll (Treasure Industries, Inc.); "Maddie Mod" clothing for dolls. (Princess Grace Dolls, Inc., of Hong Kong); "My Prayer" doll (Yuletide Enterprises, Inc.); "Plush Pals," a stuffed toy dog (My Toy Co., Inc.); the "New Barbie Doll" which has flammable hair (Mattel); so-called "Polish" dolls (imported by A. D. Sutton & Sons, Inc.); and "Teensie Baby" (Horsman Dolls, Inc.).

- Dolls and animals with dangerous pins. These are usually attached to eyes or hair ribbons and often may be long, needlelike rapiers; they may be concealed in the doll itself (stuck through into the insides) and hence may not be easily noticed. Insist on a close inspection before purchase. Some dolls that carry these risks are "The Genuine Wishnik"; the "Honey" doll (both mentioned in the preceding paragraph); "Jolly's Twistee-Softee" (Jolly Toys, Inc.); the "Nan" doll (#A719, Treasure Industries, Inc.); "Baby Sue" (Columbo Doll Co., Inc.) is promoted on the carton as a "little girl's best friend." In addition to the pin in her hair, "Baby Sue" is accompanied by a miniature plastic baby bottle which has an easily removable nipple, small enough to swallow. (Fig. 46)

- Dolls and stuffed animals with wire skeletons. These are designed to enable the figures to be bent into different postures. But repeated bending of the body or tugging on the arms and legs can force the ends of the wire through, causing nasty cuts and puncture wounds, which could lead to infection. Metal wires, of course, can carry tetanus. Stuffed animals must be examined to determine whether the seams separate. If the seams separate the stuffing might escape and be ingested. Some items to avoid are: "Gumby's Pal Pokey" (Lakeside Toys); "The Hippie Doll" (Gregor, Inc.); the Knickerbocker toy doll (Knickerbocker Co.); the "Masked Doll" (imported by the Calvert Co.); "Mop-Pets" (imported by S. Rosenberg Co.); and the "New Barbie Doll" (Mattel), which does not have a wire frame, but does have sharp plastic edges along the feet; the "Slick Chick" doll (Topper Toy). "Flexi Lorrie" (Eugene Doll Co., Inc.) has a head which easily detaches, leaving exposed the sharp wires used to make the doll "twistable." (Figs. 47 and 48)

- Dolls and animals with eyes that can be pulled off and eaten or swallowed, for example: "The Hippie"; "Mop-Pets"; and "Plush Pals"—all mentioned above.

Dolls are also sold with removable "tongues." For example, the so-called "Brat-doll" (sole importers, Parksmith Corp.), states on its label, "Squeeze me and I stick out my tongue." The tongue consists of a balloon-like red contraption that almost always becomes detached from the doll's mouth in usage.

7. *"Educational" Toys*

It's hard to decide whether some urban school systems or the toy industry has abused the term "educational" more thoroughly. The toy industry, certainly, has so flagrantly overworked the notion that it is practically impossible to draw up even a general list of dangerous toys that claim special educational value. Briefly, however, the word is simply misleading when applied to most of the toys the merchants sell under this rubric. One of the greatest surprises to me as I undertook this study was to find how many really dangerous toys were labeled as "educational"—but then my own education about toys was only just beginning.

So, until the toy industry shapes up, or is forced to, my basic advice is to maintain a fairly complete skepticism about the safety of any toy billed as "educational." Don't be lulled into a sense of security by this kind of marketing device, for it may only mean that the price has been jacked up unnecessarily. To illustrate the point, here are a few selected examples of toys that are considered educational by their promoters.

- "Etch-A-Sketch" (Ohio Art Company). Ohio Art brings in over four million dollars a year on this product, and just as regularly hears complaints and defends lawsuits about the injuries it causes. There is a transparent plate covering a sketch board filled with aluminum powder on which the child is supposed to "etch" his drawings. The plate, however, is easily broken, and the gashes it causes may be impregnated with disfiguring and scar-producing metal dust. At this writing, "Etch-A-Sketch" takes the prize as the number one subject of letters of complaint about toys addressed to the National Commission on Product Safety.
- The Lakeside Industries' "Animal House" is a plastic hut designed to house animals of different geometric shapes. It is made of brittle plastic that could easily break into sharp, hard pieces (which is exactly what happened to my son's model). Moreover, it has a lift-off resting on two spearlike struts. These could easily stab a child who happened to fall on them.
- The Fisher-Price "Telephone Pull-Toy," although intended for very young children, is easily disassembled into a collection of various pieces small enough to be swallowed. If the wheels come off or are removed, they expose the child to dangerously pointed spokes.
- The Playskool "Hammer and Nail Sets" (#510, #511) are advertised for three-year-olds, yet include hammers with metal heads, three-quarter-inch-long metal nails, and small and easily ingested pieces of wood. How learned one would have to be to recognize the dangerous quality of each of these components in the hands of a three-year-old is not clear; but we ought to expect at least this minimal intelligence from the

makers of educational toys. Moreover, the hammerhead is not well attached to the handle, and may fly off with predictable consequences.

- Another "educational" toy with dangerous features is the Kenner "Spirograph" (#401). This is a complex set of transparent plastic wires, rings and racks with holes in them through which a child is expected to insert different colored ball-point pens; by manipulating the wires, rings and racks he may draw beautiful patterns immediately. The kicker is that the rings are attached by pins to the paper on which the drawing is made. The box in which the toy comes insists it is suitable for all ages, but one well might ask whether any toy that includes sharp functional parts as essential components is truly suitable for young children, or in households where young children might have access to it.
- The Playskool magnetic inlaid plastic puzzle (recommended for ages 2 to 6 has sandwiched between two pieces of cardboard a metallic center sheet which is as sharp as a razor. The center sheet is easily exposed since the cardboard which holds it separates in normal play. The author received a letter from one irate mother describing how her child's finger was sliced by this "educational" toy. (Fig. 49)

8. Electrical Toys

Playthings that require household current are hardly toys and should not be bought for or given to children under ten, if indeed they should be bought at all. There is altogether too much danger of shocks and burns simply from the use of the household outlet, not to mention those hazards inherent in the toys themselves.

Electrical toy appliances for little girls seem to be particularly popular at the moment, in spite of the dubious publicity that some have been getting of late. Many of these reach temperatures higher and more dangerous than those attained by adult household appliances. My contention is that if a girl

Fig. 49. "Educational" puzzle with razor-sharp metallic insert.

Fig. 50. Real-life, 110-volt electric oven containing dangerously sharp metal parts.

is old enough to play safely with a toy electrical appliance, then she is doubtless old enough to be taught how to use the real thing, and probably she should be. Regular household appliances are better designed and better made, and so less likely to cause accidental shocks and burns. Furthermore, a child will usually have healthy respect for full-sized appliances for she knows that they are real and not make-believe. (Mother knows this too, and might be more inclined to leave her daughter alone with the kitchen stove than with a toy one.) Many electrical toys even fall below their own design standards and do not meet the qualifications set by the testing organizations that have lent the use of their seals on the basis of factory-supplied models. The frightening fact is that toymakers can get away with this kind of deceptive and casual, even careless, inattention to the well-being of their child consumers, while safety requirements and their enforcement are usually far more stringent for real appliances. Try to avoid any electrical toy that involves the use of household current. Try especially not to buy toy appliances, and in the case of other electrical toys substitute battery-powered or spring-driven ones where it is at all possible. Polarized contacts should be built into battery-operated toys to prevent the circuits from being completed if the battery is inserted incorrectly. The National Safety Council reports the case of a California child who inserted a battery backwards in a toy causing it to explode, just missing the youngster's face and sending the internal core of the battery twelve feet across the room. Here are some examples of hazardous electrical toys worthy of special mention:

• Corn Poppers. The "Chilton Corn Popper" (#280, Aluminum Specialty Co.); "Empire See Em-Pop" (#370, #372, #374, Metal Ware Corp.); and "Mirro Miniature Electric Corn Popper" (#T3350, Mirro Aluminum Products Co.) all present shock hazards if washed with a wet sponge or dishrag while still connected to a live outlet. The Mirro popper gets as hot as 375°F. on the underside of the unit—hot enough to char or ignite a surface it may be resting on.

- Grills. The "Suzy Homemaker Super Safety Grill" (#2017, Deluxe Topper Corp.) failed to meet strain-relief standards set by the Underwriters' Laboratories for its electric cord, even though it carried the UL seal.
- Ovens. The "Easy-Bake Oven" (Kenner Products) uses as a heat source electric light bulbs that children can too easily get to and remove (removal, of course, means an open socket), and has some sharp edges. (Fig. 50) The "Suzy Homemaker Super-Safety Oven" (Topper Corporation) has the same faults, which makes particularly curious the inclusion of the word "safety" in the title. The "Empire Little Lady Oven" (#226, Metal Ware Corporation) gets hotter than some real stoves in places accessible to children's fingers, and the "Magic Cool Oven" units (Argo Industries Corporation) warn that the ovens will smoke when first being used. But how, then, do we know whether the smoke is normal or the sign of a fire under way?
- Irons. Most of these do not get hot enough to cause burns, but there are two exceptions: the "Barby Jo" toy electric iron (#110A, Barry Toycraft) and another "Barby Jo" (#210, Sifco Toys, a division of Tal-Cap, Inc.). The other models claim to be safe, but few of them have safety plugs to prevent the child from being shocked or burned while plugging in the iron.
- Sewing Machines. Samples of the "Sewmaster Sewing Machine" (#947E, K & E Corp.) showed poor quality-control results in tests by the Consumers Union. Some of the machines worked poorly, while others had needles that could be set too far into their holders, leaving room for a child to insert a finger under the needle and thus risk being punctured by the machine.
- Casting Sets. The "Rapco Metal-Casting Sets" (#6710, #5710, Rappaport Bros., Inc.) and the "Super Thingmaker" (#4512, Mattel), both use heating molds that reach excessively

high temperatures. (See Chapter Four.) The Rapco units get as hot as 800°F., which can peal paint off their sides. They might also cause lethal shocks.
- Erector Sets. These are associated with the A. C. Gilbert Co., which was taken over a few years ago by Gabriel Industries. Two years or so before the takeover, a young boy was electrocuted when his 110-volt erector set motor shorted out. Shortly thereafter the Gilbert Company stopped using household current motors and switched to low-voltage battery equipment. Now that the erector set is being made by Gabriel, whose president, Jerome Fryer, is an officer of the Toy Manufacturers of America and a vocal defender of the toy industry's safety record and standards, the sets can once again be bought with 110-volt electric motors.
- Polishing Sets. Rapco's "Tumbling Stones" unit and similar sets are for children who have hobbies such as rock collections; the point of the set is to polish the rocks to a high gloss. A letter to the National Commission on Product Safety sums up the hazards of this kind of toy as follows: ". . . after receiving and examining it, I discovered a few nicely worded directions, such as (1) start in an out-of-the-way place, as this motor must be running twenty-four hours a day up to thirty days continuously for a finished product. (2) Heat may generate, so be careful. (3) Watch when opening tumbler container, as sometimes gases form." This box was also marked for children from seven years up.
- Child Guidance Sketch-O-Magic was advertised in November of 1970 as follows: "magical drawing/writing board, glows in the dark! wipes clean! easy & safe! UL approved!" The unit uses household current and should be avoided as an unsuitable embellishment to the plain, old-fashioned blackboard.
- Batteries. Toys that do not require household current usually need batteries, and these also present a danger—leakage, for example, may release corrosive and burn-producing

chemicals. Generally, batteries are safer and preferable, but they should always be checked out first, and again from time to time.

9. Exploding Toys

The sale of fireworks and explosives of all kinds to minors has been outlawed in most states, and with good reason. There are, however, far too many firecracker accidents reported annually. In spite of outright prohibitions or clear restrictions on their use, firecrackers still get into the hands of young children and, in those hands, burn, wound, and even kill.

The National Fire Protection Association reports that in 1969, there were more than 1,300 persons injured in firework incidents in this country. "The Class C Firework, which is 1½ inches or less in length and considered to be relatively harmless, was most frequently implicated in the injury cases." The NFPA noted that:

> The greatest number of injuries occurred to children 15 years of age and under. Twenty-nine percent were 11–15 years of age, 23 percent in the 6–10 age group. . . . Among those under 6 years of age (5.6 percent of those injured), Class C fireworks, primarily Class C firecrackers or sparklers, accounted for 61 percent of the injuries. The children were most often either holding the device or in the vicinity of the device.
>
> There were many cases of personal injury in which the victim was an innocent bystander.
>
> *Fire Journal,* Vol. 64, No. 3 (May, 1970)

The Association feels that "no fireworks are being made that are safe enough for use by the general public" (Ibid., p. 3). Surely this means that they are doubly inappropriate for children.

When it happens—and it does—that even professional pyrotechnicians have been seriously injured while handling fireworks, it seems foolish to give them to kids. I am sure that firecrackers have no social utility whatever, and I seriously question whether even large and dazzling fireworks displays really add anything of significance to our holiday celebrations. Still, if we must have them, and if you feel that you and your children must watch them, then it is a lot wiser to do so from a considerable distance and without handling them yourselves.

Even the innocent-looking cap has been a villain at times, and it, too, is illegal in some states. Caps come in two varieties, paper and plastic, of which the latter are far more dangerous. Thus, in some states plastic caps are illegal while paper ones are not. The National Fire Protection Association expressly disapproves of plastic caps. It may be worth noting (see Chapter Three) that the Ohio Art Company, one of the strongest proponents of the legalization throughout the nation of plastic caps, operates from a home state in which the legislature only recently reaffirmed its decision to keep on the books the law that makes it illegal to sell such plastic caps in Ohio.

10. "Feeding Time" Playthings

In its unending efforts to be helpful to the American mother, the toy industry has not overlooked the possibilities of taking a profitable role in the daily drama, "Johnny, Drink Your Milk." For now mother and son alike have entered the age of the "Loonie Straw" and the "Krazy-Straw" and their relatives. Television tells us that any child would be more than happy to down his milk, with or without chocolate, if only he had a straw like these to drink it through. There's nothing wrong with this, except for the fact that some of these straws are intended for reuse but cannot be sterilized—so along with the milk, Johnny might get an unhealthy dose of germs. Some of the offending items are:

- "Krazy-Straw" (F & J Enterprises); "Loonie Straw" (Newman Co.); the "Loonie Straw" (#688, Dell Plastics, Inc.); the "Romper Room Fun Straw" (#R45, Come Play Products); and the "Silly Straw" (company unknown).

There are also miniature TV dinners and play foods sold, as toys, to toddlers. These are often so realistic that a child might try to eat them. This is a potential invitation to serious injury. Knowing as we all do that youngsters may even swallow objects that taste terrible, or that have no resemblance whatsoever to food, I find it impossible to justify camouflaging solid plastics as edibles and selling them to children. Some of the plastic knives and forks sold as toys are also small enough to be easily ingested. Those that are big enough to avoid this hazard, sometimes present a different one, for many are made of brittle and easily broken materials, especially plastics, which leave hard and jagged edges when they shatter.

11. Games

On the scale of misdirected creativity, the American toy manufacturer scores very well when it comes to the production of games "for children." Violent, bloody and psychologically deleterious games of every variety are available to the country's young people—and perhaps even more discouraging than this availability is the fact that they are being snapped up by parents who ought to know better. But bought they are, and at a feverish rate. The field of sick games gives the toy merchant a marvelous opportunity to demonstrate his ability to push successfully products that have no redeeming qualities whatsoever. Consider the following:

- "Bash" (#4543, Milton Bradley). "A real KNOCKOUT game. . . . OBJECT: Hammer the BODY pieces from under the HEAD." The box has a picture showing a man holding his bashed-up head, and the thesis of the game seems to be that bashing folks is good clean fun. Imagine this in the hands of a younger child not old enough to differentiate between the fun of using the "Bash" materials and taking a genuine hammer and pounding his older brother on the skull. (Fig. 51)

Figs. 51 and 52. Two "educational" games, "Bash" and "Time Bomb."

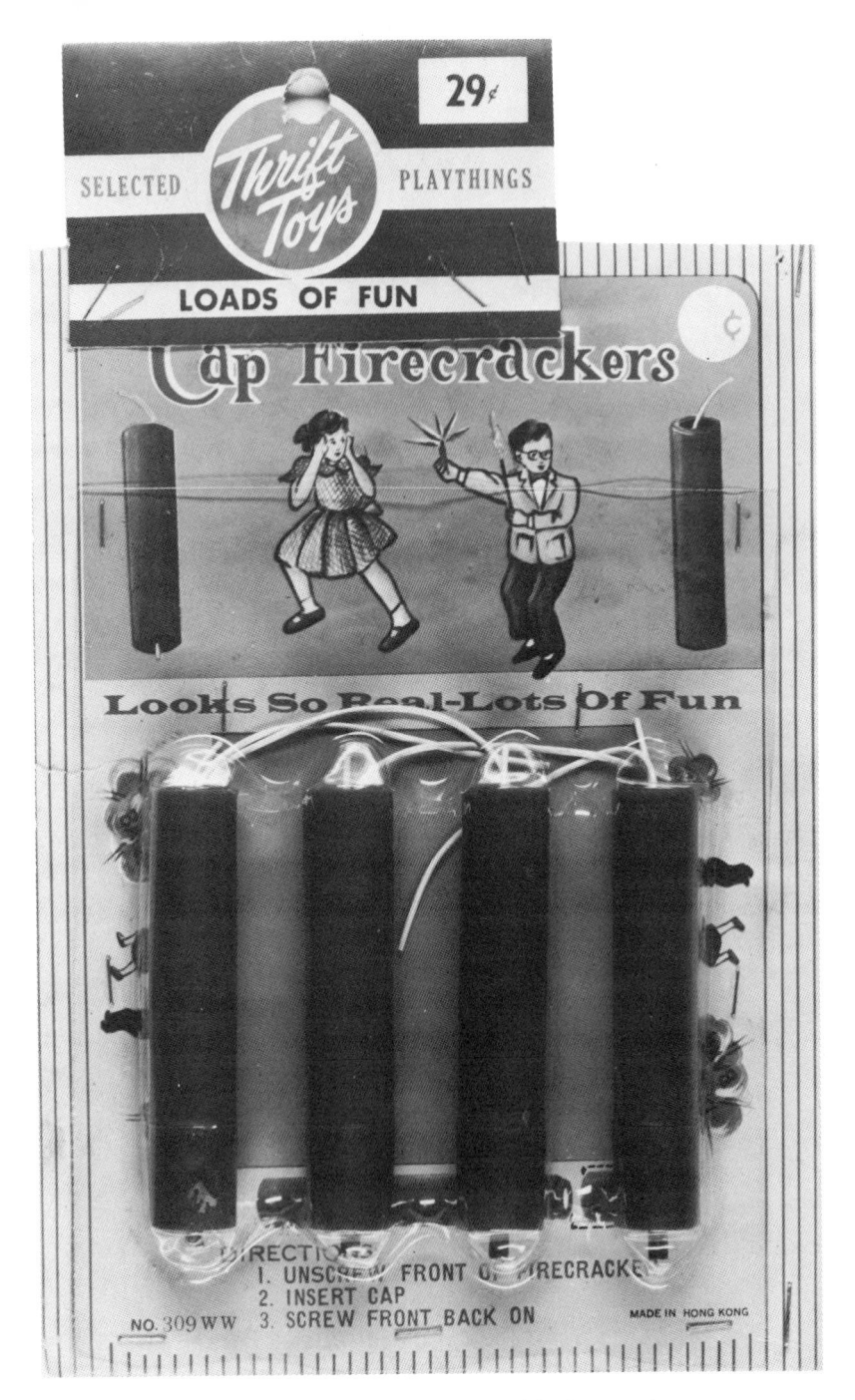

Fig. 53. Play "dynamite sticks."

- "Kaboom" (Ideal Toy Corp.), an exploding toy which, according to a letter to the National Commission on Product Safety, almost put out the eye of a young girl who was playing with it.
- "Time Bomb" (Milton Bradley), another charmingly named item. This one nearly blinded children on two separate occasions while it was being played with. (Fig. 52)
- "Dynamite Shack" (#4985, Milton Bradley) instructs players to "wear giant thumbs, try to stuff 'dynamite sticks' down chimney of shack before roof blows off. Great fun."
- "Cap Firecrackers" (Thrift Toys). These realistic-looking dynamite sticks, we are told by Thrift Toys, are "imported from many faraway lands, are carefully selected for their outstanding play value, fine qualities and child satisfaction." (Fig. 53)

Or think about the following basically acceptable puzzles with the questionable names they bear:

- "Frustration Ball" (#841, Remco Industries, Inc.). "You'll jiggle it and jiggle it until your mind bends and your nerves crack." The advertising puts this challenge: "Remain sane long enough to do it."
- "Nervous Breakdown" (Lakeside Toys). A variation on "Instant Insanity" which claims to "almost cause a nervous breakdown."

Or what of these otherwise safe toys which exploit violence (and see the section on toy weapons later in this chapter), like the following:

- "Magnetic Dart Game" (#71, Smithport Specialty Co.). This is a metal dart board with darts tipped with magnets —a reasonable idea. But the targets on the board make it a war game, shooting at aircraft carriers, tanks, ack-ack guns, guided missiles, bombers, and battleships.

- "Milton the Monster" (Milton Bradley). This simple board game is advertised for children from five to twelve. "Be the first to get to Horror Hill," is the goal of it all, and the cover shows a monster strangling a normal human while a living skeleton looks on and another human stands by in helpless disbelief.
- The "'Rat Patrol' Spin-Cycle Series: Spin to Win" (#116, Pressman Toy Co.). Like the "Magnetic Dart Game," the object here is to wipe out enemy installations, this time by spinning tops onto the field and getting them to land on positions like ammo dumps, tanks, half tracks, antiaircraft guns, and fighter planes. The television show which is the inspiration for this game is generally considered to be too violent for young children. Why is the game any different?

12. Hobby and Craft Toys

The whole point of toys in this category is that they are supposed to challenge a child to develop and to use his ability to experiment and create; and thus it is absolutely necessary that the producer give intelligent, adequate, and comprehensible instructions to both parent and child on the nature and functions of the set.

One of the most important requirements of a hobby or craft toy, then, is that the manufacturer should make intelligent age recommendations to assist the parent in making a wise choice from among the bewildering variety of alternatives available. Otherwise, it is predictable that the craft or hobby toy will be put to dangerous uses not intended by the designer or the maker.

The "Kookie Kamera" (Ideal Toy Corp.), "Lightning Bug Brand Glo-Juice" (Kenner Products), "Plastigoop" for "Thingmakers" (Mattel), and "Doodley-Doo" toymaking chemicals (Polyform Products, Inc.), are all examples of failure on this count. Each of these sets uses chemicals that are dangerous if taken internally, in spite of the fact that they may fall within the legal definition of "nontoxic" (which merely says that the test dosage of the compound kills less than a specified percentage of test rats within a two-week period). They do say, "Do not take internally," and some suggest antidotes in case of accidental ingestion, but the basic error is in failing to give adequate warning of the dangers involved and to make clear that young children should be kept entirely away from the sets. This is inexcusable.

Recently, there has been a trend toward disguising otherwise uninteresting and sometimes harmful toys and games as craft or hobby sets. Consider in this connection the "Thingmaker" series by Mattel, in which ghoulish characters predominate. The latest twist has been to invite the child to make his own monster and then exercise the privilege of destroying the creature in one of the ways described in considerable detail upon the box. This set, incidentally, requires 110-volt household current, and so presents the electrical dangers mentioned earlier.

Other companies are joining the parade. The Aurora Plastics Corporation now has a line of model monster kits that even glow in the dark. Louis Marx & Co., Inc., now offers molded plastic figures of grotesque and horrifying monsters.

Among the craft sets, there are sometimes also problems of design and of manufacture. Playskool's hammer and nail sets have been criticized for making units with small and swallowable parts, and for putting together hammers with loose heads. Ohio Art says its "Tool Chest" has "safe, vinyl tools," but in fact the equipment is heavy enough and sharp enough to do harm.

Model planes and boats powered by gasoline engines could prove hazardous. The gas vapors could accumulate and explode. Also, a child playing with a gas engine in a small room could very well be exposed to a dangerous accumulation of carbon monoxide fumes.

Little girls have "their own thing," too: knitting and sewing sets in particular. Some companies have the good and unfortunately uncommon (among toymakers) sense to supply soft, plastic, blunt needles with their sets for younger girls; others, mistakenly, do not. The Hasbro "Take-A-Long-Stitch-A-Story Set" (Hassenfeld Bros., Inc.) is obviously designed for toddlers, yet includes a two-inch, sharp metal needle. Other knitting sets, like the "Majorette French Knitting Set" (House Martin) and the "Bizzy Bee Knitter" (#4199, Transogram Co.), have unnecessarily sharp wire studs mounted on the knitting machine.

13. Hypodermic Toys

The toy industry is well aware that a popular fad or craze can be turned into a profitable toy. Perhaps it would have been naïve to expect that the industry would refrain from bringing drug addiction into the playroom. Yet incredible as it may seem, the hypodermic needle with all that it today implies has become a toy. For at least three companies make a toy syringe, complete with needle, for sale to children:

- the "Hippy-Sippy" (Alberts), which comes with a button reading "Hippy Sippy says I'LL TRY ANYTHING."
- the "Hypo-Phony" (H. Fishlove and Co., Inc.), which claims you can "fake hypo shots" with the retractable needle. Advertisements for this product have appeared in the toy industry's trade journals. (Fig. 54)
- the "Hypo-Squirt" (#5105, Hassenfeld Brothers, Inc.), which claims (or so one of their salesmen told me at the 1969 Toy Fair in New York) to be a "good answer" to the problem of selling squirting things without designing them as guns— which are currently unpopular! (Fig. 55) (See page 47, for a discussion of the design problems of this toy, which should be entirely avoided.)

14. Musical Toys

This book is not a study in aesthetics, and I make no comment on the harmonic and tonal capacities of toy musical instruments. Unmelodious though they may be (and not all of them are—some are quite well made), that is the least of our worries here.

What we do have to watch, however, are objects like wind-up musical toys with steel keys that are exposed, easily removed, and just as easily swallowed. Or pipes and whistles with sharp edges on the mouthpieces. Or mouthpieces that can fall or be pulled off and swallowed. There also are musical rattles, dolls, and baby toys with wire spokes and clappers inside which revolve to strike different tones. These, like the Fisher-Price musical lacing shoe, and the Brooklyn Museum's "Roly-Poly," may break and expose the sharp and dangerous metal parts inside. The "Roly-Poly," for instance, was recommended by *Consumer Reports* in November, 1968, but CU retracted its approval in February, 1969, after a mother complained to them about the injuries her child had received from one of the units which had broken.

As a class, the otherwise innocent xylophones tend to present the greatest number of hazards per single item. The metal sounding plates may, for example, be painted with toxic paints, or the wooden frame may be inexpertly finished with rough edges and splinters left untreated. The sounding plates may fall off, and carry with them the sharp nails used to fix them to the frame, as in the Fisher-Price xylophone. This problem arises with expensive as well as with reasonably-priced models—with the Childhood Interests/Alan Jay xylophone sold by F.A.O. Schwarz, as well as with the cheaper imported ones sold by Esco Imports, Inc. Interestingly enough, we found a ten-cent Japanese xylophone by Todai Toys in a dime store (of course), which was better made than the F.A.O. Schwarz model—one more instance where price is hardly any measure of toy quality.

15. Jewelry and Cosmetic Sets

Every little girl is trained practically from birth to want to look pretty. This is part of the national process of breaking consumers in early and preparing them for the joys of adulthood—insecurity about their hair color, their breath, their teeth, their entire physical appearance. We've gotten used to seeing little ones show themselves off, with their trinkets and make-believe makeup sets. The danger comes when they revert to a more natural children's world, and decide to eat or to taste the "jewels" and the rest. The beautiful moment could turn into a lifetime horror, for toy jewelry and little girls' makeup kits are often terribly dangerous. Some of the materials used are flammable, or toxic if taken internally, or can cause skin irruptions. Others have sharp edges that can cut and scar, while still others are so brittle and so likely to shatter into jagged pieces if broken that they present constant hazards. Many kits contain items—tiny rings and pendants, for instance—which are small enough to wind up in the lungs and throats of younger children and their infant siblings.

A few sets, such as the "Little Miss Charming Beauty Set" (#511, Henry Gordy, Inc.) and the "My Doll's Vanity Set" (#227, Standard Pyroxoloid Corp.), use real glass mirrors with the obvious danger they present of breakage, cuts, and even swallowing of the broken pieces. Others, including the following, sell very small toys to children who are not old enough to know better than to put such items in their mouths: "Tiny Toys for Little Boys" (#411, Chemical Sundries Company); "Play Dress-Up Set" (World Toy House, Inc.); "Let's Pretend Junior Miss Nurse Dress-Up Set" (#3119, Cleinman & Sons, Inc.); the "My Doll's Vanity Set" mentioned above; and the "Children's Toy Whistles" kit (sold by Woolworth's). Some units, such as the "Pretty Patty Neat and Petite Manicure Set" (#5490, Henry Gordy, Inc.) and the "Let's Pretend Junior Miss Nurse Dress-Up Set" just mentioned, include items sharp or stiff enough to put out an eye should a baby fall down on them.

16. Party Favors and Decorations

There is a special irony about most children's injuries and deaths, for many of them occur while the child is playing. Possibly the most ironic of all of these are the accidents that take place at parties and celebrations. This was brought home to me with stunning and disheartening force five days before I sat down to write this chapter, when a young acquaintance of my family choked to death at a neighborhood birthday party after accidently inhaling a balloon he was blowing up. Unfortunately this tragic occurrence is not uncommon. Balloons are especially treacherous for small children.

Even the most apparently innocent pastimes and festivities can be dangerous, even fatal. Birthday parties may go up in flames when flimsy paper costumes catch fire from the candles on the cake. Noisemakers or balloons may be swallowed or may shatter, firing pieces into children's eyes. And some so-called "party favors" are no favor at all. It is important to remember especially that in a party situation, the parental tendency is not to interfere—to let the little ones do "their own thing" (within reason, one hopes), to let them socialize with each other with a minimum of interference and a lot of fun. This is all well and necessary, of course; but it should not detract one bit from the constant parental supervision and precaution that is always necessary when children play. A wise parent can let his kids have fun without letting them in for trouble. Particularly dangerous are items that can easily be swallowed, or that explode, or that involve the use of flames or fires. Worth special mention are items which contain in prepackaged form a variety of special gifts and favors. These so-called "surprise packs" may include, for instance, tiny whistles so small that they are impossible to blow and easy to swallow. For example, the "Party Pack, 5 fringed Balloon Squeakers" distributed by American Party Favors of Pennsylvania comes equipped with a metal noisemaker so loose it can readily be ejected down a child's throat. Here are some others commonly distributed as favors at children's parties:

The Chemical Sundries Co. makes a "Wonder Plastic Balloons" kit and Hassenfeld Brothers put out "Super-Dough" with "Super-Glo," two products with some common features. The balloon kit is simply a tube of glue and a straw through which to blow. The child is supposed to daub a bit of the glue on the end of the straw and blow into it, making his own balloon. The glue, however, is extremely flammable, which makes the outfit certainly unsuitable and possibly illegal as well. The package warns, on the underside, "Do not use near flame or fire. Not a gum, do not chew," but it does not say whether the chemical is toxic or not, nor does it spell out the fire hazards in any clear detail. And while *Consumer Reports* warned about this toy as early as July, 1967, I was able to get one at the American Toy Fair in New York nearly two years later.

"Super-Dough," against which *Consumer Reports* has also issued a warning, provides an instructive lesson in the difference between a legal theorist's warning label and a practical and useful one. Outside, the package states, "Not for Internal Consumption"; this is written on a box carrying pictures of children putting the dough on their hands and faces. Inside, however—and inaccessible until after the kit has been bought, paid for, and opened up—is an elaborate instruction sheet with lengthy directions and alarming warnings, such as, "Never, never put Super-Dough (or any foreign substance) into or over your eyes, ears, nose or mouth." The box with the pictures shows it on the children's foreheads, cheeks, and chins! The inside instructions also point out that children with allergies may undergo adverse reactions. It goes on to describe

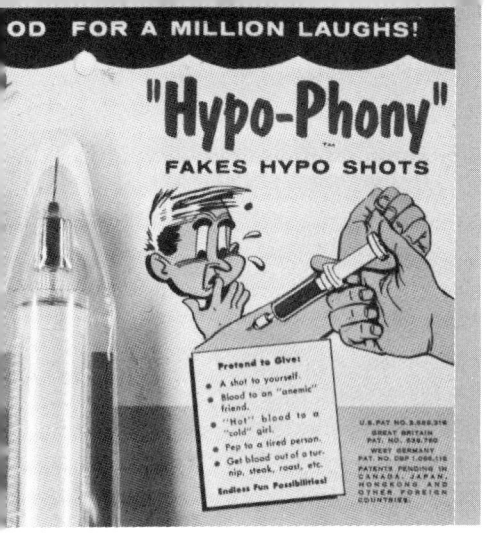

Fig. 54. Have a simulated "fix."

Fig. 55. New and exciting twist to the old-fashioned water pistol.

Figs. 56 and 57. Unsafe method of using swings encouraged by illustrations on each swing package.

the complex process of removing the stuff from walls, furniture, and anything else to which the child may have stuck it, and at the very end, tags on the following disclaimer:

Hassenfeld Bros., Inc., assumes no responsibility for the accuracy of said information and/or for any damage caused by migration and/or the results of any attempts to correct the same.

I would suggest that many of those who bought this "Super-Dough" would have left the stuff entirely alone had they known all that they eventually learned from reading the instruction sheet, which was unavailable to them when they bought the kit. As *Consumer Reports* noted, "If the precautions listed on the hidden instruction sheet are believed necessary by the manufacturer's legal staff, then in [Consumers Union's] opinion, the product should not have been marketed." This is utterly true, but of course too late—for how is the company going to get back all the packages it has already distributed around the country, or to get families to return those already bought?

17. Playground and Outdoor Equipment

These unfortunately turn up with a wide variety of design and construction flaws, despite manufacturers' claims that generous precautions are taken. A careful shopper will therefore watch for such recurrent problems as toxic paints, splintering wooden parts, and generally unstable frames. We should ask whether the units (such as swings, for instance) are spaced far enough apart from each other, and built only for a back-and-forth, and not a 360°, movement. If they are not, then collisions with other units or with inattentive bystanders are very likely. Some to avoid are: the "Monkey Swing" (#101, 20th Century Varieties, Inc.); the "Swing-A-Ling" (Moulded Products, Inc.); and the "Swing Ring" (Irwin Corp.).

Be sure to examine every aspect of any gym set to make

certain that there are no closely meshing metal parts into which children could put their hands or fingers. Long chains and bars on gym sets develop great force and pressure at their pivot points, like levers, and a hand or leg, finger or toe that happened to get in the way could easily be crushed or severed entirely. The "Sky-Rider" playground gym (Playground Equipment Corp.) did just that to a Florida three-year-old.

Ordinary back-and-forth swings have their own design defects as well. Some are made adjustable by flaring "S" hooks, which can be used to suspend the swing seat at varying distances from the ground in order to accommodate children of different ages and sizes. The problem with these is that the children may stand up on the swings or climb up the chains. These practices, of course, are dangerous enough because of the possibility of falling off, but the danger is compounded on the adjustable models by the fact that the youngsters also may take to shinnying on the chains and catching their clothes, fingers, or genitals on the S-shaped hooks. A recent report in a leading medical journal cited three separate cases of young children tearing their sexual organs in precisely this way.

Another potential danger found in swing units is typified by the "Coolvent Swing Set." I bought one of these for about $2.50 at a local hardware store. It consists of a metal swing seat, two chains, two seat hooks, and two screw-in eye hooks, used to fasten the swing to a handy tree limb or rafter. No directions, either for assembly or use, were provided, other than a drawing of two children, a boy and a girl, each on a Coolvent play swing: they are standing up and swinging back and forth toward each other. This patently unsafe behavior has been repeatedly condemned by the National Safety Council, yet the "directions" show it and thus invite it. (There is also some question as to whether or not the eye hooks supplied are adequate to support the swing, but the main issue here is that the manufacturer's promotional approach encourages hazardous misuse of his product.) See also the "Sears Swing Seat and Chain Set" which encourages similar behavior. (Figs. 56 and 57)

Some gym sets come with slides and ladders, and these have been the cause of many mishaps, too. Frequently the slides have poles or cages at the top for children to grab onto when they get up the ladder. But as the National Safety Council has remarked, these embellishments have also been the cause of more than one fatality. Children have gotten their clothing caught on the projections and, unable to free themselves, have been hanged. Therefore if there is to be a climbing or balancing aid on a slide, it should be designed so as to eliminate this possibility.

The spacing of the items included with multiple-usage home play gyms should result in stability irrespective of the number of youngsters simultaneously playing with it. Try to anticipate that several children will use the equipment at the same time. Also make sure that the spacing of various play items does not cause unnecessary bumping into one another. Play sets should contain the following features:

- Make sure all tubing is properly and securely capped.
- Sheet metal slides should have smooth, rolled or rounded edges. The author is familiar with a child who lost a finger because a slide did not conform with this standard.
- The seats of swings should be free of sharp edges and should be of a flexible soft material. Watch out for seats which have molded-in holes which might be small enough to catch a child's finger.
- The ladders of slides should have non-slip tread surfaces.
- Exposed nuts and bolts should be adequately covered or protected.
- The entire set should be balanced, level, and securely anchored to the ground at all points.
- The entire set should be treated with rust preventive.

Sears, Roebuck announces that it tests and inspects all its gym equipment, and the following notice appears in its 1969 Summer catalog: "All steel tolerances and parts subjected to Sears Lab tests. Gym sets—must meet Lab's rigid standards before approval for sale." But in September, 1968, Sears received a complaint letter about their gym sets. The letter, a copy of which was sent to the National Commission on Product Safety, pointed out that the cage atop the company's gym slide had bars that were spaced too far apart. "As a result," the mother complained, "two of our children nearly hung themselves." The bar spacing was similar to the equally dangerous design flaw in the Pride-Trimble infant's cribs. Yet, although the letter was sent in September, 1968, the same swing set with the same dangerous cage was featured in the 1969 Summer catalog.

Some physicians have criticized the fundamental concept of slides and similar equipment because of the orthopedic dangers they pose. With a properly designed slide, a child comes down on his back, and normally will drop off onto his feet. But if instead of landing on his feet he should drop onto the base of his spine, he might well injure his spinal column and even paralyze himself. There are slides sold for indoor use by younger children that are designed so that the child almost inevitably lands on the base of his spine instead of on his feet. These should be avoided in favor of those that do lead him to land on his feet or that extend all the way to the floor with no drop at all.

For similar reasons, some toy experts have condemned inflatable trampolines like the "Dennis the Menace Jump 'n Float," which is a rubber doughnut-shaped contraption three feet in diameter. In the Sears, Roebuck catalog, there is a picture of a boy jumping up and down on it, landing on his spine. The caption suggests that children should "bounce or jump" on it. After the tragedies of a few years ago, when trampolines were a novelty and a number of youngsters were paralyzed or killed while using them, it is hard to understand why anyone would try to sell something like a "Jump 'n Float," which is potentially even worse. Also avoid the "Spring-O-Lene" which is a twenty-two-inch square wood trampoline manufactured by Creative Playthings. (Fig. 58) Trampolines, at least, were recognized as suitable only for older children and adults, and they were larger—although even then people could miss them coming down and land on the ground instead.

The Ohio Art Company is a major producer and importer of outdoor toys. Genuinely ecumenical, they make both swords and ploughshares—guns and garden toys alike. Their garden tools and their sandbox, "Shovel 'n Sand Sifter," are both distinguished by shoddy workmanship and dangerously sharp metal edges. The garden implement set, for example, consists of a rake, a shovel, and a hoe, all of which have cutting edges. So do the wire mesh strainer and the metal sand mold of the "Shovel 'n Sand Sifter." All of these items are likely to be left outside, of course, exposed to dew and rain and thus to rusting; and so to the high probability of cutting, there is added the danger of tetanus. An added hazard of the sandbox toys is that both shovel and sand mold are fastened to the strainer screen by a sharp metal wire.

In fact, almost every kind of outdoor plaything may be dangerous in varying degrees. Plastic roller skates can be bought at the local drugstore for under a dollar, but are poorly made and may fall off during normal use. There are outdoor games like "Jarts" (Jarts Company) which include, in the words of the National Commission on Product Safety, "[h]eavily weighted, steel-pointed missiles [that] can foreseeably cause severe injury to even careful young children on being hurled."

18. Premiums: Free Toys

Giving away something for nothing has become a popular way of stimulating sales and building customer goodwill. Cereal manufacturers, candy companies, airlines, supermarkets, and many other promoters have all been large-scale users of the premium or promotional toy. In many cases, the toy comes in the package with the produce; and as a result it is usually small enough to fit in a cereal box and cheap enough to be worth distributing without raising costs significantly. All of us know what the prizes in the Crackerjack box look and are like. We may be less familiar with the junior "wings" which some airlines "award" small children on commercial flights, and probably few of us see political campaign buttons as a problem. But many of these items do present special dangers. Some representative ones are listed here:

a. *Airline "wings."* Some of these are cheaply made, might be swallowed, and are possibly lethal, unless the long fastening pins are equipped with safety catches.

b. *Campaign buttons.* Again, some are dangerous because they have no safety catches on the pins.

c. *Whistles.* Some of these, those in the Crackerjack boxes, for instance, are badly designed. The whistle has to be put well into the mouth if it is to be blown; there is thus a danger of swallowing it. Larger, so-called "police whistles" are harder to swallow and so are safer, but these too should be really large enough to make this possibility quite remote.

d. *Unpackaged premiums.* These often come in boxes of candy or cereal. If they are small enough and have no wrappings, they can easily be swallowed by a hungry youngster in a hurry.

e. *Projectile premiums.* Post Honeycombs cereal has used a plastic rocket and launcher set as an incentive to purchase, and other cereals have employed similar gimmicks, such as miniature space ships. Watch out for the sharp points on these toys, and note that any projectile toy is too dangerous for unsupervised children. Furthermore, many of them use rubber bands as their power source. This means that not only can they be fired with great force (and danger, for example, to a youngster's eyesight), but they can also snap back or break off and strike the child who is firing them. Toy design experts have often spoken out against the use of rubber bands in children's playthings.

19. Riding Toys

Children's transportation comes from the toymakers in a variety of flavors. But despite the great ingenuity in the conception and design of bikes and tricycles, skate-boards, sleds, wagons, and scooters, many of them are anything but safe and dependable, either as toys or as transportation. Skate-boards, for instance, have been notoriously unstable, and there are cheap roller skates sold for younger children (who presumably will quickly outgrow them) that tend to fall apart even while the child is using them. A number of bicycles use a range of gear shifts, and some of them have the levers mounted where they can do serious injury to riders thrown against them.

The most common defects in the bicycle design are load failure, brake failure, and corrosion. Is the bike made of a metal that is likely to rust out? Is it properly welded together? Some bikes have collapsed because of corrosion or poor frame assembly—and what such collapse could result in for a child trying to ride it across a busy thoroughfare is obvious. Examine all riding toys very carefully before buying any. Can it withstand the rough treatment that is only normal at the hands of children? Have your child try out the various features of the bike before purchase, both to see that he understands them and to ensure that they work properly. Make especially sure that the gear-shift levers are not only located where they cannot injure a boy's genitals, but also that the levers can be reached easily and without losing control of the bike itself.

Buying a tricycle is no simpler, as a look at some excellent suggestions made in the 1969 Consumer Reports *Buying Guide* will show:

(1) The rear seat should be mounted well forward of the rear axle for adequate stability.

(2) The rear platform should have a short overhang. If it is long, it will give the rider too much leverage when he leans back, making it easy for him to upset the tricycle.
(3) The rear wheels should be mounted on a "wishbone" frame behind the seat, instead of a straight pipe. This will help to distribute twisting stress on the wheels and make the unit last longer.
(4) Wide-track wheels and a low seat height both give greater stability on turns. Thick wheels with balloon tires also last longer, as well as perform better and in a safer manner than the narrow ones found on some models.
(5) Avoid long streamlined fenders. They are hazardous in turns and spills.
(6) A seat with spring suspension is more comfortable and durable than one without. If the seat is made of stamped metal, feel the edges to make sure they are not sharp and unfinished.

A classic instance of inadequate safety design is the Playskool "Tyke-Bike." This popular four-wheeler for toddlers has small wheels, easily removable handlebar grips, unstable seat placement, and elevated handlebars. If a child on one of these were to strike a large enough rock, for example, the front wheel would stop and he would be thrown forward. Because the handlebars are so high, the child's head could be thrown against their ends and, if one or both of the handlebar grips had fallen off, the exposed metal end could gouge his eye out. An unlikely combination of circumstances? Perhaps, but physicians know, and members of the National Commission on Product Safety have heard testimony, that this kind of accident has happened more than once, with tragic results.

Even sleds, which have virtually no moving parts, can be dangerous. The forward ends of the runners may have sharp edges or loops or hooks on which children can slash their hands. Some sleds have similarly looped or hooked rear runners that may cause similar injuries or may catch a child's clothes and drag him downhill. Still other sleds have steering bars that are raised too high from the body of the sled—too high, because children may trap their fingers in them while making even a slight turn.

Hobby and rocking horses should be checked for stability, and pogo sticks should be very well made and their bottoms firmly capped to avoid puncture injuries.

Prevalent everywhere as toys are two-wheeled motorized vehicles (Minibikes) which are commonly seen in driveways, on playgrounds, and unfortunately on public ways. It is estimated that more than one-half million of these so-called toys will be sold in 1971. They should be avoided since they are unsafe. While the Minibike is not designed for use on the highway, their users certainly are not old enough to avoid the temptation of testing their Minibikes on public ways. Many of these Minibikes reach speeds of up to 25 m.p.h. and it is quite obvious that they should not be bought or promoted as toys. Many of them are unstable and have other design features which are patently unsafe. As a class, Minibikes should not be used by or bought for minors.

20. Swimming Pools and Swimming Toys

Swimming pools are now so common that they are hardly the status symbol they used to be. Not only is the pool itself a family toy, but with it has come a wide range of accessories, sold for children in order to ensure that the pooltime hours may be constantly amusing and delightful.

Most basic of these articles is the pool ball, which is harmless enough—unless, of course, it induces a nonswimming youngster to follow it into the deep end of the pool. There are enough different flotation devices available to satisfy a junior admiral. Some of them claim to be tipproof and thus safe for even very young children. The claims are sometimes exaggerated as the mother of a young boy found out when she had to pull her son out of the family swimming pool. "I am very concerned that some mother will buy one of these pool seats"—advertised as "tip-resistant"—"and think as I did that it is totally safe, while she goes off and leaves the child to play. If we had left our son in the pool seat by himself that day, we wouldn't have him now." (*Family Safety,* Summer, 1970, p. 20) Nothing is completely tipproof, and, particularly around a pool, nothing is completely childproof. Constant dependence on flotation devices may also retard the child's development as a swimmer. And ultimately, of course, his best protection from water safety hazards will be his ability to swim confidently and well. Watch out also for metal pool toys, which may rust and—if sharp—cause cuts and gashes, exposing the child to the risk of tetanus.

A backyard pool need not be a major excavation or a large, above-ground version of the old swimming hole, to be dangerous. Small, circular "splash" pools are being sold for under $10 nearly everywhere. But these present many of the same dangers as their larger counterparts. One reason for this is that children are often left to play in them without supervision. Parents by and large fail to appreciate that it takes very little water to drown a child! *Small children should be never left alone in a pool (or bathtub) of any size.* The few seconds it takes to answer the telephone and chat a bit, or to deal with the salesman at the front door, are enough for a child to slip and go under and drown. Furthermore, the water in many splash pools is not treated, nor is it frequently changed; and this poses obvious sanitary problems.

The dangers of using diving boards installed above poorly designed pools are well-known and need only brief mention. Every year, a significant number of young people—and older ones—are killed or paralyzed in diving accidents, the most frequent causes of which are boards that are too high or too springy for the area below, diving areas that are too shallow for the board in use, and inadequate training of the person who is doing the diving.

Water slides are a better child's toy than diving boards in

Fig. 58. Dangerous trampoline. Picture taken from a card accompanying product.

Fig. 59. Helicopter with exposed, sharp gear box.

theory and usually in practice; but they still have drawbacks of their own. There is the obvious problem of supervising the child as he climbs up the ladder, and his descent is not necessarily safe either. Since the youngster hits the water feet first, it may happen that when he goes down into it, the water is forced up his nostrils; this can also happen if he jumps into the pool feet first. The result could be an infection of the paranasal sinuses, or of the middle ear and the mastoids, caused by various organisms which may be in the water. (These complications can be avoided by resorting to the old swimming hole technique of holding the nose until the downward motion has eased up under water.)

Problems also arise when the child goes down a water slide headfirst. The National Safety Council has found some water slides so poorly designed that the youngsters could hit the water with enough speed and force to give them brain concussions.

We all know that outdoor pools have to be treated chemically to prevent algae formation and an unduly high concentration of harmful bacteria. The most common treatment is chlorination. But failure of the testing materials which report the degree of chlorine already present in the water can lead to excessive chlorination, which in turn can result in a dangerously high level of acidity, capable of causing serious skin or eye burns. The usual method of determining the chlorine level in a pool is typified by "Puropool's pH and Chlorine Test Kit" (Omega Chemical Corp.). A sample of water is drawn from the pool and treated with the indicator solution, which gives it a certain color. The precise shade reveals the amount of chlorine present in the pool. The water sample which has changed color is compared with a standard color chart, to get this information. Unfortunately, some indicator solutions are very susceptible to heat and light, and can give false readings if they are overexposed to either. Similarly, the color charts may become bleached in the sunlight, and lead to misinterpretation. These errors can result in overchlorination of the water, with its attendant risks. Puropool, for example, does warn against leaving the calibrated color chart out in the sun; but they don't tell you why.

Another problem connected with chlorination lies in the process of adding the chemical to the pool. Some powdered chlorine compounds are to be added directly to the pool water, for example, but these should be handled with great care, for they can cause skin and eye burns if brought into direct contact with either. The Sun Pools Chemical Division of Sun Cleanser Company makes such a chlorine concentrate, packaged in metal foil envelopes complete with clearly stated warnings and suggested antidotes. This is very sound, except that it is virtually impossible to open the envelope without coming in contact with the chemical.

21. Trains, Trucks, Automobiles and Flying Machines

The automobile industry belatedly discovered—under intense public pressure—that the protrusions built into cars to make them more "stylistic" were causing unnecessary deaths to people involved in vehicular accidents. Recent federal laws have been enacted to eliminate this hazard, or at least to reduce it. But the individuals in our society who are the most traumatized—who suffer more falls, bumps, bangs, and tumbles than the rest of us—are young children. I cannot understand why the toy trucks and airplanes and autos that are made for them cannot also incorporate some of the fundamental principles of intelligent safety engineering. Many of them, on the contrary, come complete with rigid and dangerous protrusions and projections capable of knocking out an eye or punching a hole in a child's flesh. Items like these have no place at all in the world of the child. But there they are, as the following examples indicate:

• Wheeled vehicles with sharp protruding fins or exposed gears. Some of these are cheap imports with no manufacturer's name upon them by which to identify their source. Others are American-made: a toy milk truck by the Buddy L. Corporation; "Coast Guard Mechanical Seaplane" (#106, Ohio Art Co.); "Mission-X Top Secret Plane"; the "Astro-Train" (Remco); and the helicopter made in West Germany (Jechnofix) with the exposed, sharp gears. (Fig. 59)

- Battery-powered and other rotor toys: Some of these have sharp-edged rotors that can slice away fingers or poke out eyes; the "Johnny Astro" (Topper Toys); the "Astrojack Flying Space Boy" (#EAJ 275) and the "Lunar Bug Flying Moon Craft" (#EB 250, both, Victor Stanzel Co.); and the "Thunderbird Stunt Plane" (#528, Chemical Sundries, Inc.), are among these.
- Free-flight toys. Some toy airplanes have been known to disintegrate in flight (just like the real ones put out at immense cost by defense contractors!), with consequent injury to bystanders. Others reach the unreasonable (and uncontrollable) speed of twenty-five miles per hour. Still others are rockets with hard noses, sometimes with soft but easily removable nose cones: the "NASA Space Twins" (#5818, Larami Corporation); "Tru-Streak Jet" and the "Pressurized Gas" fuel it uses (both, Victor Stanzel Co.); and the "V-X" rocket (BE-BU of West Germany).
- "Hot Wheels" (Mattel). The cars we examined in this plaything were safe enough, although a free "Hot Wheels" button with sharp and unbeveled metal edges was included. But the real and very risky hazard of this toy is that a young child will be fiercely tempted to send the cars around and off the track at excessive speeds or to look through the little "house" that powers the vehicles as a car is coming through from the other side. These cars do reach high speeds, and could cause serious harm to anyone they might strike while flying off the track; and, of course, a child who took one head-on in the eye could be blinded.
- The "Car Plane" (#325, Kenner Products) is designed to

"fly" alongside a moving automobile to which it is attached. While it may be safe for the child flying it (and it is safe *only* if it is well attached and if the child knows not to put his own head out the window to watch it more closely), it is still fundamentally dangerous because it tends to distract drivers of other cars, as well as the driver of the vehicle to which it is attached.

- "Super Bird" walks up and down walls. It has two stiff plastic points (crown and beak) on its head. Despite this danger the child is instructed by the manufacturer (Tennessee Industries) to "try to catch him as he falls" from the wall. (Fig. 60)

22. War Games

If the statistics that document the enormous popularity of war-related playthings are correct, one is forced to wonder how many parental critics of the American adventure in Southeast Asia have, inconsistently, brought these war toys into their own homes. Soldiers in every kind of fighting unit, with every sort of gear, in postures of attack, of defense, and of death, have long been a staple of children's play equipment. To be sure that the children are sufficiently indoctrinated, the manufacturers often put out military toys as collector's series, in which soldiers, sailors, airmen and marines are presented in their full range of uniforms. Communications units and medical teams, exploding submarines, planes, tanks and even miniature atomic weapons are all realistically depicted. It is as if we can't get our fill of violence and slaughter in the movies or on the entertainment programs on television—not to mention in the news films—and have to fill our need for destruction and killing even in our leisure time as well. Thus:

- The "Andy Gard US Army Tank & Jeep" (Andy Gard Corporation). The package says "Stage your own all-out attack," and claims to be "safe; unbreakable; educational [!] and sanitary."

- The "G.I. Joe" series (Hassenfeld Brothers, Inc.), a full collection of "movable fighting men" equipped to take on anyone, anywhere.
- Two sets by Mikephil: "Two Complete Soldier Sets" (#81134) and the "Soldier Accessories" kit (#71074); two strings of soldiers in various fighting positions, together with a kit which includes what every well-dressed product of the Pentagon should wear.
- The "U.S. Air Force Surface-to-Air Missile" (#920) and the "U.S. Armored Division" (#1161K, both by Processed Plastics Company). The first provides a spring-loaded launcher that can fire pencils, nails, or anything else that fits, as well as the hard plastic nose cone that comes with the set. The second offers an entire armored division for twenty-nine cents. (This is probably better value than either the ABM or MIRV, and very likely works better, too.)

23. *Weapons*

Eye accidents endanger the sight of approximately 160,000 school-age children each year, according to the National Society for the Prevention of Blindness. Further, the Society reports that seventeen percent of all eye injuries to children are caused by such projectile playthings as BB guns, bow-and-arrow sets, dart guns, slingshots and crossbows. Despite this, many manufacturers and retailers persist in selling many of these articles as "safe" or "harmless." The case for nursery disarmament is clear, and the need is urgent. "Disarmament" is not too strong a word, for it is possible for today's child to collect a genuinely lethal arsenal of toy weapons in short order. The fact that some of these so-called playthings have been banned in many states doesn't seem to impede the toy merchants at all. They go right on selling them in those states which have no such prohibitions, and in some cases they make slight alterations in them—just enough to avoid the bans where they are in force.

The toy merchants are not content to offer an entire range of deadly items to children; they insist—as we saw in the previous section—on linking them to war. Most toy weapons in one way or another are designed or promoted to glorify the act of killing. And to judge from the number of toy weapons based on an exaltation of battle, the toy industry has found this connection with war to be quite profitable. In fact, although they have no Department of Defense contracts that I know of, some toy companies should be classed, on the basis of what they produce, as war industries—our own micro-Military-Industrial Complex.

These toy weapons are real. Guns that fire projectiles of all kinds are sold and bought for children. Zip guns and air rifles are promoted as toys. The Daisy air rifle, which shoots small steel pellets, is merchandised as the boy's best friend. Yet *one* hospital—The Charlotte (N.C.) Eye, Ear and Throat Hospital—made a study of eighty-one cases over a nine-year period in which eye injuries were sustained through use of BB guns. A significant percentage of these came about because of ricochet, and still—to date—the Daisy Company refuses to give explicit warnings of this danger and goes on recommending the indoor use of its product, thereby multiplying the potential number of ricochet incidents.

The crossbows, slingshots, boomerangs, and swords currently owned by children would be enough to delight the martial instincts of any medieval warrior, or to chill the heart of his enemies. A child today is perfectly well able to kill or maim in any of a dozen different ways, simply by using the equipment he has right now in his playroom. Here, more than in any other area, the toy industry's insensitivity is on parade. But the era has long since passed when we felt that war is glorious and something towards which our children should be favorably disposed, and the time has come to stop letting the merchants make money from the darker urges in mankind by promoting and selling these physically—and psychologically—

Fig. 60. "Super Bird," replete with pointed beak and crown.

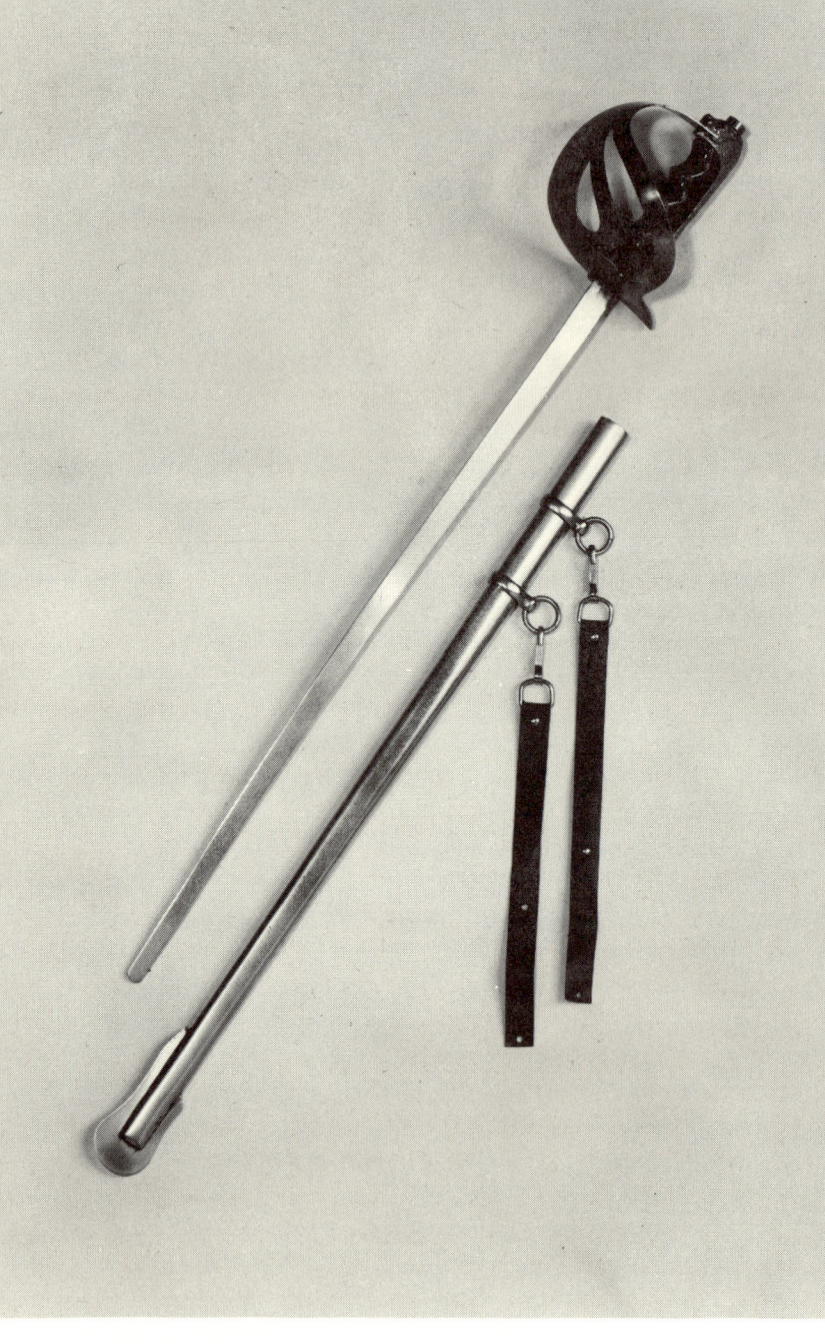

Fig. 61. Child's sword—a toy weapon which is unduly heavy, made of real metal, and altogether too realistic and dangerous.

Fig. 62. Super-caps—super-noise and super-hazard.

brutalizing toys. If you think this is too strongly put, then consider the range of weaponry below:

- Blowguns and peashooters or bean blowers.
- Boomerangs.
- Bows and arrows.
- Blood guns (that squirt "disappearing red ink," which hits the spot and looks like blood).
- Crossbows.
- Dart guns.
- Disk guns (which shoot spinning disks in lieu of darts).
- Pellet guns, of every kind and description, some of which will fire anything you can get inside.
- Rubber band guns.
- Rifles that use air power to fire BBs and similar projectiles.
- Slingshots.
- Spark guns.
- Swords and knives—including a *metal* sword (with a blunted edge) that is available at F.A.O. Schwarz and sold through its catalog. (Fig. 61)

I have not listed all the varieties of these weapons by name, since I think that the general principle ought to be this: Don't buy *any* of them. If you feel you *have* to (for whatever mistaken reason), then be especially careful of those that "work" by firing anything at all.

Some other items should also be mentioned in this section, although they do not readily fit into the categories set out above. For example, Esco Imports, Inc., and other companies, offer combination sets of military equipment, including helmets and hand grenades along with the usual firearms. Mattel used to make an "Agent Zero M Sonic Blaster" (#5530) which gave off short blasts of at least 150 decibels—loud enough to injure someone's hearing permanently. Mattel says they no longer make this, but it's interesting to note in passing that a company salesman said that this was due to a falloff in demand rather than to any considerations of health and safety for the user. The "Wasp Cap Gun" distributed by Ohio Art Co. is capable of producing sound at a level of 100 decibels or higher and likewise presents a potential hazard to hearing. The "Wasp Cap Gun" was accurately represented by Ohio Art to the trade as "super-bang," "extra-loud" and a "real noise maker." (Fig. 62) It is still possible, despite vague threats of congressional action against mail-order armaments, to purchase knives, guns, and chemical sprays by post—even if you are a child. Companies peddling these items advertise in such magazines as *Popular Science, Popular Mechanics,* and *Science and Mechanics.* The Daisy air rifles used to be promoted in *Boy's Life* as providing "safe indoor fun." We simply must disarm the nursery and the playroom.

Some General Rules and Suggestions

The specific comments in the preceding buyers' guide naturally do not cover all possibly dangerous toys and all the possible hazards they present. This section therefore sets some general pointers that can be applied to almost any toy you may be considering for your child. First, I give some things to watch for, and then I suggest some positive principles for choosing safe and healthy toys. Then, I add a few notes for all of us who see this as more than simply a problem for individual parents and finally some words addressed to the toy industry itself.

1) *Don't buy on impulse.* Decide what you want, whom you want it for, and how much you are willing and able to pay, before you go out shopping. And don't be afraid to shop for price as well as for quality. If the store hasn't got what you want at the price you want it for, then look somewhere else—and don't

assume that there is a strict correlation between price and quality; there isn't.

2) *Don't forget that children are fickle.* They have sincere, intense, but often short-lived interest in any one thing. So in choosing a toy, try to estimate how long it will really keep your child's attention, and whether it is worth the investment or just something that will be under the bed and forgotten in half a week or half a day.

3) *Don't believe the advertising claims.* Be skeptical of the toymaker's hard sell, and try the plaything out yourself or have it demonstrated for you. Be sure it performs as advertised before you buy it.

4) *Don't buy badly made toys.* Check the item for sound construction and be especially choosy about the toys that require home assembly; playthings that hang together by folding tabs, for instance, are not reliable.

5) *Don't buy metal toys without looking them over and inspecting them.* Metal toys that bend easily may be of low-quality materials, while those that are too rigid and pointed may be dangerous, too. Are outdoor toys genuinely rustproof?

6) *Don't buy wooden toys that may splinter.* Check all toys made of wood for the smoothness of the finish and the quality of the wood. Two excellent woods are Ponderosa pine, which is soft, and maple, which is hard.

7) *Don't buy painted toys unless the paint is nontoxic and lead-free.* Be especially suspicious of white paint, which has a higher lead content than colored paints. Toxicity is more often a characteristic of cheap, imported toys (usually made in Hong Kong or Japan) than of quality American or European toys. The label on the toy or on the box should state that vegetable-dye or other nonpoisonous paints were used.

8) *Don't buy anything that could cut children.* Inspect every plaything for sharp edges, points, exposed nails or screws, and for metal surfaces that can rust and might become a puncture hazard.

9) *Don't buy toys unless they are heat-resistant, nonflammable, and shatterproof.* Avoid anything that involves glass, especially glass mirrors, which may have a toxic coating. Celluloid is also a poor material for toys, for when and if it breaks, it ordinarily leaves sharp edges, and in addition, it is highly flammable.

10) *Don't buy baby toys unless they can be sterilized.*

11) *Don't buy any toys that can end up in infants' mouths.* If you have children of varying ages, remember that what you buy for the older ones will be accessible, usually, to the younger ones as well. So avoid buying the older ones such things as kits with lots of small colorful parts.

12) *Don't buy dolls with glued-on eyes* (which come off and can be swallowed), *with pop-out eyes* (the same), *or with long, sharp hair pins.* Embroidered or sewn-on eyes are best, and pins of every kind should be avoided if possible.

13) *Don't buy "action" toys with removable wheels.* They don't last very long, and the wheels can easily be swallowed by smaller children. Wheels on toys should be attached with screws or rivets, and pull-cords should be tied or firmly stapled, not tacked on.

14) *Don't buy any toy that uses household current.* Children old enough to use them would do better to be initiated into the supervised and careful use of genuinely adult products. If you *must* buy electrical toys, battery-powered versions of most toys are available and are safer. The batteries, however, should be inspected, too, to make sure there is no corrosion leakage. Should you, however, for any reason, decide on a toy that utilizes 110-volt household current, make sure it has the UL seal of approval and make sure it is equipped with transformers or converters that reduce the operating voltage to safer levels of 6 or 12 volts.

15) *Don't buy wind-up toys unless the springs are strong and enclosed in casings tough enough to contain them if they should break.* Toys that have gears should also have them enclosed. Watch out for and stay away from toys with wind-up

keys in which the key keeps turning while the toy is running —fingers and clothes can be caught in the key if the child picks up the toy before it runs down.

16) *Don't buy toys that run on batteries or friction mechanisms,* unless you are prepared to tolerate a plaything with a short life expectancy. Many of these break down very easily, or else are toys that simply perform for the child, but do not actively involve him and thus will quickly bore him. Battery toys in any case require frequent and costly replacement of the battery units.

17) *Don't buy anything breakable for an infant or a preschooler.* They are likely to do almost anything with a toy, and a fragile one will soon be of no use, and possibly of some danger.

18) *Don't forget to foresee what will happen should the toy break down or fall apart.* What will it look like then? Will it be unsafe? If you can anticipate that the plaything you are considering will present sharp points or jagged edges if it breaks, or rough inner surfaces, or a lot of little pieces, then watch out for it. Think also of what is likely to happen if the child falls on the toy: The impact of tumbling on it could force some of the fragments into or beneath his skin. Toys should not only be inspected at purchase, they should be inspected regularly for wear or damage which may prove hazardous.

19) *Don't buy any toy for a child too young to use or learn to use it.* It is no favor to present a child with something that he is too young for or too little skilled to use. The same is true of toys that require large spaces or an outdoor area—don't buy it if it can't be used. Children, incidentally, don't "grow into" toys the way they grow into ski jackets or books, and things that are too advanced for them tend to frustrate them or make them feel incompetent.

20) *Don't buy complex toys for very young children,* or for children whose play cannot be supervised. Be sure that what

you are about to bring home can and will be used safely and constructively, and personally supervise the use of things like chemistry sets and gym equipment.

21) *Don't buy weapons as toys:* air rifles, slingshots, bow-and-arrow sets, dart guns. Their educational value is quite limited, and their dangers, both physical and psychological, are considerable. It's just as important to avoid conditioning children to weapons as it is to keep them off candy cigarettes and play hypodermic needles. Certainly there may be proper adult uses for bows and arrows. But such uses *are* adult and should be taught only by competent instructors and only to young people who are old enough to understand and to observe this principle.

22) *Don't forget to buy with the whole family in mind.* Toys for older children will be passed on to their little brothers and sisters and probably circulate through the whole neighborhood as well. If there is a likelihood that a plaything you are considering may eventually be used by children too young or too naïve to cope with it, then you should forget it. Toys should be, but few really are, childproof; buy accordingly.

23) *Don't permit children to play with broken or damaged toys*—such toys present an increased risk of injury.

24) *Don't depend entirely on store-bought toys for children's amusement and education.* The natural play materials found in every home, and even such elemental things as mud, sand, and water, can often provide just as much enjoyment, perhaps more, than complex mechanical toys or elaborately constructed exhibition playthings. Moreover, if you spend a lot of money on a store-bought toy, you tend to become preoccupied with preserving it as long as possible, and this attitude gets in the way of your own and your child's normal and healthy play.

So much for the negatives. They may sound formidable and forbidding, but they are only half the story, and it is certainly possible to find good toys as well as bad ones. A good toy is one that is safe and makes a positive contribution to your child's growing up—not necessarily educational in a restricted sense, but at least fundamentally enlightening and amusing to play with. There's no easy formula for toys like this, but perhaps some qualities to look for can be suggested. Here, then, are some "dos" for the toy shopper:

1) *Do look for toys that are appropriate* to the child as he is now—in terms of his age and his present skills. If he has to wait to grow into a toy, it is only a frustration for him.

2) *Do select toys that are versatile* enough to lend themselves to different kinds of play situations and to maintain their play value for some time. Of course, this is not always possible —toddlers grow awfully fast, for instance—but it's something to bear in mind. Blocks, balls, and sports equipment can often become favorites with children who use them in varying ways and with developing skill as the months and years go by.

3) *Do buy toys that give a child room to use his imagination.* Play materials should not be closed-circuit operations, for the idea is that the *child* is *playing*, not being amused passively. Toys that are too structured and detailed restrict rather than foster the child's play.

4) *Do buy toys that allow the child to involve himself in problems and decisions in the play situation*—not complex issues that may confound and confuse him, but still situations that can give him a role. The best toy is one a child can be absorbed in and interact with; and this is what educational toys ought to be about.

5) *Do buy toys that teach or require new skills*—when the child is ready for them. A carefully selected chemistry set or a well-designed two-wheeled bicycle given at the right time can open a whole new world for the youngster and is a marvelous gift; but don't hurry him.

6) *Do look for toys that involve the child with other people.*

Perhaps the one most important thing we have to learn as children is how to get along with our peers and playmates. Toys that provide opportunities for interaction and interchange with other children of all ages, are excellent for teaching children the give and take so necessary for a healthy and full life later on.

7) *Do think of the individual child for whom you're buying.* Don't get something just because *you* like it, or because it's expensive (and thus something that will impress the child's parents or their friends). A toy that doesn't appeal to the child for whom it's bought is a waste of money. Moreover, a toy that *you* know he doesn't like will usually be one that *he* knows you know he doesn't like—and he may then think that you don't like him as he is and want to change him. This is not a very sound approach, nor does it do much for his self-identity.

8) *Do put a heavy emphasis on toys without frills, such as large soft balls and blocks with round corners.*

9) *Do look for articles and materials which would be adequate for homemade toys.*

These few rules can contribute to sound toy shopping, and I fervently hope that they do. But the drive to make the lives of our children both safe and happy cannot stop with the process of educating parents and other toy buyers to be selective in purchasing individual playthings. Some people will never be able to master the art of toy shopping, and so there will always be a market for unsafe toys—especially when they are promoted unscrupulously with hard-sell advertising and spurious and deceptive claims of safety. As long as the toy industry is running its own show, free of effective federal regulation, there will remain companies still willing, ready, and able to take advantage of people whose kindliness exceeds their ability to spot open or hidden dangers involved in many toys. For this reason, I offer some suggestions that all of us

—concerned parents, civic-minded adults, educators, physicians, lawyers, and the rest of us—might wish to follow:

1) Write to your state and federal representatives and senators and urge passage of effective toy-safety legislation. This is especially important at the federal level, and any bill that is to be at all useful should provide for premarketing controls and testing.

2) Join the campaign to educate the rest of us about dangerous toys. If you know of an accident or an injury caused by a plaything, take all the details of the episode, along with the trade name of the toy and the full name of the manufacturing concern, to your attorney and ask him to inform the proper authorities. Don't dismiss toy accidents as minor —for while *your* child may have been lucky, the same design flaw could be fatal to someone else's son or daughter.

3) It is especially important that the Federal Flammable Fibers Act be given stricter standards and a wider range, either by congressional amendment or through administrative regulations, to include *all* children's articles. Blankets, dolls, dolls' clothing, bedding, and other items commonly used by children are not presently covered by the act and this is foolish. Write to your congressman and inform the local press about this.

4) State and local laws can be valuable stimuli to toy safety. Find out whether your state, for example, has strict health laws (which could be used to ban disease-carrying toys, such as the contaminated stuffed ducklings recently seized in Connecticut), fireworks laws (the sale of fireworks to the general public should be wholly banned), antifraud legislation (which would impose criminal sanctions on the makers and sellers of dangerous toys advertised or represented as "safe" or "harmless"). Some states *do* have laws banning slingshots and restricting the sale of air rifles, and such legislation should be more universal. The Massachusetts law is an example and

could at once be adopted with some modification elsewhere. And there is no reason why states could not forthwith adopt legally binding flammability standards, which, like the British norms, bar the sale of *any* children's article that is capable of *sustaining flame*. Imaginative lawyers can find plenty of ways to act *now*, using creatively the laws we already have.

5) We need a centralized approach to nationwide toy safety, and a central authority to supervise the toy industry by instituting premarketing testing and control. Such an agency should have broad and flexible powers, including the right to keep dangerous toys off the market and the right to institute civil and criminal proceedings against deliberate and consistent violators. The National Commission on Product Safety has proposed such an agency, and the Congress is now considering it. Make your views known.

6) One of the keys to toy safety is control of the content of toy advertising, much of which is misleading, inadequate, or so confusing as to constitute a separate danger. One way to eradicate these promotional practices—which has been described as "a rape of our children's minds"—is to ask for and obtain stiff federal legislation outlawing advertising abuses connected with children's products. What we have now is an uneven collection of state and local laws that are completely unable to deal with a nationwide—and therefore federal—problem. Again, here is a field in which public pressure on the Congress could be enormously productive.

Finally, let me address a few thoughts to the toy industry itself—to the manufacturers and retailers who may think that I've treated them all very harshly. Let me say first of all that I don't at all believe that toymakers and sellers are invariably unscrupulous fiends with a desperate urge for profit and no concern for the welfare of the children who constitute their clientele. But let's look at the record:

TOYS THAT DON'T CARE 263

- There are hundreds of unsafe and unsuitable toys currently on the market and many of them are being promoted by questionable advertising.
- Industry self-regulation, while in many respects well-intended, has just not been effective in protecting the children.
- England, West Germany, and other countries have managed to do very well making and selling toys even with premarket testing, higher safety standards, and stricter regulations. Sound but firm federal legislation poses no threat to those manufacturers in this country who are genuinely conscientious and truly concerned about the health and safety of the country's youngsters.

All this being so, the toy industry could do itself a great service by being frank with the American people: by admitting that far too many of the toys for sale in the U.S.—and made in the U.S.—are hazardous. The industry could take an active part in cooperating with parents' groups, the public media, and government at all levels, both in encouraging safety education programs and in developing ways and means to ensure the safety of the toys sold in this nation. If they don't, they will acquire an unfavorable public image, like the one presently worrying major American automobile manufacturers, who, many of us believe, only began to get serious about safety engineering *after* their efforts to discredit Ralph Nader had totally failed, and *after* the public had begun to view them as entirely cynical and devoted solely to corporate profits and government contracts.

This means that the manufacturers of toys and children's playthings will have to use their imaginations not only to develop new and quick-selling products, but to *design child-proof toys*. They will have to undertake systematic research on children's behavior, and to anticipate, much more than they now do, the creative and unorthodox ways in which children can reasonably be expected to use their goods. Lamentation over the inevitability of certain kinds of toy abuse is no substitute for intelligent safety engineering, and for concerted effort to prevent such abuses.

It also means that toymakers should devote more attention to informing buyers about their wares. Clear instructions are always necessary when a toy has to be operated. But they are not a substitute for warnings, where needed. This should be stressed: operating instructions should be simple and comprehensible; their function is explanatory. Warnings should be loud and plain and unmistakable; their function is cautionary. No one expects a warning to give positive directions on how to run something; nor should directions be allowed to replace a warning, where a warning is in order. Furthermore, if warning *is* in order, then it should be made known to the prospective buyer *before* he lays his money down—not after he has taken the toy home and opened it up.

Related to this problem of providing warnings on the outside of the package so that the customer is fully informed of the hazards as well as of the joys he is about to bring into his home, is the question of advertising practices. If a toy will sell well only because its foreseeable uses are dangerous, then it should not be sold at all; and advertisers should be scrupulous not to promote dangerous toys or dangerous uses of otherwise reasonable playthings. Toy advertising works especially on children, and does so by appealing to their thirst for excitement, novelty, and even for danger; and toy advertising that induces youngsters to take unnecessary risks, or to play in dangerous ways, is morally irresponsible and wholly unnecessary. A good toy will sell without the use of misleading or risk-inducing advertising, and a toy that depends on deceptive promotional practices for its commercial success is not a good toy.

Retailers, too, have a responsibility to their customers. It is true that in many cases, all they do is hand over prepackaged toys. But they should take energetic and positive steps to assure themselves that the toys they stock and sell are safe ones, and that their customers are fully aware of whatever hazards a particular item may present. No honorable toy store, for instance, will knowingly sell a sophisticated chemistry set to the parents of a four-year-old; and every toy seller should ask prospective buyers some gently probing questions to make sure that the toy is really suitable for the child in question. Retailers should join in public safety education campaigns, should help press for truly effective legislation, and in particular should put pressure on the manufacturers by refusing to stock dangerous or defective toys. They can regain public confidence by taking a stand on the side of the child instead of the toymaker, in those situations where a choice has to be made.

Our courts, for the most part, have been increasingly responsive to the growing needs of a highly mechanized and industrialized society. This growth must continue if the law is to protect adequately the rights of our children in products liability litigation. Courts that have not yet done so should adopt the concept of strict liability referred to in Chapter Six. Once strict liability is adopted, the determination of whether a product is "defective" should be expansive enough to include the various categories of dangerous toys described in Chapter Two. In a strict liability suit, contributory negligence should not bar the plaintiff's right to recover for injuries sustained as a result of a defectively made product. This last point is especially important in cases involving children and their toys that don't care.

All of us, manufacturers, retailers, consumers, should be alert to suggestions for improving the safety and the overall quality of our children's toys. Sometimes simple ideas can have important consequences. For instance, physicians have been bedeviled by children swallowing plastic bits and pieces, for plastic does not show up on X rays. The admixture of some radio-opaque but inert (and therefore harmless) substance with the plastics used in children's things could eliminate this problem entirely. The more research all of us do, the more we will benefit from it.

The toy industry is not a marginal one. Our economy is consumer-oriented, and children are consumers like the rest of us. Toymakers can afford to invest in safety engineering and to tell their customers the truth—giving warning where warning is due, instruction for use where it is required, age recommendations where this is necessary. But if they do not, then the public will eventually smarten up, and the profits will start swinging down. When this happens, it will not be any new legislation that is to blame, or "overcautious" parents or "zealous" men, as I have been called. It will be the fault of the toy industry itself, and the name of that fault which may prove its undoing is shortsightedness.

Conclusion

THE ARGUMENT OF THIS BOOK IS PLAIN ENOUGH: HUNDREDS OF thousands of children are needlessly injured, and many killed, each year in the United States. These children are wounded and maimed and put to death, not by sex fiends, or invading armies, or maniacal and sadistic parents or ravaging diseases; they are the victims of their own playthings.

Let me repeat, to emphasize it, the statistic I referred to earlier: 700,000 children are injured by toys in America every year. Half a million more are hurt by swings, and still another 200,000 by slides. The sum of all of these injuries, in pain and suffering, grief and bereavement, permanent disability and physical and psychological disfigurement, is impossible to calculate. And much of it is *totally* unnecessary.

All the social engines that are supposed to protect us from this kind of national scandal have broken down. The manufacturers do not protect us. No independent agencies are equipped to give us adequate forewarning. The government, with only limited authority at law, and too often with only limited enthusiasm and energy as well, does little, almost nothing. And the parade of injuries and deaths goes marching on.

Something has to be done, and done at once. First we need an urgent, nationwide, and forceful cry of protest and alarm: Beware of the toys! The cry sounds overdramatic, perhaps, but if anything, it is insufficient. For protest and alarm are not enough. Action is required, too.

So it is left to us, the people, the parents, to raise the kind of fuss about the way our children run these superfluous risks for other people's profits that will shake the industry and the government out of their inertia and into positive, constructive, vigorous response. We need a Paul Revere mentality, to call a warning to us all that "the toys are coming and they can burn and blind and kill." It seems almost ludicrous to say that, but the evidence has just been presented to you; the facts are plain; there is no exaggeration of the problem.

Most of us wish our environment well, but are rarely forced to come to grips with it. We don't always see, and can rarely hear, the pollutants being cast upon our fields and into our streams. Most of us feel the same way about our children's toys. We haven't until now been made aware of the dangers they threaten, nor of the potential for great and lasting harm they bear. But, just as our silence has let us chop away our forests, kill our plants and flowers, and pour poisons into our rivers, lakes, and harbors; so also our ignorance and silence about playthings has quietly allowed the carnage to go on and on.

Enough. We have no more time for the luxury of expecting that these things only happen to other people's kids. We have no more time for the luxury of believing that each of us, alone, is powerless to do anything that counts. This book —and this is its apology, the excuse for all the omissions— is the work of *one* man, who was forced both as a parent and as a lawyer to see the problem whole. I like to think that lawyers are especially well equipped to lead this campaign for safer toys. They are skilled in the ways and means of drafting legislation, they certainly understand the realities of state and federal politics, and they are often blessed with a fierce and fighting sense of righteousness. If there is any cause that deserves the description "righteous," it is this one

—and so I hope that my own colleagues will be among the first to take up this challenge and serve it well.

If this book stirs us up; if it helps the rest of us parents to protect our children; if it motivates a lot of us to action; if it opens, not a debate, but a national call for child protection, then all the work will have been truly worth my while.

And, after all, if it saves the health or happiness or life of just *one* child, then that alone would justify this whole study and would make me very grateful, indeed.

If we begin to act responsibly at once, we may see again the day when children can give their toys the unqualified love, affection, care, and trust that children have in such abundance; not to toys that gash or burn or kill, but to the kind of toys that every child deserves—safe, delightful, stimulating, inexpensive, lasting toys: toys that care.

SELECTED REFERENCES

Accas, Gene, and John H. Eckstein. *How to Protect Your Child.* Simon and Schuster, Inc., Essandess Special Editions, New York, 1968.

American Guide to Infant and Child Care. Robert McMichael, Inc., New York, 1969.

Backett, E. Maurice. *Domestic Accidents.* World Health Organization, Geneva, 1965.

Dickerson, F. Reed, ed. *Product Safety in Household Goods.* The Bobbs-Merrill Co., Inc., New York, 1968.

Edge, Patricia. *Child Care and Management.* Faber and Faber, Ltd., London, 1968.

Fire Protection Guide on Hazardous Materials. National Fire Protection Association, Boston, 1967.

Fire Protection Handbook. National Fire Protection Association, Boston, 1967.

Fraser, Antonia. *A History of Toys.* Delacorte Press, New York, 1966.

Fritzsch, Karl Edward, and Manfred Bachmann. *An Illustrated History of Toys.* Abbey Library, London, 1965.

Fromme, Allan. *The ABC of Child Care.* Simon and Schuster (Pocket Books), New York, 1960.

Frumer, Louis R., and Melvin I. Friedman. *Products Liability.* Vol. I–III, Matthew Bender & Co., Inc., New York, 1967.

Goulart, Ron. *Assault on Childhood.* Sherbourne Press, Inc., Los Angeles, 1969.

Gruenberg, Sidonia Matsner, ed. *The New Encyclopedia of Child Care and Guidance.* Doubleday & Co., Inc., New York, 1968.

Hellyer, David T. M.D. *Your Child and You, A Pediatrician Talks to New Mothers.* Delacorte Press, New York, 1966.

Hillier, Mary. *Dolls and Doll-makers.* G. P. Putnam's Sons, New York, 1968.

Hurlock, Elizabeth B. *Guideposts for Growing Up.* Standard Education Society, Chicago, 1954.
Hursh, Robert D. *American Law of Products Liability.* The Lawyers Co-operative Publishing Co., Rochester, 1966.
Lausanne, Edita, ed. *The Golden Age of Toys.* New York Graphic Society, Ltd., Greenwich, Conn., 1967.
Matterson, E. M. *Play and Playthings for the Preschool Child.* Penguin Books, Baltimore, 1965.
Schwartz, Alvin. *A Parent's Guide to Children's Play and Recreation.* The Crowell-Collier Publishing Co., New York, 1963.
Shoemaker, Rowena M. *All in Play.* Play Schools Association, Inc., 41 West 57 Street, New York, 1958.
Stack, Herbert J., and J. Duke Elkow. *Education for Safe Living,* Prentice-Hall, Inc., Englewood Cliffs, N.J., 1959.
L. Joseph Stone, and Joseph Church. *Childhood and Adolescence, A Psychology of the Growing Person.* Random House, New York, 1957.
The Boston Children's Medical Center and Elizabeth M. Gregg. *What to Do When "There's Nothing To Do."* Delacorte Press, New York, 1967.
Your Child from One to Six. Universal Publishing and Distributing Corp., New York, 1968.

"A Doctor's Warning: Watch What Baby Eats." *Family Safety,* Winter, 1961.
"Accident Facts." National Safety Council, Chicago, 1968, 1969.
"Any Complaints Against Santa Claus?" *Home Safety Review,* Winter, 1960.
"BB Guns: Yes or No?" *Family Safety,* Fall, 1965.
Bush, Lucile. "'What Can Women Do About Home Safety?" Vol. 6, *NSC Transactions,* 1967.
Carper, Jean. "At Last—Clothing That Won't Burn." *Family Safety,* Spring, 1965.
Carper, Jean. "Plastic—Frightening New Child-Killer." *Home Safety Review,* Summer, 1959.

SELECTED REFERENCES

Carper, Jean. "The Deadly Playhouse." *Family Safety,* Spring, 1963.

Cavender, Marilee B. "Fire Retardant Materials—One Approach to Preventing Burns to Children." Vol. 27, *NSC Transactions,* 1965.

Christian, Arthur H. "Fibers—Fabrics—Fire." *Home Safety Review,* March, 1958.

"Children Can Make It." Association for Childhood Education International, Washington, D.C., 1954.

Dooley, Allan E. "Product Liability—Precautionary Labeling of Petroleum Products." Vol. 11, *NSC Transactions,* 1968.

"Don't Be a 'Torch Tragedy.'" *Farm Safety Review,* November, December, 1968.

Dykstra, Phil. "Survey of Injuries Involving Toys and Playthings Sustained by Children in Florida, June 1960, February 1961." National Safety Council, Chicago.

"Equipment and Supplies Tested and Approved for Preschool, School, Home." Association for Childhood Education International, Washington, D.C., 1968.

"Estimates of Injuries from Consumer Products." Epidemiology and Surveillance, Injury Control Program, National Center for Urban and Industrial Health, Cincinnati, Oct., 1968.

Fawcett, Howard H., "The Hazards of Home Safety." Vol. 6, *NSC Transactions,* 1964.

Garrison, Mrs. Ethel L. "A Plea For Child Safety." *Home Safety Review,* January, 1958.

"Head Start on Safety," *Family Safety,* Winter, 1967.

"Hearings Before the Subcommittee on Commerce and Finance of the Committee on Interstate and Foreign Commerce, House of Representatives, 91st Congress on H. R. 7509, A Bill to Amend the Federal Hazardous Substances Act to Protect Children From Toys or Other Articles Intended for Use by Children Which Present Any Electrical, Mechanical or Thermal Hazard." U.S. Government Printing Office, Washington, D.C., May 20, 22, 1969.

Hopkins, H. P. "Accidental Injuries to Children." Vol. 6, *NSC Transactions*, 1963.

"How to Take the Danger out of Child's Play." *Family Safety*, Summer, 1962.

"Interim Report Recommending Enactment of the Child Protection Act of 1969." National Commission on Product Safety, Washington, D.C., February 24, 1969.

Kahn, S. J. "Let's License TV Advertisers." *Reader's Digest*, April, 1969.

Keiser, Marjorie B. "Safety and Consumer Products." Vol. 27, *NSC Transactions*, 1965.

"Kids Eat the Darndest Things." *Home Safety Review*, Fall, 1960.

Kronish, S. D. "Dangerous Toys—How Big a Threat?" *Home Safety Review*, Fall, 1959.

Lin-Fu, Jane S., M.D., F.A.A.D. "Lead Poisoning in Children." U.S. Department of Health, Education and Welfare, Social and Rehabilitation Service, Children's Bureau, Washington, D.C., 1967.

Lund, Doris Herold, "Choosing Toys for Children of All Ages," American Toy Institute, New York, 1962.

Manheimer, Dean I., Joanna Dewey, Glen D. Mellinger, Ph.D., and Leslie Corsa, Jr., M.D. "50,000 Child-Years of Accidental Injuries." Public Health Reports, Vol. 31, No. 6, Jan. 1966.

Murtfeldt, Pat. "Putting the Lid on Child Poisonings." *Family Safety*, Summer, 1968.

"National Commission on Product Safety Final Report Presented to the President and Congress, June, 1970." U.S. Government Printing Office, Washington, D.C.

"New Warning on 'Death Boxes.' " *Family Safety*, Spring, 1965.

Newcomer, Carole. "Play Safe with Playthings." *Family Safety*, Winter, 1965.

"Obedience Means Safety for Your Child." American Academy of Pediatrics, Inc., Evanston, Illinois, 1965.

SELECTED REFERENCES

Oblesbay, Floyd B. "Getting Rid of Home Fire and Burn Hazards." Vol. 6, *NSC Transactions*, 1964.

Olds, Sally. "What Toys Mean to Your Child." *Today's Health*, December, 1969.

"Perilous Playpen." *Family Safety*, Summer, 1967.

"Play Areas." National Safety Council, Safety Education Data Sheet No. 29, National Safety Council, Chicago, 1948.

"Playground Apparatus." National Safety Council, Safety Education Data Sheet No. 69, National Safety Council, Chicago, 1964.

Pollack, Jack Harrison. "Homemade Toys to Tame Your Child." *Today's Health*, July, 1968.

"Preventing Accidents to Young Children." Connecticut Health Bulletin, May, 1955.

"Probe of FTC Given Congress." Congressional Record, January 22, 1969.

"Requirements of the Federal Hazardous Substances Act." F.D.A. Publication No. 35, U.S. Government Printing Office, Washington, D.C., March, 1968.

Rusk, T. L. "Textile Product Safety." Vol. 25, *NSC Transactions*, 1968.

"Santa, Be Careful." *Family Safety*, Winter, 1962.

"Special Handling of Children's Cases." 12 AM Jur Trials, Products Liability Cases S 132, et seq.

"The Dangerous Things People Eat." *Family Safety*, Summer, 1965.

"The Trouble With the Toddler." *Family Safety*, Fall, 1961.

"Toys and Play Equipment." National Safety Council, Safety Education Data Sheet No. 4, National Safety Council, Chicago, 1966.

"Toy Buying in the United States, a One-Year Study, Part I—Summary of Findings; Part II—Detailed Tables; Part III—Detailed Tables, Selected Toy Categories." Prepared for Toy Manufacturers of the U.S.A., Inc., by A. J. Wood Research Corp., Philadelphia, November, 1965.

"Tremendous Fight Against Plastic Bag Deaths." *Home Safety Review*, Fall, 1959.
Tuttles, Alexander J., M.D., M.P.H., Roland Bonato, B.A., M.A., and Bruce D. Waxman, B.A., M.A. "Preliminary Epidemiological Findings of the Family Injury Survey." *Connecticut Health Bulletin*, Vol. 72, No. 6, June 1958, pp. 189–195.
Tuttles, Alexander J., M.D., M.P.H., and Bruce D. Waxman, B.A., M.A., "Preliminary Findings of the Family Injury Survey on the Relationship Between Home and Environmental Conditions and Accidental Injuries," *Connecticut Health Bulletin*, June, 1960.
Verhulst, Henry L. "Beware of 'Harmless' Poisons That Can Kill Your Child." *Family Safety*, Spring, 1964.
Walton, Milfred H. "Toys and the Hospital Nurse." American Toy Institute, New York.
"What's Up with Skateboards?" *Family Safety*, Summer, 1965.
Wheatley, George M., M.D., ed. "Sitting Safety, A Brief Guide for Teen-age Baby Sitters," Metropolitan Life, 1966.
Wheatley, George M., M.D., ed. "Your Child's Safety." Metropolitan Life, 1968.

American Trial Lawyers Association News Letter. American Trial Lawyers Association, Cambridge, Massachusetts.
British Toys. Regent House, 89 Kingsway, London, England.
Consumer Bulletin. Consumers' Research, Inc., Washington, D.C.
Consumer Reports. Consumers Union of the U.S., Inc., Mt. Vernon, New York.
Family Safety. National Safety Council, Chicago, Illinois.
Fire Journal. National Fire Protection Association, Boston, Massachusetts.
Good Housekeeping. Good Housekeeping, New York, New York.
National Society for the Prevention of Blindness, Inc., *News*.

SELECTED REFERENCES

National Society for the Prevention of Blindness, Inc., 79 Madison Ave., New York, New York.

Playthings. Geyer-McAllister Publications, Inc., 51 Madison Ave., New York, New York.

Parents' Magazine. The Parents' Institute—A Division of *Parents' Magazine* Enterprises, Inc., New York, New York.

Product Engineering. McGraw-Hill, Inc., New York, New York.

Toys and Novelties. Harbrace Publications, Inc., 757 Third Ave., New York, New York.

Numbers in boldface type refer to pages between which illustrations appear.

A. Barry Toycraft: iron, 224
ABC of Child Care, 189
A. C. Gilbert Co.: chemistry sets, 211–212; erector sets, 225
A. D. Sutton & Sons: dolls, 45, 219
Advertising, 202, 262; and pressure on parents, 12; amount spent on, 13; irresponsible, 22–44. *See also* Television advertising
Age of children, 29, 51–53
"Agent Zero M Sonic Blaster," 253
Airline "wings," 242
Air rifles, 28, 32, 51, 150, 182. *See also* BB Guns, Daisy Air Rifles
A. J. Renzi Plastic Corp.: spray gun, 72
Alpert, Dr. Joel, 189
Aluminum Specialty Co.: corn popper, 223
American party favors, 236
American Standards Association, 84
Amsco Industries, Inc.: Hooper Dooper, 45; playfood, 209
AMT Corp.: hearse, 74
Andy Gard Corp.: tank and jeep, 71–72, 250
"Animal House," 55–56, **56–57,** 221
Animals. *See* Stuffed animals
Archery sets, 31–32, **32–33,** 60
Arco Falc, Milan, Italy, 31
Argo Industries Corp.: ovens, 110, 224
"Arrowcopter," 210
Arrows, **32–33,** 57
"As seen on TV," 37–39
"Astrojack Flying Space Boy," 249
"Astro-Train," 249
Aurora Plastics Corp.: monsters, 64–65, 231
Automobile industry, 49, 74, 263

Automobiles, play, 248–250
Azrak Hemway Corp.: squeeze toy, 205

Babies. *See* Infants
"Baby Playthings Little Angel Swing Me Suction Toy," 205
"Baby Sue," **218–219,** 219
"Bags 'n Things," 112
Balloons, 235
"Barbie Doll," 188. *See also* "New Barbie Doll"
"Barby Jo" electric iron, 224
"Bash," 68, 192, 228, **228–229**
Bashing toys, 68
Basic Products Development Co., Inc.: arrowcopter, 210
Batman, 40, 42–43
"Batman Cave Tunnel," 43
Batmobile, 43
Batteries, 225–226
Battery-operated toys, 223, 249
BB guns, 27–28, 51, 73, 251, 252
See also Air Rifles, Daisy Air Rifles.
Beads, 205
Bean blowers, 253
"Beauty Queen Electric Iron," **24–25,** 26
BE-BU of West Germany, 249
Beth Israel Hospital, Boston, 193
"Betty Crocker Easy-Bake Oven," 104
Bicycles, 120, 243
"Billy Blastoff," 188
"Bird of Paradise," 49, **50–51**
"Bizzy Bee Knitter," 232
Blocks, 205
Blood guns, 253
Blowguns, 50, 253
"Blo-Yr-Top," 54, 183

280 INDEX

"Blue Angel Stunt Plane," 210
Bluestone, Stephen, 43; on UL seal, 112–117
Boats, 231
"Bodysnatcher" hearse, 74
Bombs, 69–70
Boomerangs, 30–31, 51, 252, 253
Boston Globe, quoted, 65, 70
"Bounce Your Eyeball," 66–67, 67
Bow and arrow sets, **32–33**, 51, 179–180, 251, 253
Boy's Life, 27, 28, 254
"Brat Doll," 220
Breach of warranty, 162, 168
British Code of Safety Requirements for Children's Toys and Playthings, 89
British Medical Association, 89
British Standards Institute, 89
British Toy Manufacturer's Association, 89
Brooklyn Museum, 54–55, 233
B. Shackman & Co.: "Bird of Paradise," 210
Buddy L. Corp.: milk truck, 249
Bureau of Product Safety, 128
Bureau of Standards, 87, 128
Burns, and clothing, 213–218, **218–219**
Business and Defense Service Administration, 128
Buying: things to look for, 202; what not to buy, 254–258

Calvert Co.: masked doll, 219–220
Campaign buttons, 242
Candy "toys," 208–209
Cap-firecrackers, 105 **228–229**, 229
Caps. *See* Plastic caps
Cardinal Glennon Children's Memorial Hospital, St. Louis, 43, 70
"Car plane," 249–250
Casting sets, 224–225
Catapault toys, 210. *See also* Projectile toys
Charlotte (N.C.) Eye, Ear and Throat Hospital, 27, 252
Chemcraft, 211, 212
Chemical Sundries Co.: peashooter game, 33; catapault toys, 210; cosmetic kit, 234; balloons, 236; rotor toys, 249
Chemistry sets, 14, 25, 52, 210–213
Chemtoy Corp.: eyeball toy and "People Pieces," 67, 68; and *Parents' Magazine,* **104–105,** 105–106
Child Guidance "Sketch-O-Magic," 225
Childhood Interests/Alan Jay-Clarolyte: infants' toy, 35; swing toy, 205; rattles, 207; xylophones, 233
Child Protection Act of 1966, 134
Child Protection and Toy Safety Act, 1969, 86, 215; quoted, 136; enforcement, 138–139
Children: number of toy injuries, 8, 267; selling direct to, 13–14; and TV advertising, 39–40; age of and toys, 51–53; creativity, 56–58, 183–184; love for toys, 75; and contributory negligence, 172; individual needs, 196–197
Children's Hospital Medical Center, Boston, 40, 189, 196
"Children's Toy Whistles," 234
Child Study Association of America, 118–119
"Chilton Corn Popper," 110, 223
Chlorination of pools, 247–248
Cigarettes, candy, 73–74, **74–75,** 208, realistic, 74, **74–75**
Clay sets, 37
Cleinman & Sons, Inc.: dress up set, 234
Clothes, and burns, 213–218
"Coast Guard Mechanical Seaplane," 249
Code Authority National Association of Broadcasters, 43
Cole, Donald, 30
Cole, William G., 30
Coliform, 62
Columbo Doll Co., Inc.: "Baby Sue," **218–219,** 219
"Come Play Products": straws, 227
Commercial Standard 191-33, 132

INDEX

Commission on Product Safety.
  See National Commission on
  Product Safety
Compton, Berkeley, 10
Consumer Bulletin, 119
Consumer Council (Britain), 89
Consumer Product Safety Act of
  1970, 146, 149
Consumer Reports, 119; on thing-
  makers, 113; and chemistry sets,
  211–213; on "Roly-Poly," 233;
  on super-dough, 236–237; *Buy-
  ing Guide* on tricycles, 243–244
Consumer safety advocate, 147
Consumers' Research, 98, 119–120,
  122
Consumers Union, 94, 98, 112,
  119–120, 122, 130
Contributory negligence, 170–173,
  265
"Coolvent Swing Set," 236–237,
  238
Corn poppers, 109, 110–111, 223
Cosco, exerciser, 207
Cosmetic sets, 234–235
Craft toys, 230–232
Crash helmets, 55
"Crashmobile," 74, **74–75**
Creative Play Things, 241
Creativity, and safety hazards, 56–
  58
"Creeple Peeple," 112, 117
"Creepy Crawlers," 112
Cribs, 205–206, 240
Crib toys, 205
Crossbows, 12, 51, 106, 251, 252,
  253

Daisy Air Rifle Co., 252; BB guns,
  27–28
Daisy air rifles, 252, 254
Dark Shadows, 65
Dart guns, 48, 150, 251, 253
Darts, 57; metal-turned, 51; lawn,
  139. *See also* "Jarts"
Dawes, Dr. Lidia, quoted, 193–
  194
"Defective" toy, defining, 182
Defendants, selecting proper, 164
Dell Plastics, Inc.: straws, 227

Deluxe Topper Corp.: oven, 23,
  110; 224; grill, 223–224
"Dennis the Menace Jump 'n
  Float," 240–241
Dept. of Agriculture, 128
Dept. of Commerce, 127–128, 131
Dept. of Health, Education and
  Welfare, 128, 135, 137, 142
Design, 44–50; deviation from
  standards, 50–51
Deterrent effects of product lia-
  bility suits, 155–157
Directions, improper, 22–44
"Discovery Playthings," 118
"Discovery Set" series, 212
Disease and toys, 61–62
Disk guns, 253
Distribution, 16
Diving boards, 246
"Dizzy Doodle" doll, 205
Dollhouses, 194
Dolls, 139, 218–220; and bad de-
  sign, 44–45, **218–219;** flammabil-
  ity, 219
"Doodley-Doo," 230
Ducklings, stuffed, 61
Dueling pistols, **32–33,** 34
Durability, 17–18, 53–56
"Dynamite Shack," 68, 229

"Easy-Bake Oven," 23, 110, **222–
  223,** 224
Edibles, toy. *See* Playfoods
"Educational toys," 220–222
"Eeeks!," 112
E. K & E Corp.: sewing machine,
  224
Eldon Industries, 188
Electrical toys, 23–27, 50–51, 52,
  62, 84, 109–112, 222–226, 256;
  British standards, 90
Electric metal-casting sets, 14
Elkind, Arnold B., quoted, 20
"Empire Little Lady Oven," 109,
  224
"Empire See Em-Pop," 223
Erector sets, 225
Escapism, 192
Esco Imports, Inc., 233, 253
"Etch-A-Sketch," 46–47, 221

282   INDEX

Eugene Doll Co., Inc.: "Flexi Lorrie," **218–219,** 220
Europe, 9
European Toy Institute, 91
Exploding toys, 226–227
Eye protectors, 211

Family Safety, on synthetic fabrics, 216; on pool seats, 246
F & J Enterprises: straw, 227
F. A. O. Schwarz, 139, 233, 253; archery set, 31–32; and *Parents' Magazine,* 104–105
Federal Food and Drug Administration, 100, 128, 136, 138–139; and tunnels, 140–145, **144–145**
Federal government: regulatory agencies, 76–77, 128–129; and product safety, 121, 123–149
Federal Trade Commission, 97, 100, 118; and Flammable Fabrics Act, 131–132, 133
"Feeding Time" playthings, 227
Figurines, flexible, 55
Firecrackers, 51, 177, **228–229**
Fireworks, 150, 155, 226–227, 261
Fisher-Price toys, and *Good Housekeeping,* 101–103; "Musical Lacing Shoe," 205, 233; pull telephone, 221; xylophone, **104–105,** 233
Flammability, 52–53; and packaging, 60; and European Toy Institute, 91; of children's clothes, 213–218; of dolls, 219
Flammable Fabrics Act, 126, 131–133, 158, 215, 261
"Flexi Lorrie," **218–219,** 220
Flying machines, 248–250
Foreseeability, 173–175
Free-flight toys, 249
Free toys, 241–243
"Fright Factory," 66
"Frustration Ball," 64
Fryer, Jerome M., 87, 225; quoted, 20
"Fun" card, 66, **66–67**
Fun straws, 37, 39
Funtastic, 10

Gabriel Industries, Inc., 87; irons, 26; chemistry sets, 211–212; erector sets, 225
Games, 228–230
Garden implement sets, 241
Gasoline engines, 231–232
"The Genuine Wishnik," 219
Gibney Harriet N., 189
"G.I. Joe" series, 188, 251
"Gobble-de-spooks," 208
Goggles, 55
Go-go cars, 53
Good Housekeeping, 26, 97, 120, 121, 202; Consumers' Guaranty Seal, 97–103
"Graveyard Ghoul Duo," 74
Great Britain, 9, 27, 85, 263; regulation of toy industry, 89–90; and clothing, 215
"Green Beret Pistol and Target Set," 48, 72
Gregor, Inc.: hippie doll, 219, 220
Grills, 223–224
"Gumby's Pal Pokey," 55, 219
Guns, 51, 69, 139, 252
Gym equipment, 50, 57
Gym sets, features to look for, 239

"Hammer and Nail sets," 221, 231; Playskool, 96
Hammers, 50
Hardman vs. Helene Curtis Industries, Inc., 176
"Harmless," 202
Harnesses, baby, 207
Hartsook vs. Owl Drug Co., 183
Hasbro, and advertising, 13; GI Joe, 188; stitch set, 232
Hassenfeld Brothers, Inc.: "Hypo-Squirt," 232; balloon kits, 236; war toys, 251
Hazardous Substances Act, 81, 126, 127, 133–136, 158, 212; and "nontoxic," 36, 37
Hearing injuries, 253–254
Helicopter, **246–247,** 249
Henry Gordy, Inc.: cosmetic kits, 234
H. Fishlove and Co., Inc.: "Hypo-Phony," 232

INDEX 283

"Hidden Hazards in the Nursery," 144
"The Hippie Doll," 219, 220
"Hippy-Sippy," 47, **60–61**, 63, 192, 232
Hobby toys, 230–232
"Homelab Chem-sets," 211, 212
Homemade toys, 187, 192–197, 260
Home Safety Review, 89
"The Honey Doll," 219
"Hooper-Dooper," 45
Horsman Dolls, Inc.: "Teensie Baby," 219
"Hot Wheels," 53, 74, 249
"Hour Glass Action Toy," 205
House Committee on Interstate and Foreign Commerce. Subcommittee on Commerce and Finance, 86–89, 136
House Martin: knitting set, 232
Hula hoops, 45
Hypodermic needles, 47, 62, 232; psychological harm, 63
"Hypo-Phony," 47, 232, **236–237**
"Hypo-Squirt," 47, 63, 232, **236–237**

Ideal Toy Corp., and advertising, 13; doll, **218–219**; "Kookie Kamera," 36–37, 230; "Kaboom," 229
Identity, developing sense of, 195
"Impact," 166
Improvisation, 196
Impulse buying, 15–16, 18, 254–255
"Imputed" negligence, 172
"The Incredible Bird of Paradise," **50–51**, 210
"Incredible Edibles," 209
Infants toys, 34–37, 204–208. See also Cribs: Harnesses
Injuries, toy industry attitude to, 29–30; number of, 122, 267
"Instant Insanity," 64
Instructions, 264
Insurance, 156
Intervening cause, 178; and proximity, 180–181
Irons, **24–25**, 26–27, 224

Irwin Company: swings, 58, 237

James, Professor, 165
"Jarts," 139, 241
Jarts Co., 241
Jechnofix, 249
Jequirity beans, 62, 193
Jewelry sets, 62, **234–235**
Johnny Astro, 188, 249
Johnny Toymaker, 112
Jordan Marsh Company, 118
"Jolly's Twistee-Softee," 219
Jolly Toys, Inc.: dolls, 55, 219
"Jupiter and the Go-Go Gun," 10

"Kaboom," 229
Kaplan, Morris, 130–131
Kenner Products Co., and advertising, 13; oven, 23, 110, 224; "Glo-juice," 99, 230; "365-day toys," 104; "Spirograph," 222; car plane, 249–250
Kentucky Dept. of Health, 60, **60–61**
"Kiddie Koop," 206
Kites, 50
Kits, Inc.: archery sets, 60
Knickerbocker Co.: doll, 219
Knitting sets, 232
Knives, 253
Kodel, 216
Kohner Brothers, Inc.: nervous breakdown series, 63–64
"Kookie Kamera," 36, 37, 230
"Kooky Eyes Squeaker Toy," 205
"Krazy-Straw," 227

Laboratories, testing, 95–96
Lakeside Toys: animal house, 55–56, **56–57**, 221; dolls, 55; neurotic numbers, 64; tunnels, 144; "Pokey," 219
"Land of the Giants," 37–38
Lanolin Discovery, 176
Larami Corp.: "Space Twins," 249
Law, 1, 125, **157–158**; state, 124, 150–151, 261; federal, 131, 261; local, 150, 261; need for reform, 185

INDEX

Lawson vs. Benjamin Ansehl Co., 176
"Let's Pretend Junior Miss Nurse Dress-up Set," 234
Light bulbs, in electric ovens, 110
Lighter, cigarette, 73
"Lightning Bug Brand Glo-Juice," 99, 230
Lionel-Porter, 211
"Little Angel" rattle, 207
"Little Angel Swing Me Suction Toy," 35
"Little Miss Charming Beauty Set," 234
"Little Miss Playfood" series, 209
Locker, Aaron, 86–89
"Loonie Straws," 39, 40, **42–43**, 62, 227
Los Angeles Times, 67
Louis Marx & Co. Inc.: rifle, 48, 72; "socket-mallet," 68; monsters, 231
Love, and giving of things, 190
"Lunar Bug Flying Moon Craft," 249

"Maddie Mod" clothing, 219
Magazines, seals by, 98–106
"Magic Cool Oven," 24, 110, 224
"Magnetic Dart Game," 229
"Magnetic Inlaid Plastic Puzzle," 222, **222–223**
Mail sales, 18
"Majorette French Knitting Set," 232
Major Matt Mason, 188
"Makit and Bakit," **208–209**, 209
Man from U.N.C.L.E., 40
Manufacture, defects in, 50–51
"Masked Doll," 219–220
Massachusetts: law on air rifles, 32; law on peashooters, 33; and plastic caps, 78; regulations of, 150
Mattel, Inc., 65; growth of, 10; and advertising, 13; thingmaker series, 66–67, 112, 208–209, 224–225, 230; "Barbie Doll," 188, 219, 220; "Hot Wheels," 249; weapons, 253

Matterson, E. M., 194
"Memorability," 13
Mental illness, 63–64
Merry Manufacturing Co: lighter, 73
"Merry Play Lighter," 73
Metal staples, 60
Metal Ware Corp.: oven, 109, 224; corn popper, 223
Mikephil: war toys, 251
Milk, in straws, 40; trucks, 249
Miller vs. Sears, Roebuck & Co., 167
Milton Bradley: monsters, 65–66, 230; "Dynamite Shack," 68, 229; "Bash," 228, **228–229**; "Time Bomb," **228–229**; 229
"Milton the Monster," 65–66, 230
"Miniature Electric Corn Popper," 109, 110–111, 223
Minibikes, 245
Mirro Aluminum Products Co.: cornpopper, 109, 110–111, 223
"Mission-X Top Secret Plane," 210, 249
"Miss Petite Electrical Iron," **24–25**, 26
M-1 rifle, 48, 72
"Monkey Swing," 57, 237
Monsters, 64–66, 112, 231
"Mop-Pets," 220
Mosaic tile kits, 49, **50–51**
Moss, Rep. John E., 86–89
Moulded Products, Inc.: swings, 58, 237
M. Shimmer Sons, Inc.: sky diver, 210
"Musical Lacing Shoe," 102, 205, 233
Musical toys, 233
"My Doll's Vanity Set," 234
"My Prayer" doll, 219
My Toy Co., Inc.: toy dog, 219, 220

Nader, Ralph, 74, 147, 263
"Nan" doll, **42–43**, 219
"NASA Space Twins," 249
National Board of Fire Underwriters, 108

INDEX

National Commission on Product Safety (NCPS), 2, 34, 56, 81, 111, 112, 262; and ovens, 24; Cole testimony, 30; and dolls, 44; and self-regulation, 77, 92–93; on TMA guidelines, 80; and seals of approval, 97; and "Musical Lacing Shoe," 102, 205; on durability, 103; and super grill, 111; Bluestone report, 112–117; on jump shoes, 119; final report, 123–124, 126–127; on agencies, 128–129; and Hazardous Substances Act, 135–136; Product Safety Act, 1970, 146–147; on products liability suits, 153, 159, 160; on deterrent effects, 157; on cribs and playpens, 206; and baby harnesses, 207; and "Etch-a-Sketch," 221; polishing sets, 225; on gym slide, 240; on outdoor games, 241; and "Tyke-Bike," 244
National Fire Protection Association, 213, 217; and plastic caps, 78, 227; on fireworks, 226
National Safety Council, 24, 129–131, 223; and swings, 238; on water slides, 247
National Society for the Prevention of Blindness, 251
Nationwide Consumer Testing Institute (NCTI), 106, 121
Needles, toy, 47
Needs of child, 196–197
Negligence, 162, 166, 181; and privity, 167–168; problems with, 170–173; and proximity, 179–180
"Nervous Breakdown," 63–64
"Neurotic Numbers," 64
"New Barbie Doll," 219, 220
Newman Co.: straws, 40, 227
The New York Times, 13
"Nonflammable," 202
"Nontoxic," 202; meaning of, 35–37
Norstar Corp.: playfood, 209
Novelty, 18, 188

"Nursery Land. Best for Baby" rattle, 207

Objects swallowed by children, 56, **56–57**
Obsolescence, planned, 16–17
Ohio Art Company, 79, 92; irons, 26–27; dagger toy, 33; "Etch-A-Sketch," 46–47, 221; plastic caps, 77–78, 227, **252–253**; tool chest, 231; outdoor toys, 241; seaplane, 249; cap gun, 252–253, 254
Omega Chemical Corp., 247
Outdoor equipment, 237–241
Ovens, 23–24, 109, 110, 224

Pacifiers, 208
Packages, 58–60, 85
Pactra, Inc.: stunt plane, 210
Paints, 255
Parents, 8, 13–14; and advertising, 12; what they want from toys, 14–15; and blame for injuries, 29–30; responsibilities and NSC, 130; and product liability suits, 161; suggestions for, 261–262
Parents' Magazine, 26, 97, 104–105, 107, 120, 121, 144, 202; Commendation Seal, 97–99
Parksmith Corp.: squeeze toy, 205; "Brat Doll," 220
Parks Plastic Co.: pistol and target set, 48
Party, noise-makers, 139; favors and decorations, 235–237
"Party Pack, 5 fringed balloon squeakers," 236
Paul VI, Pope, 70, 71
PBI, Inc.: "Zooper," 31, **32–33**
"Pea Shooter Game," 33
Peashooters, 33, 51, 105, 150, 253
Pellet guns, 253
Penney, 217
"People Pieces," **66–67**, 67, 68, 105
"The Phantom of the Opera," 65
Phillips, Lonnie, 180
Phoenix House poster, **60–61**
Physio-Chem Corp., 211, 212
Picadoos, 112

INDEX

"Pieces of Body," 66–67, 67
Pitts, Dale, 180
Pitts vs. Basile, 180
Planes, 53, 83, 179, 231
Plastic: caps, 51, 77–78, 227; rigid, 55; bags, 59, 85; soft, 59–60; toys, British standards, 90; 102; cooking crystals, 209; pieces, 265–266
"Plastic Cooking Crystals Makit and Bakit" kit, 208–209, 209
Plastic wrapping, 60
"Plastigoop," 208–209, 230
Plate glass, 46
Plato, 178
"Play Dress-Up Set," 234
Playfoods, 50, 209, 228
Playground equipment, 50, 57–58, 237–241
Playground Equipment Corp.: gym, 238
Playpens, 205–206
Play range, limiting, 188–189
Play sets. *See* Gym sets
Playskool, Inc.: testing laboratory, 96; "Tyke Bike," 96, 244; hammer and nails set, 221, 231; plastic puzzle, 222
"Plush Pals," 219, 220
Pogo sticks, 50, 245
"Polish" dolls, 219
Polishing sets, 225
"Polly Pretty's Play Iron," 24–25, 26
Polyform Products, Inc.: "Doodley-Doo," 230
Pool ball, 245
Popular Mechanics, 254
Popular Science, 254
Portland cement, 49
Post Honeycombs, 242
Premarket testing, 141, 148–149, 202, 262
Premium toys, 84, 241–243
President's Committee on Consumer Interests, 127
President's Council on Consumer Affairs, 127
President's Special Assistant for Consumer Affairs, 127

Pressman Toy Co.: "Rat Patrol" game, 230
"Pressurized Gas," 249
"Pretty Patty Neat and Petite Manicure Set," 234
Pride-Trimble Corp.: "Kiddie Koop," 206; cribs, 240
Princess Grace Dolls, Inc.: doll clothing, 219
Privity, 165, 167–170
Processed Plastic Co.: missile, 47–48; war toys, 251
Products liability suits, 153–186; reasons for, 153–154; deterrent effects of, 155–157; types of, 162; problems of, 163–177; and privity, 167–170; and tampering by third party, 183
Projectile toys, 30–34, 57, 182, 242, 251
Protrusions, 49, 56, 83
Proximity, 178–181; and negligence, 179–180; and intervening cause, 180–181
Psychological harm, 62–74; and hypodermic needles, 47; and war toys, 47; and burns, 214
Public opinion, 76
Purchasing rules, 254–260
"Puropool's PH and Chlorine Test Kit," 247–248

Quality Certified Seal, 107
Quincrafts Corp.: playfoods, 209

Rapco, Inc.: tunnels, 14; metal casting set, 111, 224–225; polishing sets, 225
Rappaport Brothers, Inc.: play tunnels, 82; casting set, 224–225
"Rat Patrol" Spin-Cycle series: "Spin to Win," 230
Rattles, 35, 37, 62, 139, 194, 206–207; British standards, 90; musical, 207
Ray Plastics, Inc.: gun, 40, 105; letters from Dr. Walton, 41–42
"Reasonable man" test, 173–174
Recall of toys, 45, 141, 148
Reliance Products Corp.: rattle, 35

INDEX

Remco Industries, and advertising, 13; "Land of the Giants," 37–38; "Frustration Ball," 64; "Silly Soapmaker," 209; chemistry sets, 211, 212; trains, 249
"Remoteness," 178, 179
Retailers, 8, 264–265
Riding toys, 50, 243–245
Rifles, 253
"Rings 'n Things," 112
Ricochet, 27
Rockets, 57
Rocking horses, 245
Roller skates, plastic, 241
"Roly-Poly" doll, 54, 122, 233
Romper Room, 39; "Fun Straw," 39, 227
"Ronson Repeater," 167
Royal Society for the Prevention of Accidents," 89
Rules for buying, 254–258
Rubber band(s), 45, 243; guns, 253

"Safe-Play Dagger and Sheath," 33
Safety, how to judge, 21–22; and advertising copy, 28; goggles, 28, 56–57
Salmonella, 61
Sandboxes, 241
"Sanitoy," 205
"Satellite Jump Shoes," 119
Saturation, 37
Science and Mechanics, 254
Scissors, electric, 24
Seals: third-party, 96–97; magazine, what they mean, 98–103; how they are used, 105–106
Sears, Roebuck, 217; gym sets, 240; trains, 249
Sears Swing, **236–237**, 239
Self-regulation by toy industry, 76–93
"Series" principle, 188, 189
Sewing: machines, 224; sets, 232
"Sewmaster Sewing Machine," 224
Shopper, Dr. Moisey, quoted, 43, 70
Shopper's guide, 201–266
"Shovel 'n Sand Sifter," 241
Shriners Burns Institute, 213

"Shrink Machine," 209
Sifco Toys: iron, 224
"Silly Soapmaker," 209
"Silly Straw," 227
Skate-boards, 243
Skil-Craft Playthings, Inc., 211, 212–213
"Sky Diver," 210
"Sky-Rider" gym, 238
Sleds, 121, 244–245
"Slick Chick," 55, 220
Slides, 239–240, 267; water, 246–247
"Sling Launch Skydiver and Paratrooper," 210
Slingshots, 49, 50, 51, 79, 105, 150, 210, 251, 252, 253
Smithport Specialty Co.: dart game, 229
Smith vs. Nussman, 167
"Snippy Safe Electric Scissors," 24, **24–25**
Society of the Plastics Industry, Inc., 60
"Socket-Mallet," 68
"Soldier Accessories" kit, 251
Space rocket, 49, **50–51**
Spark guns, 253
"Specs 'n Things," 112
"Spirograph," 222
"Spit devil," 177
"Spring-O-Lene," **246–247**
Squeeze toys, 205
Squirt guns, 62
S. Rosenberg Co.: "Mop-Pets," 220
Stahlwood Toy Manufacturing Co.: rattle, 35, 55, 207
Standard Pyroxoloid Corp.: cosmetic kit, 234
Star Baby Toys: rattle, 206–207
Star Manufacturing Co.: rattles, 206–207
Star Trek, 40; Gun, 105; Jet Disk toy, 41–42; rapid-fire tracer gun, 40
Stevens Manufacturing Co.: plane, 210
Store-bought toys, dangers of, 189–193
Stoves, 11. *See also* Ovens

288 INDEX

Strahendorf vs. Walgreen Co., 179
Straws, 39–40, 62, 227
"Strict liability," 162, 181–183; and privity, 170
Stuffed: animals, 61, 218–220; toys, 82, 133
Sturdiness, 17–18, 183; as safety factor, 53–56
Sun Cleanser Co., 248
Sun Pools Chemical Division, 248
"Super Bird": 250, **252–253**
"Super-Dough," 236–237
"Super-Duper Outdoor Water Spray Gun," 72
"Super-Glo," 236
"Super Thingmaker," 224–225
"Suzy-Homemaker Super Grill," 111, 223–224
"Suzy-Homemaker Super-Safety Oven," 23, 110, 224
Swartz, Edward M.: letter on Rapco tunnels, 142–143
Swimming: pools, 245–248; toys, 245–248
"Swing-A-Ling," 58, 237
"Swing Rings," 58, 237
Swings, 57–58, 119, 237–239, 267
Swords, 51, **252–253**, 252, 253
Synthetic fabrics, 216

"Take-A-Long-Stitch-A-Story" set, 232
Tal-Cap, Inc., 224
"Target Catapault," 210
"Teensie Baby," 219
Teething rings, 37, 61–62, 208
"Telephone Pull Toy," 102, 221
Television advertising, 12, 37–40, 43
Television Bureau of Advertising, 37
Tennessee Industries: "Super Bird," 250
Testing agencies, 94–122
Tetanus, 35
Thauer, Ernest, M., 32
Thingmaker series, 66–67, 112–117, 208–209, 224–225, 230
Thriftee "'Fast Draw' Dueling-Pistol Kit," **32–33**, 34

Thrift Toys: dynamite sticks, **228–229**, 229
Thunderbird Stunt Plane, 249
"Time Bomb," **228–229**, 229
"Tiny Tot Exerciser," 207
"Tiny Toys for Little Boys," 234
"Tip-resistant" pool seats, 245–246
Todai Toys, 233
Today's Health, 43
"Toddlers' Toy Musical Chime Rattle," **32–33**, 35, 55, 207
"Tool Chest," 231
Topper Toys: doll, 55; heating mold units, 112; "Johnny Astro," 188; "Slick Chick" doll, 220; rotor toys, 249
Tops, 54, 183, 208, **208–209**
Toy Fair, 1969, 13, 63, 79, 236; 1970, 79
Toy industry: annual dollar volume, 7; volume of sales, 9; growth of, 9–11; and advertising, 12–13; distribution, 16; and obsolescence, 16–17; attitude to injuries, 29–30; advertising budget, 37; and war toys, 72–73; self-regulation, 76–93; number of companies, 79; what it should do, 262–266
Toy Manufacturers of America, 76, 79, 86–89, 149, 136; study on who buys toys, 13, 15; guidelines for toy safety, 80–86
Toy parties, 12
Toy Pistol, Holster and Paper Cap Association, 77
Toys: reform in marketing, 4; types and number of injuries by, 8; amount spent on, 11; definition of, 11–12; inherently dangerous, 52; play function of, 191; desirable, 192–193; to avoid, 187–197, 201–266; rules for buying, 202, 254–260; "dos" for shopper, 259–260
Toys & Novelties, 43, 66, 113
Toy Trade News, 65
Tracer guns, 40–42, 46
Trains, 248–250; wind-up, 53
"Traffic Jam," 144, **144–145**

INDEX

Trampolines, 240–241
Transogram Co.: knitting set, 232
Traveler Trading Co., 67
Treasure Industries, Inc.: honey doll, 219; "Nan" doll, **42–43,** 219
Tricycles: points to look for, 243–244
Triple Thingmaker, 112
Trucks, 248–250
"Tru-Streak Jet," 249
"Tumbling Stones," 225
Tunnels, play, 2, 34, 82, 118, 139, 140–145
20th-Century Varieties, Inc.: swings, 57, 237
"Twistee-Softee," 55
"Two Complete Soldier Sets," 251
"Tyke Bike," 96, 244

Underwriters' Laboratories, 25, 84, 94, 108–117
Uneeda Doll Co. Inc.: "Wishnik," 219
U.S. Office of Education, 128
U.S. Public Health Service, 8, 73, 128, 208
United States Testing Company, Inc. (USTC), 106–107, 121
United States Testing Laboratories, 106–107
"U.S. Air Force Surface-to-Air Missile," 47–48, 251
"U.S. Armored Division," 251
Use, normal and abnormal, 174

Verel, 216
Vesey, Charles, 32
Victor Stanzel Co.: plane, 249; rotor toys, 249
Victory Sparkler & Specialty Co. vs. Latimer, 155, 177
Victory Sparkler & Specialty Co. vs. Price, 155, 177

Violence, and war toys, 68–73
"V-X" rocket, 249

Walton, David S., 46; letters to Ray Plastics, 41–42
War games, 250–251
Warnings, 264; inadequate, 22–44
War toys, 192; design problems, 47–48; psychological effects, 68–73. *See also* Weapons
"Wasp Cap Gun," 254
Water pistols, 62
Weapons, 51, 251–254. *See also* War toys
West Germany, 263; on flammable toys, 82; safety standards, 91
"The Westinghouse Play Electric Iron," **24–25,** 26
Wertham, Dr. Frederic: on war toys, 71
"Wham-O," 209
Wham-O Manufacturing Co.: boomerang, 30–31
What to Do When "There's Nothing To Do," 196
Whips, 51
Whistles, 242
"Winnie-the-Pooh Crib Mobile," 205
"Wonder Plastic Balloons," 236
Wooden toys: British standards, 90
Woolworth's, 234
World Candies, Inc., 74
World Toy House, Inc.: rattle, 207; dress up set, 234

Xylophones, 102, **104–105,** 233

Yuletide Enterprises, Inc.: doll and doll clothing, 219

"Zoofie Goofies," 112
"Zooper," 31, **32–33**